Oh Happy Day

By the same author

Bad Faith
A forgotten history of family and fatherland

with Colm Tóibín
The Modern Library
The 200 best novels in English since 1950

Oh Happy Day

THOSE TIMES
AND
THESE TIMES

Carmen Callil

JONATHAN CAPE
LONDON

1 3 5 7 9 10 8 6 4 2

Jonathan Cape, an imprint of Vintage,
20 Vauxhall Bridge Road,
London SW1V 2SA

Jonathan Cape is part of the Penguin Random House group of companies
whose addresses can be found at global.penguinrandomhouse.com

 Penguin
Random House
UK

First published by Jonathan Cape in 2020

penguin.co.uk/vintage

A CIP catalogue record for this book is available from the British Library

ISBN 9780224090308 (hardback)
ISBN 9780224090315 (trade paperback)

Typeset in 12.75/14.75pt Garamond MT by Jouve (UK), Milton Keynes
Printed and bound in Great Britain by Clays Ltd, Elcograf S.p.A.

Penguin Random House is committed to a sustainable future for
our business, our readers and our planet. This book is made
from Forest Stewardship Council® certified paper.

 MIX
Paper from
responsible sources
FSC® C018179

For people who lived and live like this

Contents

PART IV
PORT MIDDLEBAY

APPENDICES

List of Illustrations

Family Tree

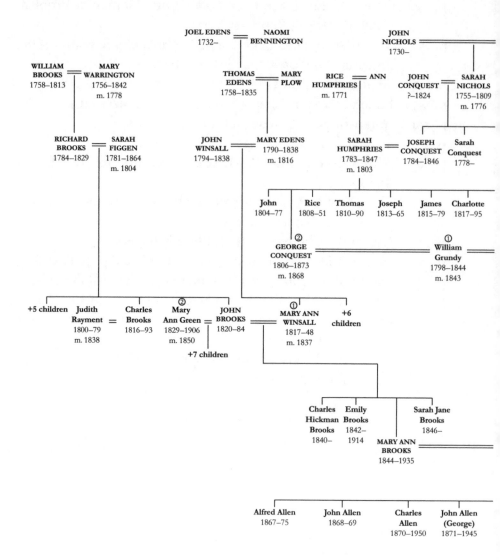

For fuller family trees see Appendices, pages 283–7.

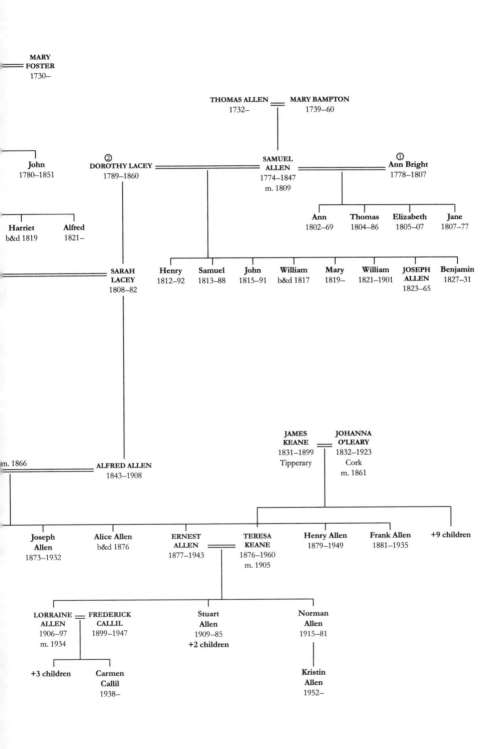

Preface

◄○►

A BOOK SUCH AS THIS, both story and history, requires a different approach to history and a different way of writing about it. My account of the lives of George and Sary, Mary Ann and their families is the result of copious investigation. But sometimes I have had to intuit things, make connections and suppositions. Any mistakes are mine alone, and I will happily correct them.

When I began the research for this book, I intended to write about all my diverse emigrant ancestors, English, Irish and Lebanese, who were sent or emigrated to Australia in the nineteenth century. Many of us are the descendants of people like them, the poor, the criminal, the 'surplus' population of the world, then and now. But I decided to concentrate on my English forebears because, as I wrote, that English construct, the social pyramid, rose again before me. The wealthy and entitled few at the top continue to prey on the much larger number of the poorer beneath them: not lost, not gone before, but in vigorous health, and as strong as ever.

I was fortunate. My English ancestors were the busy insects of the early Industrial Revolution, and so they were observed, because wealth and profit depended on their good behaviour – all too rarely provided. The British governing classes of the early Industrial Revolution feared the influence of the revolutionary French, and for this reason – and others – kept a keen eye on those beneath them. They needed them to fight in wars, to work in factories, to breed adequate children, and later, to people the empire. And so my ancestors' stories, with some surprises, were waiting there to be discovered – in newspapers, in church, court, civil and workhouse records.

In our own time, the economic crash of 2008 was used by the British government to introduce the policy of austerity: cutting, removing, destroying the justice of the social arrangements called for by the British people after the Second World War. Using, as the pretext, what they called 'the damaging culture of welfare dependency', they introduced the system known as Universal Credit. This is only one turn of the austerity screw gifted by English persons of consequence to the necessitous classes, installing the social system the British live with today, which, put most simply, requires those who have not, to pay for the sins of those who have. The malady of Brexit followed.

So I decided to tell only the story of Sary, George and Mary Ann, natives of England's labouring poor – the paupers, asylum seekers and refugees of their day. Their story raised a question: had so little changed in Britain in the last 200 years, that generation could succeed generation, each one repeating their grim experiences?

Australian history, Indigenous and emigrant, settler and refugee, is not only an account of that continent; it also delivers a history of England, whose people live today with the results of empire, in a culture marked by an almost wilful forgetting of its dual inheritance. Many convicts, like George Conquest, survived to live better lives than anything their motherland could offer them. Others were tortured and lashed to pieces, their ghastly deaths in many cases carefully recorded by the bureaucracy of empire. But this is also a story of migration, of those despatched from the British Isles as economic refugees, a species of forced resettlement familiar to us as it is repeated throughout the world today.

For the British poor, what they found in return for being consigned to the other side of the earth, apart from work and full bellies, was something their ancestors and the family members they left behind had never known: power. This was not the power of money or position, but that of citizens rather than subjects.

And for my Irish and Lebanese ancestors, it was much the same. They fled – or were forced to leave – the British and Ottoman empires, and when they reached Australia, they were accepted for the work they could do. Their robustness, energy and ingenuity demonstrated that in surviving and thriving, as many of them did, they may well have been a loss to the countries they left behind. What they did with the opportunities they were given is another story, one Australians still have time to make it their own. As the English do, too.

I

HARD TIMES

Something to be worked so much and paid so much, and there ended; something to be infallibly settled by laws of supply and demand; something that blundered against those laws, and floundered into difficulty; something that was a little pinched when wheat was dear, and over-ate itself when wheat was cheap; something that increased at such a rate of percentage, and yielded such another percentage of crime, and such another percentage of pauperism; something wholesale, of which vast fortunes were made . . .

Charles Dickens, *Hard Times* (1854)

1

Sowing

The Peterloo Massacre at St Peter's Field,
Manchester, 18 August 1819

THE STORY BEGINS WITH Sary,* as it must, because she was
the first to leave. Pursuing ancestors previous to the Sarahs
and Mary Anns, to Johanna and Henineh, or the numerous
Johns, Josephs, Jameses, Samuels and Alfreds, is of no use. The

* Sarah Lacey called herself Sary when she was young. I refer to her as 'Sary' throughout
in order to distinguish her from all the other Sarahs in this story.

records of their lives, if any, have mostly disappeared, as have the unmarked graves in which they are buried.

Sary was born in 1808, on the cusp of the Regency, as George III's long reign, marked by intermittent mental illness and many wars and conquests and by discoveries both scientific and imperial, saw his final descent into madness. In 1770 Captain James Cook claimed the east coast of Australia for Britain, which viewed the unknown south land as belonging to no one, though there were something in the region of 500,000–750,000 people living there at the time. The loss of Britain's American possessions in 1782 was one of the many reasons it decided to ship off its criminal and pauper classes to its strange and distant new possession in 1787.

Throughout the eighteenth century, Britain and France were constantly at war, circumstances exacerbated by the French Revolution and the rise of Napoleon Bonaparte. By 1808, Napoleon was at the height of his powers. He had conquered much of continental Europe, and was about to invade Spain and begin the long Peninsular Wars which marked the beginning of his downfall. Until his final defeat at Waterloo in 1815, the early years of my great-great-grandmother Sary Lacey – as she signed herself on her first marriage certificate in 1843 – were dominated by the spectre of Napoleon, as every force was marshalled to remove the emperor and his threat to Britain's colonial and maritime power. But after Waterloo and Napoleon's exile to St Helena, the United Kingdom, as formally created in 1801, turned its attention to invention and industry, and to the creation of unprecedented wealth and prosperity. And to its empire.

In 1811 George III's son the Prince of Wales became Regent, giving his name to the period so exquisitely chronicled by the novelist Georgette Heyer. Regency England was a land of precise social gradations. The 16 million human beings who inhabited the United Kingdom at that time formed various strata of impermeable rock, shaped into a pyramid: at the top a precious few, their lives a very heaven; at the bottom a heaving multitude, hell kept precariously at bay, if at all:

Monarch
Royalty
Aristocracy

Gentry
Middle Classes
Artisans and Tradespeople
Servants
Labouring Poor
Paupers

Sary hovered between the last two categories. Although she spent fifty years trudging along at the foot of the pyramid, she had two distinctions. She belonged to the largest class of British subjects, and she was emancipated, as the women above her were not to be for more than a century: she was a working woman from the day she was born.

Sary's mother, Dorothy Lacey, was born in Rearsby, Leicestershire, around 1786. In Dorothy's first year the eleven ships of the First Fleet set sail from Portsmouth, departing for Botany Bay with their allotment of 770 convicts on Sunday 13 May 1787. Two years later the storming of the Bastille in Paris heralded the French Revolution. Both these events were to affect the lives of many millions, none more so than those who lived on less than nothing, of whom Dorothy and her offspring were prime examples. Dorothy, an unrecorded class of person, was probably illegitimate: what is certain is that her firstborn, Sary, certainly was. Dorothy contrived for her daughter what she had not had herself: a baptism in the Church of St John the Baptist in Hungarton, a tiny village about eight miles from Rearsby, where Sary was born.

On 20 November 1808 Dorothy Lacey had her firstborn christened as Sarah Eglesfield Lacey, no father's name given. Eglesfields, Eaglesfields, Egglefields and others of this name, variously spelt, abound in Leicestershire, and many of them are to be found on the register of baptisms of St John the Baptist in Hungarton. There are many Laceys in the region too, but no male Eglesfield ever acknowledged the birth of Sarah. Throughout her life Sary Whatever-her-name-was chose a series of fathers when official documents required them. It may well be that Dorothy Lacey was as careless with names as her daughter was to be, and picked a father for Sary to suit herself.

At this time, Leicestershire was, and had been for centuries, a rich, farming, arable county, famous hunting land. Hungarton lies at

the heart of this pursuit: the Quorn hunts there to this day. When
Sary was baptised, the master of the Quorn was Thomas Assheton
Smith the Younger, also a notable cricketer, the high point of whose
career were his scores of 4 and 8 in the inaugural Gentleman vs Play-
ers match at Lord's in 1806. Hunting brought excellent employment
to this tiny rural community, whose self-sufficient subsistence on
common land was entirely thrown over by the land enclosures of the
eighteenth century. These began as early as 1730 in Leicestershire,
more enthusiastic than most counties in ruining its peasant farmers
and thus preparing a body of men and women ready to serve the
Industrial Revolution, already on its way.

Industrial Revolution or no, the gentry's horses and dogs had to
be fed and tended, and many of the locals were employed to serve
their hunting owners. Someone helped Dorothy. If not the sports-
man Assheton Smith, it could have been someone from Ingarsby
Hall, from Baggrave Hall, the seat of the Burnaby family, or from
Quenby Hall, the seat of the Ashbys. These were the three families
who ruled the area, the rural poor who worked for them, and most
particularly the small Church of St John in Hungarton. The population of the parish – around a hundred – would fill the small church,
its rustic charms carefully divided into four sections. The Ingarsby
interest sat on the left, the Ashbys on the right, and the Burnabys
occupied the nave. The hoi polloi, divided from their betters by a box
pew, sat at the rear and did so, it is said, until recent times.

Perhaps Dorothy was in service at one of the manors, or worked
at one of the local hostelries, and a benevolent employer, in the manner of Mrs Gaskell's novels, aided her in her sin. Whoever assisted her
enabled her daughter to be baptised before Dorothy herself was made
an honest woman by marrying a journeyman framework knitter,
Samuel Allen. A widower from Thurmaston, a village a few miles
away, with three young children, his wife and another child having
died within months of each other, he could not be too fussy about
Dorothy's base-born child. He needed a mother for his children, and
he married Dorothy twice, first in Rearsby on 5 August 1809, and
then again three days later in Thurmaston, presumably in order to
celebrate with his family there. And in Thurmaston she lived thereafter, as, for many years, did Sary.

The Industrial Revolution brought advantages as well as monstrous harshness to the lives of the poor. It was a time of medical and sanitary advances, but in the early years such benefits were for the few, rarely for the many. People lived longer, but for those at the bottom of the pyramid, longer was often nastier. The Leicestershire hosiery industry was one of the very last to turn to powered machines and factories: it was many decades before improvements in sanitation and any increase in life expectancy reached them. Death threaded through the life of my ancestors: babies and children, all too numerous, mothers and fathers dead too young.

Families such as that of Samuel and Dorothy Allen could claim – but did not – a history of cottage framework knitting that went back to the seventeenth century, though 'cottage' is not the word that properly describes their dwellings. In 1684 a petition to Leicester Corporation stated that it employed '2000 poore people, Men, Women and Children of the Towne of Leicr & the adjacent villages'. Fifty years later Leicester had 13,000 stockingers,* 'the typical knitter' being 'an artisan with little more property than his frame, a few pieces of furniture, and here and there a few sheep, a pig or a cow'. Every village in Leicestershire resounded with 'the indescribable sound of the stocking frame'. This village industry was paradise in comparison with what was to come after the Napoleonic Wars.

Historians still argue about the origins, trajectory and processes of the Industrial Revolution, but what is tentatively agreed is that the eighteenth century saw its first murmurs, and that it was in its most noxious period in the 1830s and 40s, though not yet harnessed to the imperial wealth under which it flourished from 1870 onwards. Thus the early phase of these industrial changes, from 1800 to 1850, coincided exactly with Sary's young womanhood, but improved it not at all. James Hargreaves' spinning jenny had already replaced the spinning wheel. Richard Arkwright's throstles, flying shuttles and power looms transformed traditional knitting work. Coal and steam engines, canals and roads, railways and factories revolutionised working lives, and the lives of the men and women of fortune for whom they toiled. And there were so many more of the former.

---

* A stockinger is a knitter, a person who knits on a stocking frame.

From the beginning of the nineteenth century, the population of
England and Wales exploded, with the first whispers of medical discoveries and better hygiene. The census of 1801 recorded a population
of 9 million; by 1851 it was nearly 18 million: a great migration moved
large numbers of them from the country to the town. Most English
cities and towns doubled or trebled in size, but from 1740 to 1842 the
population of the counties of Nottingham, Leicestershire and Derbyshire, home to the framework knitters of the East Midlands – a
regional description that came into being only in 1965 – increased by
sixteen times as land enclosures propelled farm labourers and village
cottagers to the towns. In the days of my great-great-grandmother
these were knitting towns, served by the villages and villagers surrounding them. Before the coming of factories and workshops, many
stockingers worked at home. The town to which they walked to collect yarn and return finished goods was the centre of their universe.

Thurmaston, four miles north of Leicester on the eastern banks
of the River Soar, then on the turnpike road to the hunting town of
Melton Mowbray, was the kind of English village in which the black-
smith was always called Smith. It was home to some 800 souls when
Dorothy and her baby went to live there in 1809. Many of them were
Allens, a common name in those parts – to which Allen-a-Dale in
Robin Hood bears witness – though it was often spelled Alin or Allin,
as most could neither read nor write. Some could, of course: a Thomas
Allen was a curate during the Commonwealth, and the lord of the
manor of Thurmaston was an Allen, always called Thomas, until the
last Thomas Allen was killed in the First World War.

Then there was John Bishop Allen, brother of the squire Thomas
Allen of the time, who on 25 November 1822 shot William Lane, a
drummer boy recruiting in the village for the army. A few weeks earlier the squire had suddenly dropped dead, and their mother had
followed days after. John Bishop Allen, distraught from these losses
and irritated by the modest noise, appeared at his window at about ten
o'clock in the evening, dressed in his nightshirt and aiming his gun.
He shot the poor drummer boy twice, an event so extraordinary that
all the inhabitants of Thurmaston poured out of their hovels and cottages to witness the furore as the boy's body was moved to the Old
Plough Inn, where the inquest was to be held. Sary was fourteen at

the time. It was a moonlight night; the family's cottage was just a stone's throw from the Old Plough (which Sary's half-brother Joseph was to run in due course). Hard to believe that she and her half-brothers and sisters, so often out on the village lanes after dark, were not in the crowd outside too. Of the accused John Bishop Allen, the sergeant told the court:

> I believe that some parts of his family, though not very near relatives, have been insane, so that there may have been some hereditary taint running through the family.

In the long line of wealthy Allens there are no Samuels and no Alfreds. However, Thomas Allens were common in the family of the journeyman knitter Samuel Allen, into which Dorothy Lacey had married. Samuel's father was a Thomas Allen, and Samuel's eldest son was thus named too. The next Squire Thomas Allen (1818–88), of Sary's time, was the last to live in the manor house, but Samuel Allen's long line of ancestral Samuels, Thomases, Williams, Anns, Marys and Sarahs, who could only sign their names with a cross, had lived in the village for as many centuries as their squire.

———————— ⟨∿⟩ ————————

Samuel Allen's three living children, Ann, Thomas and Jane, were aged between two and seven when Dorothy came to live with them, bringing Sary, a baby of one year old. So it is not surprising that the new family Samuel and Dorothy started did not begin until 1812, when the young Allens were old enough to take on their parents' knitting work. In the following fifteen years there were eight more children – the parish register records Samuel Allen's family as one of the largest in the village. Seven sons: Henry, Samuel, John, William 1 (died at six months), William 2 – the replacement – Joseph and Benjamin; and one daughter, Mary Ann. Mary Ann's name, and those of most of her brothers, were to continue through generations of the family.

Throughout Sary's life in Thurmaston, the family lived in a framework-knitter's cottage near the Church of St Michael and All

Angels. Many of them are buried there, albeit in nameless graves, though grander Allens are duly recorded. My mother, Lorraine Allen, was very partial to the poetry of tombstones, and would have loved the well-used words with which Hannah Allen recorded the death of her husband Thomas, who died at the age of thirty-one in 1753:

> Stay, Reader, prepare; reflect, whilst this you view,
> Who next shall die, – uncertain – why not you?

Few stockingers owned their own cottage or stocking frame, but rented both, and the whole family worked at, on and around the machine. The stocking frame was a large wooden construction, replete with thread carriers, sinkers, jacks, pulleys and treadles; the work was back-breaking, fourteen hours a day if lucky, seventeen hours and more if not, in ill-ventilated rooms, crowded around or hunched over the frame. In the stockinger's cottage it was usually done by the man of the family, or by the older sons; they needed both feet to work its

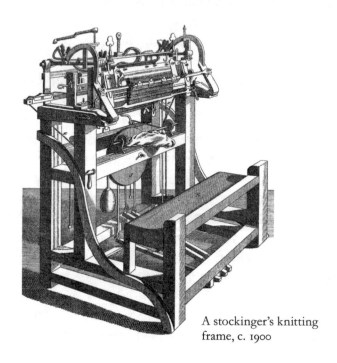

A stockinger's knitting
frame, c. 1900

treadles, both arms to manoeuvre the iron carriage in its frame. Some
women worked the frames, but mostly it fell to the women and children of the family, whose fingers were nimble, to seam the fabric into
fashioned stockings and hose, using needlework and embroidery until
modes changed.

The large, heavy frames could take up an entire ground floor,
with a winding wheel inched in, or be 'crammed into basements, or
attics, with the family occupying at the most two rooms elsewhere in
the house'. They could also be housed in a crude shed or an outhouse
thrown up in an alley or the yard. Many families lived in just one
room, almost their only furniture being the frame itself. Keen eye-
sight was required, candles were expensive, work hours long: for that
reason many knitters' cottages had elongated, low windows at ground
level and a low-eaved space upstairs for sleeping or for the yarn,
reached by a rickety ladder.

In time windows were added to these attics, the roof raised to
accommodate yet more frames, and thatched roofs gave way to slate.
No curtains – shutters if anything; doors rough planks; floors brick or
dirt; walls lime plaster and reeds; an open fire kept stoked with coal to
keep the temperature high for the knitting machine and the yarn. How
did they keep their hose clean for their middlemen and manufacturers –
if they did? In time, some workshop rooms were moved to the upper
floor of the house, to make as much use as possible of what light there
was. Look up in any Leicestershire village, and see the windows on the
upper floors – these are the larger of the framework knitters' cottages.

The children of knitters generally began winding and sewing
between the ages of three and seven, with the seats and treadles raised
for them. They carded the fibre and wound the yarn onto bobbins,
and older daughters and wives spun yarn and seamed and embroidered the stockings. Hands, eyes and feet all had to be in good order,
but going to bed supperless as often as not meant that this was rarely
the case. The child moved on to the frame at about nine years of age.
By the age of twelve they could work the frame as well as an adult, but
were paid much less. Parliament could regulate child labour in factories, but this domestic industry meant that as late as 1862 Mary Thorpe
described the treatment of children in her Nottinghamshire village to
the Children's Employment Commission: 'Mother will pin them to

her knee to keep them to their work and if they are sleepy give them a slap on the side of the head to keep them awake.'

Dorothy had seven children's heads to slap by 1815. Her youngest baby, John, was a month old when the Treaty of Paris ended the Napoleonic Wars. For the next four decades, until 1854, almost the entire period of Sary's life in England, a most unusual period of peace descended upon Europe. But for knitters at the level of the Allen family, these were desperate times. The golden years of framework knitting – if such there ever were – were ending just as Dorothy and Sary arrived in Thurmaston, as food prices and taxes rose during the wars. What had been for centuries a cottage industry, allied, for survival, to a small farm or allotment, had fallen victim to a host of malpractices and misfortunes well before anything resembling the Industrial Revolution paid its first call on the Midlands knitting counties.

The knitting machine, first invented in 1589 by a country parson, William Lee of Calverton, near Nottingham's Sherwood Forest, was improved and tinkered with over the centuries. It became more flexible as the requirements of breeches and hose called for embroidery and decoration for the wealthier male leg, but essentially the parson's invention was used in one form or another until the timid advent of steam-powered machines in the mid-1840s. The range of goods these knitting machines could make extended eventually to gloves and mittens, socks, pantaloons, braces, cravats, shirts and drawers, vests and shawls, jackets and under-waistcoats, nightcaps, knitted caps and many varieties of fancy hosiery.

In Leicestershire mainly worsted hose was knitted, just as Derbyshire specialised in silk and Nottinghamshire at first in cotton hose, until its famous lacemaking came to predominate. Local sheep provided the wool, and by the 1850s, the skins for the boot and shoe industry of Leicester, the trade of my great-grandfather. By 1800, what had been a rural occupation had created a middle class of hosiers in the knitting towns. Master hosiers, worsted manufacturers, merchants or wholesalers owned the yarn, the machines, the warehouses and workshops. They employed most of the populace of the county as 'framework knitters, spinners, bobbiners, sinker-makers, needle makers, woolcombers, dyers, framesmiths, combmakers, winders, sizers, seamers'. There were setters-up, pieceners, menders, embroiderers – or cheveners as they were called – for the decoration they gave to the stockings and half-hose. The lovely names of these forgotten skills faded too, with the coming of machines.

Only Charles Dickens could adequately describe the conditions of those who worked in the framework knitting trade in the early nineteenth century. Unfortunately he did not apply his genius to it. It lacks the attention paid for so long to Lancashire lasses and Yorkshire lads of mill and factory, perhaps because at its worst, the poverty of the stockingers beggared belief. Villagers would walk to the nearest large town on a Monday morning – for the framework knitters of Thurmaston it was to Leicester – to collect the yarn from the masters, and would bring back the finished goods on the following Saturday. The process of settling up, the checking and weighing and final payment, could take all day. On Monday they walked back again to collect the following week's yarn, and on it went. These laborious procedures gave the framework knitters a strange week. No knitting could be done on Saturdays, Sundays or Mondays. Saturdays and Mondays were occupied with plodding to and fro, Sundays often divided between a church or chapel and the tavern, with no one benefitting much from either, except perhaps the taverners.

As the Napoleonic Wars came to an end, an interminable trail of middlemen began to surface to deal with these antique practices. They took on a variety of tasks for masters and merchants – 'takers-in', 'putters out', 'undertakers', 'bagmen' or 'bag hosiers' – and by 1820 they controlled and manipulated to their own profit the lives of the domestic stockingers. Often they rented out frames, or became hosiers themselves. They saved time for the master and the knitter, but the cut for their services was, of course, taken from the knitters' portion. 'Stinting' was their preferred abuse: when orders were low they spread the work around, a few hours' work here, a few hours' work there, creating a vast pool of underemployed, half-starved men and families. And even with the arrival of the middlemen, the knitters still had to wait until late Monday, or even Tuesday, for the yarn to arrive.

Most attempts at change were half-hearted because the master hosiers benefitted from the old-style intense four-day knitting week. They could rent out more frames, spread the yarn between more and more knitters, pay each less, and have them begging for work. Those on high accused the knitters of laziness for 'Honouring Saint Monday', as that workless day was called, for the tradition of not working on Saturdays or Mondays lingered on. For the stockingers, who most likely had had nothing to eat on the preceding Thursday or Friday, those sacred days were spent using what cash they received to buy food, reclaim the clothes they had pawned when the money ran out the week before, or wasting some of it on a relieving visit to the inn or beerhouse.

Renting frames was good business for everyone except the knitters. Frame rent, which was deducted from the knitters' earnings, was usually extortionate, and had to be paid whether or not the knitter had work. Thus the owners of frames had little concern as to whether work was available or not – they still received their rent from the unemployed knitters. Sometimes frame owners charged a 'standing' fee for allowing the machine to be housed in the knitter's home. So profitable was this that it became a business in itself, with all and sundry investing in frames and renting them to knitters, or to hosiers who then rented them to bagmen who then rented them to the stockingers, a minestrone of financial nitpicking that left the knitters at the very bottom of an empty soup tureen.

Then there was the practice of 'trucking', by which stockingers were forced to accept their wages in goods, such as potatoes or bread, often at inflated prices, rather than in the hard cash they had earned. Though Parliament abolished the practice in 1831, the stockingers' rage continued as the law was ignored. Sometimes the middleman or hosier supplying the knitter with work owned the shop that 'trucked' such goods. William Smith, who employed over a hundred stockingers in Thurmaston, was an arch exponent of this system. His grocery shop was attached to his workshop, and there he doled out potatoes or tobacco instead of money. Deducting expensive food from their weekly earnings meant that some knitters saw never a shilling.

Another trick was to supply the knitters with damp yarn, which weighed more, but produced less. Some fabric inevitably went to waste: the knitters had to pay for it. Owners were meant to maintain their machines; knitters often could not afford to wait for them to do so. Retaliation by stockingers took the form of pilfering yarn or stealing finished goods, making socks and stockings on the side, petitioning and agitating. They were known as 'most expert poachers', snaring hares, stealing sheep, filching mushrooms in season, any vegetable or fruit unobserved by its owner, any animal that wasn't tethered.

After 1815, new problems arose. The wars had offered constant employment, but also high taxes, and increased prices and rents. Depression followed the end of war, and for the stockingers it continued with only rare periods of respite until the 1850s. With the war, fashions had changed. Fancy hose, knitted pantaloons and 'inexpressibles' – those tight-fitting trousers designed to present every portion of the male sexual organ – fell out of favour. Imitating the sans-culottes of the French Revolution and the Prussian military uniform, ankle-length trousers replaced such garments, and the exquisitely embroidered or striped stockings and smooth knee breeches of the Georgian era. Trousers required only half-hose or socks. Women took to wearing boots and longer dresses, and simpler requirements replaced the fine 'fancy work' of the Leicestershire framework knitters, the branch of the trade that had been the best paid.

With the end of war competition from Europe increased. Even as wages and the amount of available work fell in the first half of the nineteenth century, the rent for the machines still had to be paid. Army and navy requirements had provided considerable work during the wars, now it fell to nothing. Soldiers returning from the war swelled the numbers looking for work, and thus the number of unemployed. There is a sense in which both owner and knitter were hostile to any change to the domestic system: the stockinger and his family led an independent life within their home, while the merchants made money from it all, well removed by middlemen from the disagreeable aspects of supervision.

Still further calamities were to strike the domestic frame-workers. Their stocking frames could produce only a flat piece of material of varying widths. In the pursuit of increased production, alterations and improvements were made to the knitting machine. It became wider, more adaptable, capable of knitting more than just one stocking piece.

Spinning mills became common in the early nineteenth century and small-scale employers set up workshops to house the larger frame, which could not fit into a knitter's cottage.

From the wider piece of fabric produced by the new frames, the curse of the domestic framework knitter – 'cut-ups' or 'spurious articles', as they were known – could be made. Traditionally, fashioned hose had been knitted to fit the shape of a leg. The stockings produced from the wider woven cloth were cut up with scissors and sewn. Cut-ups were cheaper to manufacture, cheaper to buy, and the wider frames could produce far more of them. They could also turn out gloves, socks, drawers and much else. Worse for the traditional stockingers, little skill was required to operate the new machines, and little skill meant little pay.

The stockingers' cries of hatred for nasty cut-ups, and their laments for the loss of their old ways, reached the heavens. This first intimation of mass-market procedures meant an end to the way of life of framework knitters such as Samuel Allen. At the same time the old traditions of apprentice and journeyman fell out of usage, as untrained knitters took their places. Women workers fared better. They were paid less, and could seam cut-ups and adapt their spinning, stitching and embroidery skills to the mechanised new world that was coming. In London, larger warehouses began to appear, using the canals and the new railways to transport their merchandise. They bought in bulk at the lowest prices from the East Midlands hosiers, further depressing the rates paid to the knitters at the bottom of the pile. The London warehouses soon moved to the top of the pyramid, making their owners 'millionaires in both the first and second generations'.

It must not be thought for one moment that persons of the class of the Allen family took to this altered life without a struggle. Framework knitting was an independent way of life, albeit with curious procedures and traditions peculiar to itself. In 1788, when attempts were made to introduce the spinning machine in Leicester, the framework knitter John Allen was indicted for riotous assembly after attempting to incite a riot by carrying around a spinning wheel bedecked with ribbons – he was acquitted. He was not the only curmudgeonly eighteenth-century stockinger: hostility to any machine that might produce more but employ them less began well before the nineteenth century. The knitters fought constantly for fixed-price agreements for their work. In truth, however, all they had to defend their way of life were their fists and the implements they could wield. By 1811, a bad harvest, the loss of the American market and high prices caused by the war had already heralded the end of the good years. In that year, in Nottingham, destitution gave rise to the Luddites, so named after a mythical Captain or General 'Ned Ludd', purportedly headquartered in Sherwood Forest, though the word is actually Leicestershire dialect for machine-breaker.

Wages were less than they had been a hundred years earlier. Desperation, allied with a rapid rise in the price of wheat, formed gangs of men who set out to destroy the new wide-frame machines, the workshops that sprang up to house them, and the cut-ups they produced. The riots grew, spreading to nearby Derbyshire and Leicestershire, and north to Lancashire and Yorkshire. Their fury extended further than mere machine breaking; men were hanged or transported for robbery, larceny, assault, extortion, and, most particularly, and understandably, for rioting for food.

By the Framework Knitters
A Declaration

Whereas by the charter granted by our late sovereign Lord Charles II by the Grace of God King of Great Britain France and Ireland, the framework knitters are empowered to break and destroy all frames and engines that fabricate articles in a fraudulent and deceitful manner and to destroy all framework knitters' goods whatsoever that are so made and whereas a number of deceitful unprincipled and intriguing persons did attain an Act to be passed in the 28th year of our present sovereign Lord George III whereby it was enacted that persons entering by force into any house shop or place to break or destroy frames should be adjudged guilty of felony and as we are fully convinced that such Act was obtained in the most fraudulent interested and electioneering manner and that the honourable the

Parliament of Great Britain was deceived as to the motives and intentions of the persons who obtained such Act we therefore the framework knitters do hereby declare the aforesaid Act to be null and void to all intents and purposes whatsoever as by the passing of this Act villainous and imposing persons are enabled to make fraudulent and deceitful manufactures to the discredit and utter ruin of our trade. And whereas we declare that the aforementioned Charter is as much in force as though no such Act had been passed . . . And we do hereby declare to all hosiers lace manufacturers and proprietors of frames that we will break and destroy all manner of frames whatsoever that make the following spurious articles and all frames whatsoever that do not pay the regular prices heretofore agreed to [by] the masters and workmen – All print net frames making single press and frames not working by the rack and rent and not paying the price regulated in 1810: warp frames working single yarn or two coarse hole – not working by the rack, not paying the rent and prices regulated in 1809 – whereas all plain silk frames not making work according to the gage-frames not marking the work according to quality, whereas all frames of whatsoever description the work-men of whom are not paid in the current coin of the realm will invariably be destroyed . . .

Given under my hand this first day of January 1812.

God protect the Trade.

Ned Lud's Office

Sherwood Forest

The war with the French did not prevent the government from savage reprisals. Twelve thousand troops were sent into the Luddite areas, and breaking frames was made a capital offence. Six Luddites were convicted and hanged in Leicester in 1817: in all 1,000 frames were broken, seventeen men were put to death and twenty-five transported. In 1812, before the bill was passed, Lord Byron, whose ancestral home was in Nottinghamshire, made a passionate defence of the frame breakers in his maiden speech to the House of Lords. He described

circumstances of the most unparalleled distress . . . these men
never destroyed their looms until they were become useless, worse
than useless . . . a starving population . . . famished into guilt . . .
I have been in the most distressed provinces in Turkey; but never
under the most despotic governments of an infidel country did
I behold such squalid wretchedness as I have seen since my return
in the very heart of a Christian country.

When the prime minister, Spencer Perceval, was assassinated in
May 1812 there were 'great rejoicings on this melancholy event in both
Leicestershire and Nottinghamshire, the Bells were set ringing in
several towns in both counties'.

The Luddites were unfortunate, because the excesses of the later
years of the French Revolution quite put to an end to any British parliamentary belief there might have been in political or social reform,
unsurprising perhaps in a country whose wealth and increasing
empire had depended for so long on the slave trade. Slavery was
finally abolished throughout the British Empire in 1833, but the drive
for domestic and political reform faltered decades before that, as the
Members of Parliament, and the lucky few whom they represented,
dominated by fear of any repetition of the French experience on their
own soil, used authoritarian tactics and laws to suppress French
notions of liberty or rebellion in the British Isles.

In Sary's early years, all families such as hers suffered from the
rise in food prices caused by the war. After its end, a combination of
useless rebellion and the struggle for subsistence dominated the lives
of the poor as, to pay off the debt generated by the war, the government placed heavy duties on beer, soap, tea, sugar and tobacco.
Income tax was abolished at the same time, of great benefit to some,
but of no use at all to the poor. A familiar pattern, repeated today.

Luddites struck in Loughborough, only a few miles from Leicester, in 1816, a year with an excessively bad harvest which led to food
riots throughout the country. The Combination Acts of 1799 and 1816
had prohibited workers from forming unions, associations or taking
strike action. These Acts were repealed in 1824, but the Combinations
of Workmen Act of the following year exerted much the same restraint.
To finagle the laws, in many hosiery villages they formed sick clubs,

clothing clubs and quasi trade-union 'friendly societies', at meetings of
which they read the work of the radical journalist William Cobbett,
and from which they constantly petitioned Parliament. Women's
friendly societies fared better than men's, as women were not, in general, paid any attention by the state or by local government, unless
their wombs or genitals were involved. Agitation, legal or not, continued, as did death sentences and transportation. But the domestic
and scattered nature of home framework knitting often meant that
workers were unwilling to join a union, or to strike and lose what precious work they had. A cussed lot, their outrage sometimes got the
better of them.

This post-war period was a time of swaggering boom, elegance
and luxury for the people of consequence at the top of the British
pyramid. For those not so positioned, all through these years the
price of bread was a festering sore. During the war, when corn could
not be imported, more British wheat was farmed. At the end of the
war, wealthy landowners and farmers wanted to protect their bailiwick, and so in 1815 Parliament introduced the first Corn Law on
their behalf.

The Corn Laws were fought tooth and nail throughout the country.
In 1838 Richard Cobden and John Bright harnessed the national rage to
form the Anti-Corn Law League, which struggled on behalf of the
underfed and starving throughout the following decades, but statutes
to enforce the Corn Laws continued until 1846. They kept the price of
grain high, prevented cheap foreign imports, and brought comfort and
security to the aristocracy, large landowners and those who did not live
on bread alone. From the day the first of the Corn Laws was passed,
when angry crowds gathered outside the Houses of Parliament, to the
time the last of them was repealed, they were as hated as the poll tax
would be for Margaret Thatcher in Britain in 1990.

Matters worsened particularly in 1819, when there was a strike
after knitters' wages fell by a third, but to little end. Bread and potatoes
were the staple food of the poor, tea the staple drink, and beer if possible; meat was a treat worth risking seven years' transportation for
poaching, and rarely obtained by any other way. On 16 August 1819,
over a hundred miles to the north of Leicester, more than 60,000
men, women and children gathered in St Peter's Field, Manchester, to

demand parliamentary reform and to protest against the high price of bread and the Corn Laws. A cavalry charge of local militia sabred eleven of them to death. A further seven died, and 600 or more were wounded, many severely. This was the Peterloo Massacre which became instantly notorious as popular outrage spread throughout the country.

The Peterloo Massacre was the precursor of the unrest that was to mark the first half of the nineteenth century in Sary's England. Two months later, the government's reaction to it, and the rumble of fury heard throughout the country, led Parliament to pass six Acts intended to deter any further political agitation: 'A conspiracy existed for the subversion of the constitution in church and state, and the rights of property.' The 'measures designed to meet this evil' ushered in more unrest in the 1820s as forbidding blasphemy, sedition, misdemeanours, and taxing newspapers did nothing to fill empty stomachs, or clear the ordure from the streets.

2

Reaping

A sardonic view of the English workhouse after 1834

ANY STOCKINGERS CONTINUED TO work at home in their traditional ways throughout the early decades of the nineteenth century, their refusal to march with the industrial times always a major cause of complaint from those on high. These knitters who worked on the narrow hand frame, producing only one piece of work at a time, descended into pitiable poverty as year by year workshops, factories, truck-masters and middlemen destroyed their way of life. So it was for Samuel Allen of Thurmaston. When Sary came to the village in 1809, Samuel had at his service his children Ann and Thomas, at seven and five well into winding. By 1815 Henry, Samuel Jr and John had come along, Jane was eight and Sary seven. If money was to be made from his trade, their father had the hands to help him. But the old ways all but disappeared as his family grew. Thurmaston, in which Sary spent the first thirty-five years of her life, changed from an open rural hamlet with farms and cottages, shepherds and labourers, a church and a modest lord of the manor, into an industrial village in which two out of every three men were knitters, working for bag hosiers or masters.

William Cobbett best described the worst of these stockingers' dwellings when his *Rural Rides* took him to Leicestershire in the 1820s.

> look at the miserable sheds in which the labourers reside! Look
> at these hovels, made of mud and of straw; bits of glass, or of old
> off-cast windows, without frames or hinges, frequently, but merely
> stuck in the mud wall. Enter them, and look at the bits of chairs
> or stools; the wretched boards tacked together to serve for a table;
> the floor of pebble, broken brick, or of the bare ground; look at
> the thing called a bed; and survey the rags on the backs of the
> wretched inhabitants; and then wonder . . .

It is true that Cobbett luxuriated in celebrating the habits of an imaginary Merrie England of yesteryear, but in the handloom weavers of Leicestershire he found poverty that required no romantic exaggeration. One of the ways the village stockingers had subsisted was by keeping a cow and a pig and growing the odd vegetable, apple or plum from a piece of land rented from a farmer or landowner. Thurmaston 'had been a typical Leicestershire village with all its farmhouses and cottages clustered together and surrounded by huge open fields until the enclosures of 1763'. Samuel Allen came from this old way of life in a village cottage, in which framework knitting, particularly of quality fancy goods, had provided an adequate living for a journeyman knitter. But by the time Sary was born, to a great degree survival depended on whether or not a knitter still had access to an allotment. Without it, few fruits or vegetables could be added to a diet

of gruel, coarse bread, potatoes and tea. Salt and sugar were hoped
for. When nothing was left after buying coal and candles, bread and
treacle were a staple.

There were some fine houses in the village: the Manor House,
home of the Allens, squires of Thurmaston; the Elms; the Old Hall
nearer to the river, with lovely gardens and orchards; Thurmaston
Hall at the other end of the village; Home Farm; and the fine old
Georgian farmhouse called the Grange. But for most, their rented
cottages housed as many as ten or twelve human beings, all sleeping in
one or two rooms. The old cottages were often timbered farmhouses,
divided up after the enclosures so that many families could live in
them. These might be thatched and comparatively roomy, but tumble-
down with age.

The new homes hastily put up by speculative builders for the rural
incomers who poured into the early industrial villages and towns
were meaner altogether: cheap brick cottages constructed around
small communal yards replacing orchards and gardens, front door
opening directly onto the street, back door opening onto the yard
with its single pump, which froze in winter. Yards were often inches
deep in sewage, cesspools too near dwellings; later, earth closets were
dug too close to wells. Overcrowded cottages, hovels, and contaminated water brought death: puerperal fever, consumption, cholera,
typhoid, diarrhoea, smallpox. In time the back doors opening on to
these yards became the entries to small workshops. Such cottages
survived, lived in, with cold water from a single tap, no electricity or
gas and a shared privy, until the 1950s.

In 1814, Samuel, Dorothy and their six children were living in a
household of thirteen people. Knitters often shared a house with
another family, or took lodgers or a pauper child apprentice – the latter paid for by the parish – into their already crowded households. In
December 1815 the tenure of 'three capital Messuages or Tenements'
with yards and precious gardens adjoining, inhabited by five families,
one of whom was Samuel's, was put up for sale by its owners. The
post-Napoleonic age was just beginning in England, and for its
labouring poor, the very worst decades of the Industrial Revolution.

For most of Sary's years in Thurmaston the Allens lived in Garden Street, facing the tombstones at the rear of St Michael and All

Angels and the new Primitive Methodist Chapel. Sary, her ten half-siblings and their parents lived in a cottage hazy with wool dust. The smell of human bodies and rank tallow candles wafted over the drone of the winding machine and the endless clackety-clack rattle of the frame. Passing through Thurmaston, Cobbett complained: 'the sound of the frame reminds you of the incessant toil, and the squalid appearance of the operatives show that they do not fatten by the system that propels it'. Physically, it is clear that the domestic stockingers and their families were a wretched bunch, the damage inflicted on their lungs handed on to hundreds of descendants, many of them also particularly deaf in the left ear.

In Thurmaston, all the Allen children were put to different aspects of hand-frame work. The children wound the yarn onto the bobbins, Dorothy and the older girls seamed and finished the stockings. Hose and stockings, fancy or plain, were the business of the village. By the time Sary left to marry and live in Leicester, Thurmaston produced only children's socks and gloves, the embroidered titivations of earlier times quite gone as the inventions of the 1840s adapted the home frame to increased production. Brewing and malting were also traditional trades in Leicestershire, and it is a measure of the tedium and boredom such industry evoked that pubs and beerhouses were so ubiquitous in the village. As was god, battling it out with landlords to raise the spirits, save the souls, and grasp the pennies of the Thurmaston poor.

Opposite the church was the thatched Black Horse, and there were many others – the White Hart, the Harrow, the Old Plough, the Unicorn and Star, besides beerhouses such as the Three Horses and the Generous Briton. The Beerhouse Act of 1830 and its later amendments, introduced to discourage ruination by drinking gin, enabled ratepayers and thus inn- and beerhouse-keepers to brew their own beer, with lethal results. By 1794 Leicester Navigation Canal had been completed and Thurmaston was one of the ten locks along its Loughborough Branch. There were brickworks, potteries and gravel pits in Thurmaston, as well as the bustle of Thurmaston Lock, with its three wharves and attendant pub, the Boat Inn. Stockingers needed little tempting: they were notorious for excessive bouts of drinking whenever a spare farthing or hour presented itself. But the eternal clatter of

the framework machines dominated all else by the time Sary was put
to work for her stepfather.

Until 1841 the Church of St Michael and All Angels was a chapelry
only, and there was no vicarage until 1838, but there had been a Wesleyan chapel in Thurmaston since 1792. From the mid-eighteenth
century Leicestershire had been a hothouse of Nonconformity, religion at that time occupying the British to a degree unimaginable
today – its obsessions now transferred to sport in general and football
in particular. By the nineteenth century there were a multitude of dissenting congregations in Leicestershire, ranging from Moravians, who
preached the joys of 'stillness', through many varieties of Methodism
(Wesleyan and Primitive), Baptists and Anabaptists, Independents
and Congregationalists, Presbyterians and Quakers. Primitive Methodists arrived in Thurmaston in 1833 to compete with the earlier
Wesleyan chapel in trying to attract the poor.

The marriage register of a Leicestershire village for the years
1837–50 revealed that only one knitter in three could sign their name,
fewer for women of the family. Samuel Allen marked his presence on
this earth with an 'X', as did his children, and as had his father and
grandfather before him. A National School was opened in Thurmaston in 1844, far too late for Sary – not that this mattered, as the
children of framework knitters could attend only rarely as they were
already at work. The thriving Wesleyan chapel established a Sunday
school in 1810, and held a children's writing class on Monday evenings, but it was probably the Sunday-morning writing class held by
the Primitive Methodists, so near the Allen cottage, at which Sary
learned to write. The shaky lower-case signature – 'sary lacey' – to be
found years later on her marriage certificate, was as much as she ever
achieved.

God, generally speaking, was held in little regard by members of
Sary's class. But each religion offered goods and services that eased
the life of the ungodly. Sary's world was ruled by squire, Justice of
the Peace, magistrate and parson. The curate at St Michael and All
Angels conducted a service once a week, and was occasionally on
hand to baptise children and ensure they had some access to parish
relief. Relief! How could they have survived without it? The groans
of those forced to give to those without, appear to have increased

over the centuries, the misery of those on the receiving end remaining, alas, much the same.

> Relief is continually given to able-bodied men without their
> being set to work; and the knowledge which the paupers have
> that the magistrates will order them relief, makes hundreds apply
> who would otherwise make a shift to provide for themselves . . .
> A workman has no incentive to work . . . he can do much better
> for himself by going to the magistrates.

The poor survived on strange-sounding potions – Bett's Patent Brandy, Dr Stone's Tasteless Compound Herbal Solution, Mr Howard's Patent White Succedaneum for decayed teeth – and a variety of charities.

Meanwhile the Poor Laws were constantly being tweaked as the number of paupers created by the Industrial Revolution grew like bindweed. Until the New Poor Law came into force in 1834, responsibility for the relief of the poor was based on each parish, or a combination of neighbouring parishes, administered by vestrymen or Justices of the Peace who appointed overseers or guardians, and later clergymen, men mostly at war with each other as to who constituted the worthy and industrious as distinct from the feckless poor. The Act of Settlement of 1662 had laid down the rules which required that paupers or those seeking relief must apply to the parish of their birth for assistance, unless they could present a certificate signed by a Poor Law guardian or parish overseer, which promised reimbursement from their birth parish should they become dependent elsewhere. Parson and squire supervised each town and village: a beady eye was kept on new arrivals lest they become a burden on the parish. For a pauper stockinger looking for work, travelling to find it was a hard choice to make.

Relief was given according to the price of bread and the size of the family, an excellent thing for Samuel and Dorothy Allen, less so for those who paid the Poor Rate, the annual levy imposed on householders and farm owners. Financed by this, the parish supplemented inadequate wages for large families, found work for destitute adults and apprenticeships for destitute children. Its adjuncts were poorhouses for orphans, the aged and infirm, and felicitously named

Houses of Industry – workhouses – supplying food, lodging and
other assistance in the form of money, food or clothes. Before 1834,
the near certainty of receiving relief was an assumption upon which
the poor based their lives.

It seems likely that the number of children in the family who
could work, and parish relief granted to households with four or more
children, kept the Allens out of Thurmaston's House of Industry,
gloomily placed near their cottage in Garden Street. In Leicestershire,
the parish paid some hosiers to keep men in work and thus 'off the
parish'. Unemployed knitters had no choice but to accept this minimal parish wage, the alternative being the House of Industry. Their
cheap labour meant cheaper products, thus other hosiers and knitters
had to lower their wages to compete. And so on it went. Who should
pay for the poor, the old, the sick, the unemployed? The abuse of
benefits had 'a pernicious effect on the morals and comfort of the
lower orders'. The cry of centuries. This plaint and the habit of putting the unemployed and impoverished to useful work – for example
'reducing hills on roads' – at rock bottom and decreasing wages, is as
British an institution as the monarchy.

The descent of the majority of stockingers into pauperism was
matched by the rising fury of the rate-paying classes as year after
year the population, and the Poor Rate they had to pay, rose alarm-
ingly. If relief was begrudged, as was so often the case, the needy
poached and stole, fought and lied. History in the form of hundreds
of newspaper reports of county sessions indicates that when caught,
such offenders could be wonderfully inventive liars and fabricators,
telling stories of dead birds found on the road, or handkerchiefs
which 'came their way'.

In one county session at Leicester Castle on 28 April 1827, a parade
of men, women and youths were tried for stealing a procession of
objects: a watch, ten pounds of hay, a saddle and bridle, two strikes
and a half of barley, a barrel, three pounds of clover, three strikes of
potatoes, a key, cheese, two loaves and forty-four yards of ribbon.
Assaults with a bobbin, with mud, with potatoes, with fists – flurries
of fists – were typical. A sense of stubborn refusal to accept their lot
rises up from these old newspaper accounts, as can be seen from the
row between Mary Flint, governess of the House of Industry in

Sapcote, sixteen miles from Thurmaston, with one of her inmates, Elizabeth Holmes, who told the court that

> She did not say that if Mrs Flint was there, she would throw the porridge in her face; and that if she were the cook, she would poison her . . .she did not create a riot in the house, and call the other inmates a set of poor devils . . .nor did she say that if she had a gun, she would shoot Mrs Flint.

Elizabeth Holmes, despite her vivid way with words, was indicted for perjury.

Sary was otherwise occupied in April 1827. She was pregnant with her first child. Samuel Allen's brood of children had grown to ten, providing him with relief if needed, but which forced Sary, Ann, Thomas, Jane, Henry, Samuel, John, William, Mary Ann and Benjamin to share whatever bed was available. John Thurman of the Leicestershire village of Shepshed gave evidence to the 1845 Royal Commission on Framework Knitting. He had a wife and seven children, and he describes what must have been the conditions of life of the Allen family:

> The whole nine of us lie in two beds, and for those two beds we have one blanket for both . . . Never a week goes by but I have to put my wife to bed for want of food . . . When I have got my little on a Saturday, I pay every farthing I can, as far as it will go, and then when Monday morning comes I have not got 6d to buy a loaf with and there is nothing in the house. Then whatever few garments we have about us we take them and pledge them into the [pawn] shop to get a bit of bread to go on with during the week . . . Sometimes it lasts till Thursday dinner time . . . and then we have to go without until Saturday when we get our things again.

Older stockingers went to bed when darkness fell, to save on candles, but there is much evidence that the young did nothing of the kind. These were troubled times in the lanes and back alleys of Thurmaston. Poaching and theft were regular activities, but young men were also tried constantly for riot and assault, the judges threatening that 'if these disturbances at Thurmaston were not abated, the Court would inflict a most severe punishment upon all future offenders'. Understandably, in the years she lived in Thurmaston, Sary was no better than she could bear to be, and what is known about her is measured by her womb, and by whatever official documents survive to report her use of it. One of many reasons offered for the exceptional increase in population which produced so much cheap labour for industry in the nineteenth century was that the age of marriage fell significantly, and the number of illegitimate births did the opposite.

Sary had the first of her three children when she was nineteen. Her firstborn was registered as 'Allin, Eliza, ill/e* Dr. of Sarah Lacey' on 12 August 1827, a few months after her mother Dorothy had given birth to her youngest child, Benjamin. The law required that the putative father should support his illegitimate child; he could be imprisoned if he refused to do so. The parish would have insisted that Sary reveal the name of her baby's father, then pursue him by way of his parish. If no father made himself known, the parish provided relief for mother and child, in which case Sary would have received 1s 6d from the magistrates, most probably accompanied by a lecture. Too much has been written about the fate of bastard children born into poverty in the nineteenth century for it to be any surprise that after Eliza's birth, nothing was heard of her again until Sary recorded her three children in 1868, and then only obliquely. Her report – 'Three children, two living, one dead' – tells the story.

The births of Eliza and Benjamin added to the already crowded Allen cottage. This seems to have caused some kind of explosion in the family. When Eliza was born, Jane married and left home, and Ann and Thomas swiftly followed. Also in 1827, the framework knitters of Leicester addressed a petition – a 'Memorial' as it was called – to the Privy Council for Trade in Whitehall, listing their grievances and describing how for many years they had

> endured, with the greatest patience, the most intense sufferings . . .
> Sixteen hours a day many are compelled to labour, with only a
> morsel of bread to support them through the day, and then go to

* Illegitimate, delivered of

bed weary, hungry, and almost supperless, destitute of necessities to cover them.

They received the following cheering reply from Whitehall:

I am directed by their Lordships to inform you, that they are extremely sorry to learn that the memorialists are suffering so greatly; and that their Lordships regret very much that it is not in their power to point out a remedy, nor to comply with the request conveyed in their memorial.

In 1830 there was revolution in Paris and Belgium, and uprisings in Poland and Switzerland. In England 'Captain Swing' emulated General Ned Ludd as the mythical leader of revolt after the bad harvest and the bitter winter of 1829–30, which exhausted the Poor Rate coffers throughout the land. In 1831 the Swing Riots spread from Sussex and Kent to Gloucestershire and Hereford, and then extended north through the Midlands and beyond, farm labourers rising up to break machines and burn hayricks. The British government, terrified once again of wafts of revolution from the Continent, exacted revenge on its rebellious paupers. Nineteen were executed, 600 imprisoned, and 481 transported to Australia.

Throughout the 1830s, campaigning for new laws to prevent the abuses of labour in English industries made stuttering headway. Unions being banned, the sock makers of Thurmaston formed a 'Meeting' of sock operatives, at which a Mr Dorman addressed the villagers in semi-religious terms about the villainy of the slavery under which they laboured. Such activities were dangerous. The Factories Act 1833 addressed the abuse of children, but all such Acts, and the many that would follow in the 1840s and 50s attempting to limit child labour and to improve the lives of the labouring poor, were of no use to families like the Allens, who worked at home.

Years of public pressure, culminating in riots throughout the country when it was rejected by the House of Lords in 1831, finally forced the passing of the 1832 Reform Act, called Great but considered so only by the Whigs and Tories who issued it. For the first time, the franchise was extended to inhabitants of the new centres of industrial power – Birmingham, Bradford, Leeds and Manchester. But still only one adult male in seven had the vote, corruption remained rife, rotten boroughs and constituency imbalances remained. The strength of Leicestershire's Nonconformity and the harrowing circumstances of most of its inhabitants made the county a stronghold of dissent and radicalism. Whigs imprisoned, transported and starved the poor just as Tories did. 'I make no difference between Whigs and Tories,' declared the Irish reformer Feargus O'Connor. 'Put them in a bag and shake them, and see which would come out first.'

In the grim year of 1831 Samuel Allen's eldest son Thomas began a family of seven children. His first daughter Elizabeth died in infancy, replaced by another in the following year. Dorothy and Samuel's youngest child Benjamin died in the cholera epidemic of that year, at the age of four. It may well be that it was in this epidemic that Sary's daughter Eliza too died; her death was not recorded. When cholera came, connections were made between the disease and the overflowing cesspits, the 'filth' as it was euphemistically named, in the yards and streets of the poor. Once the epidemic passed it was forgotten, but the excrement which was part of the sight and smell of so many daily lives did not go away.

Between 1814 and 1844 wages for the stockingers fell by forty per cent: it was the period of 'half work and full charges', or no work, full charges and then the workhouse, or last farthings spent in the beerhouse for solace. The Allens were surrounded by the pubs and inns of Thurmaston, and there is a whiff of alcohol in the account of Sary's arrest in June 1833, when she, her half-brother Samuel and three others were tried for riotous assembly and breaking the peace. They were found guilty but not transported, though other Leicester citizens were: David Bland, eighteen, a servant in Leicester, received a ten-year sentence for breaking stocking frames, and was sent to Van Diemen's Land (now Tasmania) in 1834; John Grimes, nineteen, a labourer, got seven years for machine breaking in 1837 and was sent to New South Wales; two brothers, John and Samuel Morris, were transported for life to New South Wales in 1840 for damaging a steam engine. There were many, both men and women, before and after them.

The last lines of Shelley's great political poem 'The Masque of Anarchy', written after the Peterloo Massacre of 1819 but not published until 1832, were to be used almost as a hymn in the centuries to come:

> Rise, like lions after slumber
> In unvanquishable number!
> Shake your chains to earth like dew
> Which in sleep had fallen on you:
> Ye are many – they are few!

The many of Leicester and Thurmaston did arise. Groups under names such as the 'Framework Knitters Friendly and Relief Society of the Town and County of Leicester' had struggled since 1819 in an endless battle to earn the stockingers a living wage. The knitters fought by way of friendly societies, trade societies and cooperatives; they tried negotiation, sometimes they dared to strike. Neighbourhood support, credit from local shopkeepers, family networks and charities kept many a pauper family alive. But hosiers remained hostile to any kind of 'union' activity. In 1825 and 1826, stockingers were reduced to starvation wages, with results which were 'beyond the power of language to express'. Constantly recurring years of depression cemented the stockingers' unwillingness to take action, and their willingness to accept whatever they could get. Matters became worse when the New Poor Law Amendment Act of 1834 seamlessly led to two decades of even more extreme suffering, with 1838–43 and 1847–8 being perhaps the worst years.

A parade of political theorists, economists and philosophers prepared the ground for the New Poor Law of 1834. Adam Smith in his *Wealth of Nations*, who viewed the old Poor Law as obstructive to natural laws of supply and demand, and Thomas Carlyle and William Cobbett, who argued for political emancipation, confronted the harsher views of Edmund Burke and economist Thomas Malthus, the mixed blessing of the radical sage Jeremy Bentham, and the laissez-faire theories of the economist David Ricardo. All influenced the new law. Malthus believed that poor relief encouraged large families, improvidence and idleness, and that its withdrawal would lead to the survival of the fittest, thus reducing the numbers of the unemployed poor, who would be forced to find work to survive. He made no provision in his theories for the Leicester-shire stockingers, for whom so little work was to be had. Cobbett, on the other hand, had, in his *Political Register*, urged the rural and manufacturing poor to fight, and not 'lie down like dogs and die with hunger' – for which support he was tried for seditious libel though later acquitted.

The utilitarian philosopher Jeremy Bentham concurred with Malthus that public assistance did the destitute no good at all, and harmed those ratepayers who were industrious enough to be obliged to provide money for it. His scheme for 'Pauper Management' envisaged a body of workhouses which would take in thousands of destitute people, who would be fed minimally and worked hard. Bentham's moral insistence on procuring 'the greatest happiness to the greatest number of people' enabled him to be anti-slavery abroad, but dismissive of it at home. Eleven million slaves were transported from Africa by European countries; Portugal was responsible for most – 4.65 million. Britain comes next in this grim league table, transporting 2.6 million human beings in 12,000 voyages, leaving all other European competitors far behind. British merchants and shipowners eclipsed all competitors in the seventeenth and eighteenth centuries, controlling over forty per cent of the trade, which was blessed from above for 'the colonial church owned slaves and supported slavery'. When the Slavery Abolition Act of 1833 came into force in August 1834, it provided a fund of £20 million (approximately £2.6 billion today) for slave owners as compensation for their loss of human labour. This was claimed by 46,000 British slave owners, in Britain and throughout the empire.

In that same month, royal assent was given to the New Poor Law Act. Its influence lives on: the belief that denial of relief encourages self-respect and independence in the poor has been a recurring theme of British life. Under this new Poor Law – 'that curse and disgrace to humanity' – paupers were to be helped only in exceptional circumstances.

> All relief whatever to able-bodied persons or to their families
> otherwise than in well-regulated workhouses . . . shall be declared
> unlawful . . . and all relief afforded in respect of children under
> the age of 16 shall be considered as afforded to their parents.

Groups of parishes were formed into 600 'Poor Law Unions'. Outdoor relief, which had provided food, clothing or money to paupers outside the workhouse, was abolished, and assistance was provided only within the workhouse, except for cases of extreme need, to be authorised by medical officers. The union workhouse was directed by a board of guardians elected by local ratepayers – from municipal councillors, politicians, clergymen and the like – with paid officials to oversee the necessary misery. To ensure no further reward for idleness, the workhouses were designed to cause so much suffering that their inmates would do anything to avoid them. This was achieved. Illegitimate children were in future to be the concern of their mothers only; inside the workhouse husbands and wives were separated, children removed from their parents.

From the age of seven all paupers in the workhouse were put to work. The poor were given clothes and food in exchange for several hours of manual labour each day. There was a nasty uniform, rules were strict, and the diet of bread, watery soup, in fact watery everything, added to all the other miseries. The inmates' fitness for work

THE MODEL UNION WORKHOUSE.

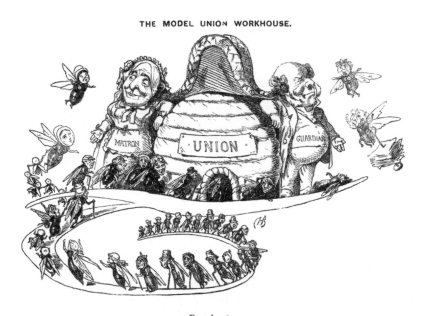

Punch, 1841

was assessed by physical tests such as breaking stones, grinding corn or picking oakum (unravelling bits of old rope, strand by strand).

Stockingers were never fit men and women and they could not afford to damage their hands in such work. Under the old Poor Law they had survived on temporary parish relief, and for them and their families the new 'Bastilles', as they called them, were a particular abomination. The new arrangements came into effect with, and contributed to, the onset of the 'Hungry '40s'. Much depended on the charitable hearts – or otherwise – of the new commissioners, as to the speed and severity of implementation of the new laws. In the case of the East Midlands, compassion of any kind was rarely apparent, and hatred of the Leicester Poor Law Union led to angry political agitation from the knitters. It also led the destitute of Leicester to devise a most inventive and professional manner of begging with which to persecute their betters, demonstrating that Dickens invented almost nothing in *Oliver Twist*.

3

Garnering

The demonstration at Copenhagen Fields, London, in protest against
the transportation of the Tolpuddle Martyrs, 21 April 1834

L EICESTER, AN ANCIENT MARKET town in the valley of the
Soar, grew from a population of 17,000 in 1800 to 68,000 in
1861. By 1843 it had handsome merchants' houses, and many
churches and houses of dissent – the Unitarians of the Chapel of the
Great Meeting, Particular Baptists and many more. It boasted a race-
course, a very popular cricket field, gas lighting, a Mechanics Institute,
a theatre, music in the New Hall and the Exchange rooms, a well-filled

jail and a much-dreaded Union Workhouse. And, of course, a surfeit of gin shops, taverns, inns, pubs and beerhouses. The main streets were paved; Leicester had a police force, a fire brigade, penny post and rumbustious newspapers.

Baptists and Independents were exceptionally plentiful in Leicester: Mrs Gaskell's Unitarians were the smallest in number, but the most influential. Primitive Methodists, Independent Methodists, Armenian Methodists, Wesleyans and Quakers made up the solid number of Nonconformists in the town. This formidable community and its long-fought sectarian quarrel with establishment Anglicans gave Leicester its radical temper, reflected in the three disputatious newspapers of the county: the *Leicester Journal*, upholder of aristocrat and Tory, the *Leicester Chronicle* and the *Leicester Mercury*, both of Whiggish and Liberal persuasion.

It is almost impossible today to understand the importance of religion to both the poor and the rich of Britain in the centuries that preceded our own. Or the brutalities bestowed by those favoured by the British class pyramid, despite their inundation in religious belief, on the people without power amongst whom they lived. For those on the lower strata of the British pyramid, the Great Reform Act of 1832 did nothing. From all these inequities and disillusions, and more, arose the Chartists, who became a mass political movement in full force from 1838 until the 1850s. The six demands of their People's Charter, proclaimed in May 1838, included votes for men over the age of twenty-one, secret ballots and other reforms.

The Chartists were not the rebels of earlier, more rural days: these were men of the new industrial towns and their weapons were words, supported by strikes, rallies and riots, marches and petitions. Leicester was home to many freethinkers and rebels of a general and diversified 'agin the government' persuasion, and at much the same time as the rise of the Chartists, the socialism of Robert Owen influenced the region. In 1839 an Owenite Social Institute was opened in Leicester, and Owen himself visited four times, preaching his message of a 'New Moral World' based on freethinking and co-operation, and hostility to organised Christianity. This inevitably led to the formation in 1842 of a Leicester Anti-Persecution Union, set up to defend those incarcerated for blasphemy and for questioning the established church.

The first petition the Chartists presented to Parliament in June 1839 was signed by nearly 1.3 million people (over 13,000 of them from Leicestershire), disillusioned by the false hopes raised by the Great Reform Act. The second petition of May 1842 was signed by over 3.3 million people – four times the number (men only) who could vote at that time. But these mass petitions never achieved the support of more than fifty MPs. Sary's early years in England saw few advances in the political sphere for the labouring poor, and none at all for women. The People's Charter demanded rights only for men, although women attended their meetings and fought alongside them. Also as usual, imprisonment and transportation remained the reward for active objection to the status quo, not only for Chartists, of whom over a hundred were transported to Australia, but also notably in the case of the Tolpuddle Martyrs in 1834. These six agricultural labourers formed a friendly society to fight local farmers who were grossly underpaying them. They were arrested, quickly tried under an obscure eighteenth-century Act forbidding unlawful oaths, and immediately shipped off to Sydney and Van Diemen's Land. The injustice of the proceedings that condemned them caused uproar throughout the country.

The early 1830s saw the establishment of the earliest trade unions, legal or not. Most prominent was Robert Owen's Grand National Consolidated Trades Union. Owen organised a demonstration in support of the Tolpuddle Martyrs on 21 April 1834, at which 100,000 people gathered in Copenhagen Fields, near King's Cross in London. Despite the presence of cavalry, dragoons, special constables and cannon, cheering spectators watched the demonstrators, banners flying, march to Whitehall to present their complaint, which, 'borne on the shoulders of twelve unionists, was taken to the office of the Home Secretary, Lord Melbourne. He hid behind his curtains and refused to accept the massive petition.' It was reported that 30,000 marched down Whitehall, although as so often today, the true number may well have been 100,000. A quarter of a million people had signed the petition to free the Tolpuddle Martyrs.

The Tolpuddle Martyrs were pardoned in 1836. After some delay they were given a free passage home. George Loveless, ploughman, Wesleyan preacher and Chartist, was the first to return. In March 1837, as he was on the high seas during his six-month journey back to

England, a small new settlement in the Port Phillip district, south of New South Wales penal colony, was named after Lord Melbourne, the British prime minister who had personally overseen the speed and harshness of the martyrs' trial and whose severity continued in his dealings with the Chartists. His family seat was in the knitting town of Melbourne, Derbyshire, twenty-eight miles from Thurmaston, just over the Leicestershire border. Not a whiff of the lives of the people who surrounded him seems to have come his way: to him, Chartists and Tolpuddle Martyrs heralded the end of civilisation as he and most Whig and Tory grandees knew it. The unfortunate name given to the city of Melbourne lives on.

Sary was twenty-eight in 1836, another exceptionally bad year for the stockingers. In August of that year she had her second child, a boy, baptised, as before, in the Church of St Michael and All Angels. He was registered as 'John Dick ill/e. son of Sarah Lacey'. Unlike Allen, Dick was not a common Leicestershire surname, but no father named Dick presented himself. The old English phrase *'Tom, Dick or Harry'* is all that comes to mind. John was born ten years after Sary's daughter Eliza and was to call himself John Allen all his life, all Dicks quite forgotten. The reputation of the young men of Thurmaston makes it unlikely that these were Sary's only pregnancies during those ten years.

After the 1834 Poor Law, Sary could no longer look to the parish for support. But the harshness of the new laws took time to harden the hearts of some overseers, used to the old ways of care. As with Sary's short-lived daughter Eliza, John was born as yet another year of depression set in; her good fortune was that the Allen family kept her and John out of the workhouse and the foundling hospital, or the dubious, and frequently fatal, care of a baby farmer – women who took into care the babies of working mothers, single mothers, desperate mothers, for cash.

Poverty, hunger and the Poor Law advanced the cause of Chartism in Leicestershire. On 19 November 1838 the People's Charter was adopted at a huge rally held in Leicester's Market Place, the first of many events in the city, which became a stronghold of the movement.

First it drizzled, then it poured with rain, but undaunted, the stockingers of Thurmaston's 'Union and Friends' followed the band
carrying their banner. Anti-Corn-Law and Chartist hymns were sung.
The Leicester Chartist leader John Markham, a Methodist preacher
and shoemaker, and the radical Irish Chartist leader and orator Feargus O'Connor, brilliantly held forth to 2,000 drenched listeners. 'My
friends,' declaimed O'Connor:

> You have been living for centuries under a constitution made
> to govern manual labour, but we are now living under a new
> system – under a system of machinery; and that system which
> ought to have made men's happiness has been made men's curse.
> It has broken up small rural districts, and shut you up in the
> infernal rattle-boxes by thousands at the caprice of one great
> manufacturer . . . We will beat the press, the army, the navy, and
> both houses of Parliament (cheers) . . . we will beat all the Town
> Councils, too . . . (Renewed cheering).

The next leader of Leicester's Chartists, Thomas Cooper, caused
a far greater stir. He had been born in Leicester, but raised in nearby
Lincolnshire. On his return in 1840, he 'saw the rags and bones of
the Leicester stockingers'; the fire entered his belly, and carried him
beyond the Methodist calm of John Markham into a furious embrace
of the Chartist cause. Cooper dominated the town from the Market
Place on Sundays, led great meetings throughout the county, lec-
tured on Milton and Liberty, opened a Sunday school, a coffee room
and much else, and collared an invalid framework knitter and a
glove-maker to write the hymns for his Chartist Handbook. Not-
withstanding their marked inferiority to Shakespeare, Cooper's
Chartists called themselves 'The Shakspereans' (*sic*). Cooper was a
teetotaller, and added that 'ism' to his phase of the Leicester Charter
movement, an innovation not attractive to many.

But the songs and hymns, the poetry of the Chartist movement,
reached everyone. The *Northern Star*, the Chartist newspaper founded
by Feargus O'Connor, who so often favoured Leicester with his rous-
ing tones, had a circulation of 50,000 in its heyday, and printed the
songs and poems the Chartists loved to write and sing. This was a

most popular one, with the best tune, and perhaps the best words, often sung at Chartist meetings in Leicester's Market Place or on parades around the city, accompanied by cheering and shouting:

> Men of England, ye are slaves,
> Though ye quell the roaring waves –
> Though ye boast, by land and sea,
> Britons everywhere are free.
>
> Men of England, ye are slaves,
> Bought by tyrants, sold by knaves;
> Yours the toil, the sweat, the pain,
> Theirs the profit, ease and gain.
>
> Men of England, ye are slaves,
> Beaten by policemen's staves;
> If their force ye dare repel
> Yours will be the felon's cell.
>
> Men of England, ye are slaves;
> Ev'n the House of Commons craves
> From the Crown, on bended knee,
> That its language may be free.
>
> Men of England, ye are slaves –
> Hark! the stormy tempest raves –
> 'Tis the nation's voice I hear,
> Shouting 'Liberty is near.'

In 1839 there was a serious slump in trade. Bad harvests followed, and the Corn Laws kept the price of bread prohibitively high; poverty that had already been dire became abysmal – starvation followed. The struggle against the Corn Laws was another vociferous battle in Leicester, as it was throughout Great Britain. Walter Upton was the leading Thurmaston Chartist and chair of its political union. At a meeting in Leicester in February 1839, he urged further action. Nothing had changed: 'if he and his fellow-townsmen of Thurmaston were to work sixteen hours per day they could not get a sufficiency of food, to say nothing of clothes, house rent &c.'

As is ever the case, Chartists and Anti-Corn leaguers, despite having so much in common, found some nitpicking point which prevented the two radical movements from co-operating. Chartists had the better tunes and poetry. Their meetings were often preceded by 'a procession, accompanied by music' and they had a grand time speechifying to great applause. They formed reading groups, held celebratory suppers, lunches and pub meetings. The eccentric Leicestershire Chartist Thomas Rayner cheered his audience by declaring: 'I had to wait upon forty Members of Parliament, and forty such cursed fools I have never met with in my life.' The language of the Thurmaston Chartists was often violent but their action was limited, most likely due to hunger as a good quarter of them were half starving.

This state of affairs was not assisted by the royal progress of Queen Adelaide, the Queen Dowager of William IV, through Leicestershire in November 1839. The five royal carriages, followed by carriages containing pages-in-waiting and other menials, proceeded through the county with the band of the Leicestershire yeomanry leading the way, and a parade of cavalry, honourables, more carriages and equestrians behind. Queen Adelaide gave £50 to the Leicestershire Lunatic Asylum, and Thurmaston greeted her with 'a large arch-way abundantly covered with handsome evergreens, and surmounted by a well-painted crown'. The schoolchildren and inhabitants of the village lined the streets, the children being given 'a large plum bun each, marked with a crown'. Sary was thirty-one at the time, and her son John was three; Samuel's son Thomas and his three children, Samuel's daughter Mary Ann, and Samuel and Dorothy's Samuel junior, William and Joseph were all still at home in Thurmaston, and got one bun each.

The winter of 1842 was grim, and the summer was worse: there were men on the streets singing Chartist songs, begging and marching for bread and assailing the town hall and the Union Workhouse. The crowds of the starving put the fear of god into Leicester Corporation. Cavalry, police and special constables were sent out in force to break up all such gatherings; Feargus O'Connor was jailed, as was Thomas Cooper. As to the stockingers, 'imprisonment presented no terror to them. They were starving and would be better within a gaol than outside of it!' There were riots throughout the county and much of England. Called the Plug Riots, because striking textile workers pulled out the boiler plugs from factory steam engines, these were industrial protesters, half a million of them.

The revolt of these men and women of the 'suffering classes', as the newspapers of the day called them, spread throughout Lancashire, Cheshire, the Potteries, Warwickshire, Tyneside, South Wales and Scotland. Queen Victoria headed the response, pronouncing the strikes illegal and promising a reward of £50 to any subject who turned in a striker. Hundreds were tried; eighty of them were transported to Australia. In Sary's world the Sock Branch of Framework Knitters battled for their fellows, reduced to 'degradation, want, and misery'. Men haunted the churches and chapels 'with labels round their necks begging [the attendants] to remember the starving poor'. 'Many persons . . . wished to go to prison to be well fed and taken care of.' In Thurmaston the village's Independent Order of Brothers was matched by the opening of a female lodge. But Sary was otherwise engaged.

In 1843, pregnant again at the age of thirty-four, Sary left her son John behind for good – he was seven at the time, and probably already at work for his grandfather. He would pop up from time to time over the years, working as a framework knitter in Leicester in 1851, living with his uncle William in the city's slums, and often creating mayhem – among his offences in the 1860s were the breaking of fences and the assault of a constable. Three months gone, Sary married a journeyman framework knitter named William Grundy, a forty-three-year-old bachelor living in one of Leicester's insalubrious lodging houses. Many Thurmaston knitters had already left the village to find work in the larger workshops in the city; Sary's half-siblings Henry, John and Mary Ann now lived in the slums of Leicester St Margaret's, and William soon joined them. It may be that it was through her brothers or their wives that she met William Grundy, but there were Grundys in Thurmaston too.

Whether William Grundy was the father of Sary's son Alfred is hard to say. Sary was a rich fibber when it came to officialdom: at her marriage to Grundy in St Margaret's Church, Leicester, she named 'Thomas Lacey, Labourer', as her father (she would assign Samuel

Allen that role when she married a second time). Alfred was born six months later, on 9 December 1843, in Eaton Street, Leicester. What is certain is that my great-grandfather, Alfred, if conceived in wedlock would have been, as a six-month-old baby, most unlikely to survive in the condition and century into which he was born, and that Sary's twenty-year-old stepbrother Joseph married a Mary Ann Sarson in Thurmaston three months after Sary's nuptials. Both Joseph and Sary were signed off at the altar by Samuel Allen, sock maker, with his 'X'. Later in life it would be Joseph whom Alfred identified as his father, and it was Joseph's name that was passed on to his descendants.

Fornication between close relations, whether blessed by the Church or not, was not uncommon in nineteenth-century Britain. Prince Albert was the first cousin of Queen Victoria; in fact all the Hanoverians had the habit of marrying cousins of one degree or another, as did many of their descendants. The novels of Jane Austen are studded with similar couplings. Charles Darwin married his first cousin Emma Wedgwood, and so on through the novels of Trollope and Hardy. In time Darwin became concerned about such marriages, and asked his son George to find out 'by inquiry in asylums, whether the percentage of the offspring of consanguineous marriages amongst the diseased was greater than that in the healthy population'. George concluded that the rich suffered little from such arrangements, but that for the poor 'if the children were ill fed, badly housed and clothed, the evil might become very marked'.

'How can decency or self-respect be the fruit, where ten or twelve human beings vegetate in a spot 11 feet by 9?' Little has been written about incest in the congested family quarters of the labouring poor. Beatrice Webb described it fifty years later:

> Young girls, who were in no way mentally defective, who were, on the contrary, just as keen-witted and generous-hearted as my own circle of friends – could chaff each other about having babies by their fathers and brothers . . . The violation of little children was another not infrequent result. To put it bluntly, sexual promiscuity, and even sexual perversion, are almost unavoidable among men and women of average character and intelligence crowded into the one-room tenement of slum areas.

What is noticeable is that in their oral accounts the poor constantly refer to beds – dearth of beds, beds of straw or rags, the numbers of people who sleep in those beds, head to toe or otherwise, if beds there were: sleeping on the floor was common. In 1845 a commission was appointed to inquire into the Condition of the Framework Knitters, and it gave one of the many thousands of descriptions extant as to how such families lived – and slept. Samuel Hurst, a stockinger, reported that he had six of his ten children at home. 'The family slept in one room: he and his wife and two small children in one bed; three children in another, and two more in a crib-bed.' Another, William Wyatt, reported, 'we all of us lie on one bed'.

Though Leicester was a robustly Nonconformist city, its corporation was a Tory stronghold until 1836, when the dissenters who made up a large part of the Reform Society brought about the end of Tory control of Leicester and provided seven mayors over the following years. One of the first acts of the new Radical/Whig corporation was to rid themselves of the wealthy appurtenances of Tory office, including the power to bestow such sinecures as bellmen, beadles and molecatchers, as well as the rich plate, crockery, glassware and all the other trappings of the wining and dining such men considered suitable to their condition. Another was to tackle the large debt left behind by their Tory predecessors, devoted as they had been to bribery and other diverse expenses constantly required to get themselves re-elected. This debt deferred any improvement in the circumstances of the industrial poor of Leicester for many a year.

At that time, men of means, Tory, Whig or Radical, used the same spectacles to observe the industrial poor, and this approach did not exclude dissenters, however religious they might be. This was not a period of 'there but for the Grace of God go I': Leicester's poor were simply dismissed as shiftless, lazy, pesky criminals, their plight regarded as a punishment from god. So whether those who controlled the lives of the workers of the city were Tory or liberal manufacturers and merchants, dissenters or otherwise, any attempt to improve the housing of the poor and their condition of life was a long time coming.

The grace of god was entirely absent from Leicester's slums. 'Being an old walled town, its streets were narrow and tortuous, and paved with cobbles and pebbles. Its houses were crowded, its yards confined in area and paved, where paved at all, with pebbles.' The two-roomed tenements and the lodging houses, built of timber and plaster, were often windowless, facing onto a courtyard with a gully, a communal privy and muck hole. Some were built back to back, with no back door or windows. Unventilated, without sewerage or running water, with an open fire for cooking if coals could be afforded, they were plentifully supplied with bugs, lice, beetles and rats. Ventilation and culverts might have saved many: 'Out of 242 streets and 3417 courts, alleys and yards, only 112 are entirely culverted, and about 130 partially so.'

Culverted or not, fresh air was nowhere to be found. Filth adorned the maze of streets and alleys, and the ubiquity of disease bore witness to the rarity of visits from the night-soil man. Dark passages – suitable for a variety of dubious activities, and sometimes given ironic names such as Paradise Row – connected the hovels to streets and other yards. Railways had supplanted canals by the time Sary moved to Leicester, but the very name of Wharf Street, the centre of the Leicester slums and 'perhaps the most unhealthy part of the town', came from its nearness to the waterway system which had made possible the early industrial world in which she laboured. Open ditches ran along the slum streets which tentacled off it, and in two of them, Eaton Street and Metcalf Street, both now long gone, Sary and Alfred would live for the next fifteen years.

Leicester was not the most crowded industrial city of that time. There were still vestiges of the old medieval spaces for orchards and gardens when Sary went to live there, though they had all but disappeared by 1850 as tenement housing spread to cope with the never-ending influx of those looking for work. The repeal of the Corn Laws in 1846 brought one battle to a close, and, encouraged by the Nuisances Removal Act of the same year, Leicester Town Council appointed two medical officers and an Inspector of Nuisances. Together with voluntary and religious agencies, their work to improve the lives and conditions of the city's industrial poor was only one of the reasons Leicester was to become, in due course, proud of its radical history. The Board of Guardians of the Leicester Union, despite the strictures of the New Poor Law, was on occasion forced to provide out-relief – any attempts not to do so were met by riots in the bad depression years of 1848 and 1849.

Under the new Poor Law the destitute could apply for medical help, or apply for free tickets to the Leicester General Dispensary or the Leicester Infirmary, but the stigma attached to any '*bastille*', and particular fear of the Leicester Union Workhouse, were almost universal deterrents. No artist could do justice to the *galère* of worthy men (no women were appointed until 1875) who ran the Union and faced those unable to work or to find work, and the paupers, widows and prostitutes who needed their help. Tentatively imposed in the early years after 1834, by this time the New Poor Law was in full force, and it consigned countless numbers to perdition. The explanation for Leicester's exceptional number of denominational chapels, churches, meeting houses and drinking holes lies here.

With or without the city's charitable efforts, Leicester also provided one particularly efficient killer of its poor: the absence of sanitation caused by a minimal water supply, toxic drains and the resulting omnipresence of excrement and other effluvia. It is impossible properly to convey the full extent of the 'nuisances' – the word chosen for such excrement at official level – that runs through the history of Leicester and its attendant villages at this time. Low-lying, with ancient, uncovered and oozing cesspools, and drains full to overflowing, the city's streets were dotted with stagnant pools. It was worse in the narrow streets and overcrowded tenements where Sary lived, and where the keeping of pigs and the presence of slaughter-houses in the vicinity, often adjacent to the privies, added a final pestiferous touch, exacerbated by the nasty habit of collecting the filth and selling it as manure to the very few who had an allotment, and the even nastier habit of converting pigsties into single-room dwellings for the desperate.

This all-pervasive stench should be, but is not, represented in every historical drama which recreates those times, both as something constantly complained about and agonised over, and as a miasma covering everything. That this was so is demonstrated by the fact that so many believed the stinking, malignant air itself was the source of all illness. Though slum dwellers trudged through by far the worst of it, it was not mud that dirtied the aristocratic boot when a person of consequence ventured out into the streets of the time, but the 'nuisances' of man and beast.

When the River Soar flooded in winter, as it was wont to do, quantities of 'nuisance' were forced into the low parts of the town; it rose through gratings, and spread through the streets and the ground floors of buildings. And there it lay. 'Nuisance' complaints for the twelve months beginning in October 1848 record almost every insalubrious practice spotted by one intrepid inspector (he failed to note the odour of tripe boiling):

For foul and offensive and badly constructed privies and soil pits	814
Filthy dwelling houses	443
Swine keeping	278
Foul and offensive drains	90
Foul cesspools and ditches	29

Dickens wrote of this world, but most often of London. However, in the league table of death rates in the early nineteenth century it was 1. Bristol, 2. Manchester, 3. Liverpool and 4. Leicester. But for the death of children, Leicester led the field. It is surprising that Alfred survived at all, for 1844 was another year of great hunger. A stockinger's plea appeared in the *Leicester Chronicle* on 3 May: 'I have had no meat, sugar, tea, coffee or butter for three months, and for one month I entirely lived upon bread and water, with a little salt and potatoes, and had neither blankets nor sheets, and five of the family lay in one bed.'

Fevers flew through the tenements. The word covered many major epidemics which afflicted these years: cholera again, summer diarrhoea inevitably, consumption, typhus, influenza, scarlatina and smallpox. From one of these afflictions, most probably typhus, much complained of in that year, William Grundy died in March 1844, nine months after his marriage to Sary, when Alfred was just three months old. He was forty-four when he died, well above the life expectancy of the average stockinger, which was just twenty-six years and three months.

The circumstances of the stockingers were so grim that in 1843, 25,000 framework knitters had petitioned the House of Commons demanding a Commission of Inquiry. The petition complained about wages, unemployment, frame rents, new machinery and imports from abroad. Richard Muggeridge was appointed to head the commission, and his officials spent several months in the East Midlands taking evidence from the many beautifully named knitting branches – 'the cotton berlins, brace and cravat branch, German pieces, shirts, the ribbed branch, worsted imperials and lisle thread gloves, &c.' The report which followed in 1845 achieved nothing, but it well described the 'defenceless poverty' of families like the Allens. Muggeridge reported to both Houses of Parliament that only a quarter of all framework knitters were in work, with the rest underemployed, unemployed, or on parish relief.

His report concluded that 'the supply of Frame-work Knitters has almost invariably exceeded the demand for them', and implied that the employment of so many women and children in the trade permitted their masters to pay pitiful wages. The most notable modern historian of the hosiery industry has concluded that 'all that was needed was more flexible response to changing market situations', and bemoaned the sense of self-pity that permeates virtually all first-hand accounts of the lives of the knitters of the first half of the nineteenth century. The stockingers 'were less a lumpen proletariat, than a rump. A residual group largely composed of older workmen, semi-skilled women, and juveniles.'

Framework knitters, it is clear from this account, lacked the sort of masculine presence that elicits higher wages, the entrepreneurial skills to rise up from their condition, and any proper enthusiasm for the innovations of the Industrial Revolution. But it is difficult to satisfy historians of this persuasion when your stomach is empty, your bed is shared with ten others, and you have to lie in it while your clothes are washed. And, that done, when your ragged clothes are in stark contrast to those of the men who employ you. That said, the knitters did cling on too long to their traditional ways of working: nothing changed for them until factory production took them by the scruff of the neck and shook them into mechanisation.

With William Grundy's death in 1844, Sary was left to fend for herself, joining the most undefended of Leicester's precarious poor. It is most unlikely that she could have afforded to rent a frame or continue paying the rent due on that of her dead husband. But in December 1844, nine months after William Grundy's death, a piece of luck came her way. An Outdoor Relief Prohibitory Order was enacted – one can but hope that Leicester's voluntary and religious officials were on hand to explain its mysteries to Sary – which gave a widow with a fatherless child entitlement to six months' out-relief, without the necessity of entering the workhouse. This was dependent on the child being incapable of work, which, at the age of one, Alfred happily was. Before the amendment to the law Sary would have been required to pick oakum, or do something even more disagreeable, in a yard attached to the Leicester Union Workhouse.

Merchant hosiers often had a frame workshop and warehouse adjoined to their handsome properties. Others had built rows of houses of two or three storeys, with twenty or so frames for rent on the second or third floor, or set up in the yards behind. These buildings had rows of elongated windows to let the light in – but not air – and living quarters of a most dismal kind below, with everything to be paid for, or deducted from earnings. Working on a stocking frame at home continued, but more than a third of the old frames in Leicestershire had fallen idle by the 1840s, and by 1847 competent hosiers had begun to take up circular and rotary frames which could knit tubular fabric and had tentatively moved on to power-operated machines. For the conservative Leicester hosiery trade these moves were adopted slowly but by the 1850s the manufacturers employed hundreds of stockingers in their factories. The 1847 Factory Act permitted only a fifty-eight-hour working week for women and for children under eighteen, but for the lives of the domestic knitters, where stockinger bid against stockinger to get work, it brought what they could earn to rock bottom.

Sary could have walked to a workshop and lived in some insalubrious lodging nearby. 'Those pest-holes called ready furnished rooms' as they were described by a most excellent human being, Joseph Dare, who came to Leicester in 1845 to set up a domestic mission to work among the poor on behalf of the Unitarians of the Great Meeting. He served as a devoted and practical missionary in the city for thirty years, and his work there was a constant blessing for many of Leicester's poor, though not necessarily for Sary and her undeserving ilk. For Joseph Dare grieved about the lot of the poor, but seems to have been equally unhappy about their diversions. Drinking holes, snuggeries, gambling dens, beer and public houses were constant temptations. Dog fighting, rat hunting and the rat pit gave the poor the opportunity to abuse those weaker than themselves. (The rats' teeth were knocked out before they fought.) The Leicester Fancy Rabbit Club, however, was kinder to its animals.

Penny dreadfuls, religious pamphlets, political pamphlets and a deluge of cheap weeklies, broadsides and news-sheets did the rounds of pubs and drinking holes. There were fetes and fairs in May and at Michaelmas, cricket in summer and dancing on the cricket ground when the game was over, circuses, pantomimes at the Amphitheatre, fighting of all kinds – bare-fisted bouts, street fighting in groups – swimming naked in the Soar ('nothing else but a meeting place for all kinds of vice and filth'), gambling, betting, music (a good sing-song), dancing and a Pleasure Fair which presented 'Wright's wild beast-show and Holloway's company of theatricals'. All these kept life in their hearts, if not food in their bellies, though 'scarcity of money' kept most stockingers away.

When cricket was not being played, the Wharf Street cricket ground, so near to Sary's lodgings, was open to the public, and spectacular balloon ascents, fireworks and much-loved brass bands could be watched and heard. The Wharf Street slums were alive with pawn-shops, credit shops, bakeries, slaughterhouses, lodging houses and brothels. Shops, like the pubs, stayed open late, and sold everything from rabbits to concertinas. Above all, the hustling community was ferociously irreligious, and took little notice of the sabbath. The holy water of alcohol eased their days: unlike their water, alcohol at least was not contaminated.

A mite would buy you a small beer, and you could buy it most hours of the day or night. Food was available in the pubs, or could be brought in to be heated up; parents and their children lingered in the light and warmth. Young men filled the public houses and the streets, up to as much mischief as they could manage. In such pot-houses and in the streets nearby, wives were beaten, men and women assaulted, watches stolen, money filched, but top of the list of charges dealt with by the County Office was that of being 'drunk and disorderly'. Wharf Street rang throughout the night with noisy brawls and song and the activities of bawdy houses. How the good Joseph Dare bemoaned it all, most particularly 'mothers addicted to drunkenness ... When this vice lays firm hold, it is like the coil of a deadly serpent; destruction is almost inevitable ... I felt it necessary to dismember the "Female Friendly Society" for it turned out anything but friendly.'

The charitable missionaries of the nineteenth century wanted to seek out the worthy and deserving poor, and bring them god and salvation; the poor, as is eternally the case, wanted food, work, shelter, clothes, money and alcohol. God came a long way behind, and the wretchedness caused by continuing economic depressions made mockery of such quibbling. Dare visited the poor, and ran a mission that educated and helped many, but always within the 'blessed promises of the gospel of Christ'. With so many in need within that category, he 'came to the determination of rejecting all applicants from the common lodging house and ready furnished room'. Fortunately, in practice his sympathy often overrode this decision, and like those amongst whom she lived, Sary was more than capable of making a pretence of piety if needs must.

The ranks of the destitute in Leicester increased as Irish immigrants who fled the famine of 1845 filled up the lodging houses of the slums. An Irish child described his impoverished Leicester childhood in the 1850s:

> What filthy little wretches we children were, and how could it be
> otherwise? Not Papuans nor Basutos nor Fijians could I think
> be more degraded. And this was in the middle of the nineteenth
> century. O great and glorious empire! What chance to be clean
> was there in a house on whose only floor bags of dusty rags and
> putrescent bones were spilled out to be sorted? Nevertheless, we
> were used to this, and before going to bed we all knelt down on the
> bare uneven brick floor and recited the rosary, Father leading off.

Sary's young son Alfred would not have played with these Irish ragamuffins, because the Irish poor and the Leicester poor fought from dawn to dusk. Nevertheless, he was just as dirty as any Irish boy, as not only was water barely available except from canal or river, but there were no municipal baths until 1849 – and then, who could afford to pay to use them? The rosary, however, loomed ahead for many of Alfred's descendants.

It is impossible to know what Sary would have looked like, although there are clues in the noses, eye colour (blue) and height (short) of many of her progeny. The clothes of the industrial under-class were often rags, and what she wore would have largely depended on what she was given by charity and Church. Neither the crinolines, muslins, silks and comfortable layers of Mrs Gaskell's heroines nor the exquisite raiment of Georgette Heyer's heroes would have been part of the stern Nonconformism of Leicester charities such as the Ladies' Working Society, who distributed old clothes among the poor. If not from them, clothes could be had from the slop-shops: hooded cloaks, drab shawls, flannel petticoats, gowns, woollen stockings and lace-up short boots.

The Leicester women could sew, and clothes, ragged or not, were mended, patched, and passed on. Sary survived a decade of the end-less battle between bare subsistence and the workhouse, perhaps because Leicester's framework industry so depended on female and child labour. Cut-up goods meant that the hosiery trade came to be dominated by women, who seamed and sewed, and could be paid much less than a man. Her looks, and her height, would have been much affected by her pauper's diet, as reported in a framework knit-ters meeting in Leicester in 1845:

> We principally live on taters; we have taters for breakfast, taters
> for dinner, taters for tea, and taters for supper, and when them are
> gone, I get some turnips from the farmers, and chop them up
> with cabbage sprouts, to make a stew, and we get along as well as
> we can with the bits and sups given us.

Women of Sary's condition were forced to turn their hands to anything: scavenging, filching, baby-minding, and, if necessary, taking to the streets or alehouses and offering themselves for sale. But kin kept together, and Sary had many half-siblings and other relations to hand. Jane Allen was in Humberstone, then a small village just outside Leicester, as were William Grundy's mother and sister Ann, a cotton-winder. Sary's half-brothers Henry, William and John all lived nearby in the slum streets of Leicester's St Margaret's parish with their families. And in Thurmaston, by 1841 her stepfather Samuel had bettered himself, probably from taking on glove-making, the best-paid goods stockingers could produce, which came to be the 'salvation' of the village. He now rented a larger cottage into which more frames could be squeezed, and which had an allotment garden behind. Once again, a pig and the growing of vegetables could keep the family, including Sary's son John, still living with Samuel and Dorothy, out of the poorhouse. Samuel's oldest son Thomas, a knitter, lived in Thurmaston and was an excellent gardener, although a violent man: in 1846 his stepmother Dorothy charged him with assaulting her in the street.

In 1847 Sary's stepfather Samuel Allen died: he was seventy-three, a very good age. Thomas inherited the tenancy of the Thurmaston cottage, and immediately dumped Dorothy on the parish. She was sent to live at the lower end of Garden Street in Thurmaston with her sister Ann, to be listed as paupers of the parish until their deaths. Twelve years later Thomas would come home drunk, beat his wife and four daughters, threaten them with a knife, and lock them out of the house. Sary's John went to live with his step-uncles in Leicester.

If help was to come to Sary, it could no longer come from her mother, or from what was left of her family in Thurmaston. Could matters get worse? They could. 1848 was a turning point. After a Public Health Act was passed by Robert Peel's government, a Board of Health was set up in Leicester, its efforts much limited by dilatory and unwilling local officials, ignorance as to the medical effects of the insanitary conditions in which the poor lived, and the sheer weight of numbers invading the new industrial town. Between argumentative and disputatious members of Leicester's boards and councils, and vigorous objections to the removal of pigs, pigsties and slaughterhouses from both 'the industrious poor' and the less admired poor who also depended on everything a pig could supply, much improvement was not to come their way until well after Sary left.

However, apart from Sary's family network, living in the slums offered its own support system. There were backstreet pawnshops and credit shops galore. Neighbours could be better than kin: living hugger-mugger could be violent and desperate, but being close as peas in a pod also created invaluable support for the denizens of the Wharf Street slums. Leicester's Market Place was very near, and many of the city's poorest inhabitants were masters and mistresses of pilfering and begging, and the lifting of the odd bit of cheese or meat. Their mysterious Leicester jargon, impenetrable to those they pursued and those who pursued them, babbled through the Wharf Street slums and the city's imposing jail, noted for its attachment to flogging and hard labour, straitjackets and the crank.

The Leicester Board of Guardians, always protective of the ratepayers who elected them, constantly bemoaned the pauperism caused by the 'gross oppression and cruelty practised' by hosiery manufacturers, and by middlemen who used the circuitous and corrupt systems of the hosiery trade so much to their own advantage and to the gross disadvantage of the ratepayers required to fund this pauperism. The result:

> depravity and licentiousness are increased to an alarming extent,
> habits of prudence and frugality are almost unknown, and a
> reckless desperation is engendered, which in due time, produces
> its natural fruits – drunkenness, disease and death.

This was an accurate description of life on Wharf Street in 1847, scarcely inferior to the gruesome existence inflicted by the Board of Guardians on those whose penury forced them to enter the workhouse's frightening doors.

The wealthy and the religious of Leicester, lamenting that the labouring classes had almost entirely lost interest in god and his representatives on earth, struggled to instil the virtues on which they prided themselves: self-reliance, discipline, reason. They were not alone. In all their songs and poems, Leicester's Chartists demanded justice in god's name:

How long shall babes of tender years
Be doomed to toil for Lazy Peers
The locusts of our land?

Make bare thine arm, O Lord! defend
The helpless, and, be thou their friend,
And shield them with thy hand.

It was those for whom all these fought who seemed oblivious to the impressive array of places of meeting and worship in the Wharf Street slums. Baptists, Congregationalists, Bible societies, Methodists of every inclination and the odd Anglican fought the good fight against drink, sexual misdemeanours, irreligion and poverty, often providing soup and bread kitchens as part of their mission. Misbehaviour usually meant expulsion by these worthy men. In 1854 Leicester's Evangelical Baptist Church instructed that Delilah H 'be erased from the list of members. It is feared that her conduct agrees with her name.'

Sary and Alfred were exceptionally well placed, with a Methodist mission hall and a school opened by the Leicester Infant School Society in their own street. But for children slightly older than Alfred, most of whom worked from the age of six, little schooling was possible. Nevertheless, church, chapel and charities evangelised around the slums offering god, reformation, practical help, Sunday schools and some education to the urban poor. Despite his great labours, Dare always fretted: 'many of the poor little things fall asleep over their lessons. Some are precluded from regular attendance through want of shoes or outer garments.'

Joseph Dare kept a particularly compassionate eye on widows and their children; his mission offered a Boys and Girls Evening Instruction Society at which Alfred could have learned to read and write. Certainly he became a good deal more proficient than his mother, whose signature remained vestigial to the end of her days. Alfred may also have been a beneficiary of Dare's 'writing and summing' class. Dare's Mission Reading Room, which was open, free of charge, to the labouring classes every Saturday evening from seven to ten-thirty, offered much more than the 'Bud and Blossom' religious pamphlet he

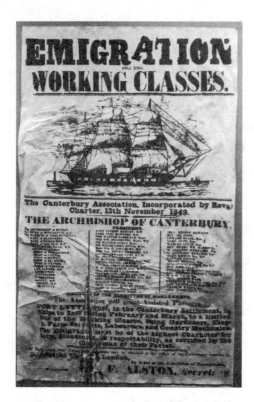

A barrage of pamphlets,
advertisements, leaflets
and posters urged
people to depart

liked to distribute to the poor. Many other 'useful works' were made available there, ranging from the three Leicester newspapers and *The Times*, to the *People's Journal* and *Punch*. Advertisements offering a better life abroad filled the newspapers of the time. Sary soldiered on until 1854. It was then that her great piece of luck, her happy day, sailed into sight.

II

THE NOBODIES

The nobodies: nobody's children, owners of nothing.
The nobodies: the no ones, the nobodied, running like rabbits,
dying through life, screwed every which way . . .
Who do not appear in the history of the world,
but in the police blotter of the local paper.

Eduardo Galeano, 'The Nobodies' (1991)

4

Independent Men

The Manchester Coach, Market Harborough Town Square, 1837

AFTER THE DEATH OF William Grundy in 1844, Sary and Alfred moved to the next street, from Eaton to Metcalf Street, both in the Wharf Street slums. Two streets away lived the Conquests, Joseph and Sarah, and nearby three of their sons, John, Rice and Joseph junior. Joseph Conquest was a brickmaker from Market Harborough, seventeen miles south of Leicester, eighteen miles from Thurmaston, and had brought up his sons, young men who were no better than they needed to be, to do likewise. In the Hungry '40s they had moved to Leicester to find work, though in 1846 Joseph senior would return to die at the home of another of his sons at Fleckney near Market Harborough. His other three sons remained in Leicester, neighbours to Sary and Alfred and many of the Allen brothers.

———————⟨∞⟩———————

Market Harborough is called thus as it began as a market, placed where the road from Northampton to Leicester crossed the River Welland, which flows on to Stamford in Lincolnshire then on to the Wash. By the eighteenth century, brooks, streams and the river watered the old market, now a village, the Welland traversed by a ford, with a chained bridge – to be used by carriages when the ford was not passable – overarching it. On the border of Leicestershire and Northamptonshire, it became a centre for the prosperous agrarian district nearby.

With some forty small villages in its hinterland, Market Harborough's Tuesday market and annual October Fair were the sources of its continuing prosperity, as were the services its inhabitants offered to the many large and gracious country houses surrounding it. Sheep, cattle and horses were bought and sold – the army and navy were major clients of Harborough market – and there could be as many as 2,000 beasts in the town on market days, such a gold mine for its inns and hostelries that by the late eighteenth century seven more fairs and sale meetings had been added to the rattle and bang of life there.

Horses were everywhere, the beautiful creatures upon which the area's aristocratic, hunting and commercial fraternities depended. Harborough was at the very centre of the Shires – Leicestershire, Northamptonshire and Rutland – and 'bruising riders' and the cream of fashionable society descended upon the town for the winter hunting season. 'Our town is frequently enlivened in the winter by the Noblemen and Gentlemen' of the hunt, stated the historian son of the Harborough Grammar School headmaster William Harrod, in 1808. Hounds were kennelled at Bowden Inn, the most famous of all the local hunts, the Belvoir and the Quorn, hunted to the north, and the Pytchley was nearby. Lord Vernon's hounds, Mr Corbet's hounds, Lord Scarborough's hounds and Mr Osbaldeston's hounds met regularly, as the rich and fashionable settled into their 'snug little hunting boxes'. The juxtaposition of such patricians with the canal navvies and framework knitters of Leicestershire is one – but only one – explanation for the strength of Nonconformity and the Chartists in Leicestershire.

The labouring classes of Harborough were not confined to one trade as in Leicester. If weavers, they were weavers of tammies and shalloons, wonderfully named cloths from the pre-industrial age, often used for curtains and linings and, in the case of shalloons, for women's shoes. The town's hosiers produced 'fancy hosiery . . . cotton and worsted net braces, worsted cravats, worsted under-waistcoats, children's shoes, stay laces, tippets etc'. There was a tannery, a brickworks and coachworks, a brewery, some silk and wool spinning. As tammy declined, Joseph Clarke's Worsted and Carpet manufactory rose to take its place, soon employing 500 women, children and men of Market Harborough.

But Harborough's splendour, such as it was, came from the rich hunting folk, lusciously described, once again, by Georgette Heyer, for whom the town was a favourite location for hunting and coaching scenes. Harborough provided them with every service, from mantua makers to gunsmiths. Roads from the town led to Corby, Kettering and Stamford to the east, Rugby and Coventry to the west, and south to Northampton and on to London. In its earliest market days, over the hill, a mile away, was the prosperous village of Great Bowden, and much nearer, though over the border with Northamptonshire until the 1890s, the tiny village of Little Bowden. Here, amongst the farmhouses, gardens and orchards, most probably in one of the village's mud cottages, the Conquest family lived. Today both Bowdens have been absorbed to lesser and greater degrees into Market Harborough.

Eighty-three miles from London, it was a thoroughfare town well before the nineteenth century, first by coach and horse, then by road, then by canal, and later, by railway. The great north/south road from the capital traversed Harborough in the shape of its long High Street. Mail wagons, curricles and stagecoaches rattled through the town, the most eagerly anticipated coming from Manchester and heading for London, turning up at 9.30 p.m. each day at the Three Swans, Harborough's most famous hotel. Changing horses at the numerous inns was a rich source of income to innkeepers and stables, but of tremendous noise as teams of horse-drawn carts and covered wagons, hauling goods to and from the town, added to the permanent tumult.

Turnpiked roads came to Harborough very early, in 1722, and the hard roads put down – despite the unpopular tolls which had to be paid – brought profit and prosperity to the dozens of coaching inns and public houses. There, ostler Conquests handed down men and women of substance from their carriages, the steaming horses cared for by them or by village children. The Bell Inn advertised its humble hopes for:

> The Honour of Waiting upon the Nobility, Gentry and Clergy, who occasionally travel through That Town . . . respectfully assuring them they will, at The Bell Inn, meet with good Beds, a well-supplied Larder, real genuine Wines, best of Liquors, roomy commodious Stables, neat Post-Chaises, with able, active Horses and experienced careful drivers . . . the Leicester Coach calls at the above Inn on Monday, Wednesday, and Friday mornings going to London: and on Tuesday, Thursday and Saturday evenings on its Return to Leicester . . . A handsome Hearse, with able Horses, ready on the shortest Notice, to any part of England.

The arrival of the splendid mail coaches, replete with guards in gold and scarlet, bearing blunderbusses and pistols, was announced by shots or the calls of the town crier as they careered down the wide High Street and through the Square – once the Sheep Market. Craftsmen and tradesmen lived and worked on their premises close to the marketplace. There were winding lanes of stone, brick and – more rarely – old timber houses, but very few other streets at the time the Conquests lived there; the High Street and its coaching inns, the Square and the elegant Georgian buildings and houses in the upper High Street were the core of the town, though its centre was Chapel Yard. The Anglican Chapel of St Dionysius, with its searching grey spire, dominated the area (and still does). St Dionysius was only a chapel then, as the parish church of the time was St Mary in Arden in Great Bowden (to be the site of future Conquest misbehaviour). Next to it was a guardhouse, stocks, a whipping post and the Old Grammar School, set on posts, its arches creating a covered market, and built in the timber and plaster which marked the town before the onset of infelicitous red brick.

Harborough Sheep Market, 1836

There were markets for much besides sheep: a beast market, a flesh market – the butchers' shambles – a pet market, a pot market, a cloth market, a butter market, a corn market, a Tripe Alley and a Tag Lane. Animals of every kind, with pigs to add to the joy of it, crowded the High Street and its squares on market days, their 'nuisances' afflicting Harborough as they did every other town. The inns and beerhouses made matters much worse:

> King's Head-yard, and another contain several stables, pigsties, a
> slaughter-house, and open refuse pits, in which is deposited soil
> and filth from the neighbouring cottages . . . There is but one
> convenience for all the inhabitants of fifteen houses . . . by far
> the most disgusting in appearance and dilapidation of any seen in
> the town.

Open tubs of human excrement were dumped in the Welland, the drinking water was polluted, and on market days the outpourings of the prodigious number of animals raised the complaints of the inhabitants to the highest decibels. Of the many images of Market Harborough at the time, none portray the stomach-churning appearance of its streets and lanes, or its excretal miasma. There was more poverty and disease in Market Harborough than in other towns, because travellers brought disease with them to such a degree that epidemics were almost constant. The rank and file, though spared the industrialised horrors of Leicester, lived in similar tenements, cottages and yards scattered behind the town centre.

By 1813 the Earl of Moira's country house in Leicestershire 'boasted two bathrooms and six water-closets and his wife even had her own elegantly appointed personal bathroom and WC adjoining her dressing room'. Market Harborough, with a population of 1,801 in 1716, had a comfortable middle-class with domestic servants, and a long tradition of charitable bequests and donations – the Town Estate, as it was known, run by its Charity Commissioners – feoffees – to sustain its well-being. Tradesmen and others of that ilk boasted privies in their yards, nicely named 'the Necessary House'.

Past the Old Town Hall, with its butchers' stalls at ground level, and the Angel Hotel, just off the High Street, was Bowden Lane, where the first Independent Meeting House was built in 1694, though Independent preachers had been hard at work in the region a good thirty years before that. John Nichols, ancestor of the Conquest family, was an original member of this chapel. In the small town of Market Harborough Presbyterianism was the dissent favoured in the seventeenth century, but by 1694 many had broken away to become Independents – called Separatists in the sixteenth century. This form of Nonconformist Christianity, with its Puritan roots, went back to the earliest years of the Bowdens and Harborough, where the Parliamentary cause was particularly strong during the English Civil War. Independents believed in a gathering of individual souls with direct access to god, rather than the Anglican hierarchy of Church, parish, bishop and Crown. For them, a group of Christians assembled in a room, field or chapel constituted a Church. Oliver Cromwell was a Separatist, as were the Pilgrims who founded the Plymouth colony in Massachusetts.

Independents formed a considerable community of some eighty families in Harborough, a quarter of its households, whereas Methodists provided only six families, Presbyterians, Baptists, Quakers, Sandemanians and Antinomian Baptists fewer still. By the time of Joseph and Sarah Conquest the Presbyterians had become Independents, and Harborough Independent Meeting House on the corner of

The Old Independent Meeting House, Market Harborough:
first used for public worship in 1694, taken down in 1843

Bowden Lane and High Street could hold up to 1,000 believers. One reason for the success of Nonconformism over the established Church in places like Harborough was that 'in most of the dissenting houses they have the good sense to keep them comfortably warm, which, no doubt, brings many customers in, while our churches, in general, lament the want of it in tears trickling down their lofty pillars'.

Members of the Independent faith appointed their own ministers, got rid of them if found unsatisfactory, and were not answerable to other congregations, but only to their own chapel. Independents were stern souls: in the early days they had to be, as they were frequently jailed for 'preaching the gospel', and were forced to meet secretly in barns, cowsheds or cottages, until the Act of Toleration of 1689 freed dissenters to preach. The Chartist Thomas Cooper found them a dry lot, and dull to boot, but the lives of many of the Conquest boys give the lie to that. Their vigorous dislike of authority may be attributed to some extent – poverty also played its part, of course – to the fact that Independent churches were self-governed. This democratic approach led to furious squabbles in many a community, but also to a sense of independence and disobedience rarely found in Anglican churches. The Independent Puritan, Oliver Cromwell, was not celebrated in Market Harborough in later years, but John Bunyan, who came to preach in Leicester, Harborough and Great Bowden in 1672, certainly was.

Schooling was much a part of Harborough life from the early seventeenth century onwards. The town's Anglican grammar school, founded in 1607, was intended to educate the poor, and considerable endowments came its way to do so, but its definition of the poor transmuted itself into providing education for the offspring of the privileged and professional classes, and for those who could already read the Bible. Religion and the pursuit of Christian godliness in its infinite varieties were all-pervasive in these years. The transgressions of the Conquest sons appear almost valiant when confronted with the amount of religious instruction to behave otherwise offered throughout Britain at the time.

Though they were free to preach after 1689, Independents could not hold public office or attend a university: thus they created their own Sunday schools and academies. They were men of commerce and business, not of the land, in practical service to the market town and the county: at the top, solicitors, architects, bankers, feoffees, Overseers of the Highways or of the Poor; in the middle, coachmakers, butchers, bakers, grocers, brewers, carpenters, drapers, tanners, shoemakers and saddlers; and at the bottom, the Conquests and their like: brick and tile makers, ropemakers, labourers, ostlers, hotel porters and canal boatmen. At the lower levels women worked too of course, as mantua makers, milliners, hosiers, hatters, charwomen, stitchers. Harborough presented a *Canterbury Tales* procession of old trades and occupations.

As the fortunes of the Anglican grammar school declined, the Independent academy flourished, and there were many other small private schools, boarding twenty pupils or so, in the town. But they were not for the likes of the Conquest children: Sunday school was their only chance to gain any sort of education, however rudimentary, and as in Thurmaston, the labouring classes were otherwise occupied on the sacred day. But the Independent Sunday school in the barn in Ratten's Yard was a generous one, teaching reading and writing, with a clothing club and the occasional offer of a good dinner for the poorest of the poor. Because of their Independent connections, some of the Conquest children could read, write or do both.

That they could do little more, and the general absence of godly obedience in the Conquest family, may have been due to the fact that the Independent minister of the time, George Gill, was 'not distinguished by grasp of mind, power of reasoning, depth of thought or extent of information. His powers, whether natural or acquired, were not of a high order.' Those who succeeded Gill after his death in 1818 seem to have been worse. From then until 1836, the Independent church of Market Harborough under Gill's successors William Gear and William Wild was in a constant state of ferocious uproar. Such disruption bears witness to how much Independents cared about their particular form of godliness, and how little tolerance they had for any deviation as to what they wanted from their men of god.

Many reasons are presented for the gradual development and final explosion of the Industrial Revolution in Britain. Some of them are admirable – the country's rich and enquiring scientific and technological culture; some repellent – the enormous wealth created by the slave trade which made so much of it possible, and the vast riches that poured into Britain from its invasion of India, first through the East India Company, and after 1858 by the British Crown, which took direct control in that year. Progress began with private entrepreneurs who financed turnpike roads, replacing earth, mud or clay tracks with hard roads. Toll roads made travel immensely faster and easier (and were of considerable importance to Harborough's coaching trade and its inns and taverns). But of all the facilitators of Victorian wealth, the creation of canals and railways – the entire transformation of the nation's transport system – was perhaps the most remarkable. Leicestershire, the county farthest from the sea, set in the undulating Midlands, profited most.

Of these two brilliant technical achievements, the creation of the canals in the eighteenth century was first, and seems the most heroic. Contemplating the backbreaking work of the horses and the navvies who, with pick and shovel, bucket and wheelbarrow, hacked out these waterways, and the genius of the inventors and civil engineers – James

Brindley, Thomas Telford and many more – who planned them, makes one wonder why it is not their images decorating the boats that still use the canals today, instead of the traditional 'Rose and Castles'. The British waterway system – there were 2,600 miles of canals by 1815 – made the early Industrial Revolution possible.

By 1700 large and heavy goods were already being moved by sea and on river, and the latter were being deepened and widened. In 1760, while on his Grand Tour, Francis Egerton, the 3rd Duke of Bridgewater, saw Pierre-Paul Riquet's seventeenth-century Canal du Midi in the Languedoc, and came home to copy it. His was not the first cut in England, but it was the most remarkable. Happily endowed with considerable wealth and rich coal mines at Worsley near Manchester, and a clever estate manager named John Gilbert, the duke hired James Brindley to cut a canal from Worsley to Manchester, complete with aqueduct, complex contouring and elevations. Brindley's invention of 'puddling clay', a watertight substance used to line canals and dams, is still used today. These years of 'canal mania', slowed down but not halted by the Napoleonic Wars, led to a remarkable fretwork of navigable waterways connecting many parts of the country, most particularly the Midlands and the north of England to London and Liverpool. Previously, goods had come to and from Leicester, by sea and river, road and wagon. For the landlocked Midlands of England, canals changed everything.

Men of wealth and power fought tremendous battles to finance and build these revolutionary water roads. Beloved landscapes would be ruined. Canal navvies, 'a restless, rootless turbulent set of ruffians', were met with suspicion and energetic distaste wherever they went. Earls, dukes, lords, MPs, coal-mine and turnpike owners, bankers, landed gentry and merchants of every order fought, sometimes to the death, to create or prevent the new canals. Poets 'wrote topical verses on the beauties and blessings of navigations'. Ancestral lands were desecrated, villages cut through, and arid farmlands suddenly found themselves with a limitless water supply. Wharves and warehouses, locks and tunnels, footbridges and inns transformed the countryside. So great was the fervour for these new creations that genuine canal promoters took to meeting in secret to avoid the crush of would-be shareholders who pursued them on foot or horse to grab a piece of the action.

Market Harborough was at the centre of this passion. By the end of the eighteenth century the thunder and bustle of the goods wagons and coaches and horses rumbling through the town had become unwelcome to all but the hoteliers and innkeepers. In 1793, as Louis XVI was guillotined in Paris, the meeting to set up the Leicestershire and Northamptonshire Union Canal Company had to be held in a field because so many country gentlemen, knights and lords and businessmen turned up to buy shares that no room in the town could hold them all. The subsequent developments were 'pleasantly complicated', studded with fierce arguments and constant stoppages as funds ran out. The Harborough Canal Basin and its new wharf to the west of High Street, with wharves at Great Bowden and Gallow Hill just outside the town on the Leicester Road, were opened on 13 October 1809. The occasion was marked by a magnificent ceremony with a 'barge and two boats decorated with flags, from Gallow to Harborough, between banks lined with enthusiastic spectators . . . and the convoy entered Harborough Bason [*sic*] to the cheers of thousands of spectators'.

Waterway connection from Leicester to the East Midlands and the coalfields of Derbyshire and Nottinghamshire was completed in 1814 by a magnificent engineering creation: Foxton 'Staircase' – a series of ten locks via which the canal ascended a steep hill, lifting the narrow boats an astonishing seventy-five feet – and a tunnel cut through the high ground of the old village of Foxton, about five miles north-west of Market Harborough, to join the aptly named Grand Union Canal. The Grand Union provided a direct route from the River Trent in the Midlands to Leicester, which thus became 'the centre of extensive navigable lines' directly connecting the north of England to London. The ports of Liverpool and Bristol were now connected by this national water network to the industrial Midlands: a weekly boat service left Leicester on Thursday mornings, and arrived in Harborough on Monday evenings. Canals now connected the Humber to the Thames.

The driving impetus for the building of these canals was the search for quicker access to the collieries of the Midlands. Canal transport meant that the cost of coal was halved. But in their heyday the canals transported everything: timber from Boston, salt from Middlewich, gravel from Mountsorrel, and the produce of the Midlands – bricks, wool, corn, flour, hosiery. In 1817 the committee and proprietors of the Grand Union Canal celebrated their success with haunches of venison, passing an afternoon at Harborough Wharf's inn 'with a hilarity, temperance, and good humour, that blended conviviality with rational enjoyment'.

Sarah Ann Nichols (every woman in my English family seems to be called either Sarah or Mary, with Ann following close behind), the great- or great-great-granddaughter of John Nichols, a founder member of Market Harborough's Independent chapel, married a John Conquest there in 1776. Her husband, the first discoverable Harborough Conquest, seems to have been a member of a family of labourers or small farmers from nearby Buckinghamshire – the class of worker who poured into the market town each week to trade with or to service the surrounding gentry. Harborough was full of such immigrants.

Sarah Ann and John had three children: Sarah (again), born in 1778; John (again) in 1780; and Joseph in 1784. Each of them was baptised in the Independent chapel, each following the English naming customs of the time: the eldest son was given his father's name, the eldest daughter her mother's, then grandparents' and maiden names came into play. By 1791 the family were living off Bowden Lane, near the Independent chapel and the beerhouses which graced this lane, amidst their Nichols and dissenter neighbours, some of whom, unlike Sarah Ann and John, were wealthy enough to qualify as ratepayers.

Into the calm waters of these dissenters, John Conquest brought traditions that were to be passed on to his children and grandchildren. Local newspapers record that the Conquest tribe were at constant war with the powers that be. One illuminating despatch – probably concerning cousins of the Harborough Conquests – was published on 15 July 1820:

> We, the undersigned, William Conquest of Great Linford in the
> County of Buckinghamshire, Labourer, and William Conquest
> the Younger, and Joseph Conquest of the same place, Labourers,
> sons of the said William Conquest, having had a Prosecution

commenced against us by the Constable of Newport Pagnell, for a violent Assault upon the said Constable, on the 22nd Day of June last, which, at our earnest Entreaty, he has consented to suspend on our expressing our Contrition for our Offence and paying the Charges incurred; now we do hereby express our great Sorrow for having unguardedly committed such crime, and do offer our sincere Thanks to the said Constable, for his Forbearance and Kindness for proceeding no further in his Prosecution against us.

Witness our Hands on the 13th day of July 1820

The mark X. of WILLIAM CONQUEST

The mark X of WILLIAM CONQUEST, Jun

The mark X of JOSEPH CONQUEST

In 1803, Britain declared war against France. The government called upon volunteers every time fear of revolutionary France shook king and Parliament, and Napoleon was now threatening invasion, massing his Grande Armée at Boulogne – it could be seen from the English coast. The sans-culottes of Market Harborough, for the most part, spent their lives servicing the quality and the aristocratic presence in the town and its environs, and despite the town's dissenting tenor, were not of Leicester's radical cast of mind. Under the influence of its aristocratic patrons, all the good and great of Harborough subscribed to pay for the volunteers; and nineteen-year-old Joseph Conquest signed up as a private in the 1st Harborough Volunteer Regiment, one of nearly half a million Britons who were to offer their services by the following year.

In Harborough 150 men volunteered to take the king's shilling. Those accepted for service were supposed to be among the 'most substantial inhabitants' of the town, with 'no labourers or paupers allowed'. But by 1803 the government was desperate. Only the intense dread of invasion could have reduced Parliament to arming with musket or pike men such as Joseph Conquest and his fellows, belonging as they did to that class which, particularly since the French Revolution, was both feared and repressed. That the fathers of the villains later to be found in company with the Conquest boys – John Garlick and Thomas Cort among them – joined up in Harborough attests to the great hardship that the Napoleonic Wars and their aftermath brought to those shakily loitering just above the hand-to-mouth classes. There were financial incentives to enlist: uniforms, clothes and shoes were on offer, the men were paid during training, 'wit and wine' and food were provided. And so Joseph Conquest now found himself rubbing shoulders with the officers drawn from the meritocracy of Market Harborough and the surrounding squirearchy.

Dread of Napoleon and the longing for his defeat conquered all fears of 'labourers or paupers'. Volunteers like Joseph were feted with feasts, balls, dinners and military parades. The Harborough men were toasted: 'May the Volunteers of Harborough have the Wisdom of Solomon, the strength of Sampson, and the Spirit of a Game Cock.' The infantry band, comprising drums, fifes and a triangle, provided martial accompaniment. These Volunteers were to be guerrillas on home territory, formed to harass the invading French forces; in practice the local nature of these civilian forces, and the disarray that went hand in hand with such motley crews, had much in common with the Second World War comedy *Dad's Army*. The roll call of the Duke of Rutland's Volunteer Infantry who offered themselves to their king is a perfect replica of those splendid men.

Greed, jostling with the right to resign if displeased, and innate indiscipline, meant this was but a passing phase for men such as Joseph Conquest, and his company forayed out only twice, once to Melton Mowbray and once to Daventry in Northamptonshire. It seems fortunate that Napoleon turned his attentions elsewhere, the British volunteers melted away, and French ambitions for invasion were finally ended by their defeat at the Battle of Trafalgar in 1805.

With the lump sum of £4 or £5 provided by his military endeavours, such as they were, in 1803 Joseph Conquest married. He chose yet another Sarah, the daughter of Ann and Rice Humphries – he a labourer in the town. The bride's father was not the only Rice Humphry, Humphreys, Humphrey – the name was spelled every which way. A few streets away lived a more affluent Rice Humfrey, a baker who left £300 at his death and was officially described as a yeoman, a commoner who owned a little land. Since the eighteenth century, wealthier and variously named Humfrey/phrey/phreys families were to be found throughout Leicestershire and Northamptonshire. 'Rice' is probably an anglicisation of the Welsh Rhys, suggesting that the large number of Independents in Harborough may have been due to a diaspora from Wales, where adherence to the Independent Church was both early and strong, providing passionate preachers. But more likely the first Rhys Humphries was one of the Welsh cattle drovers who had ferried their animals to the Midlands cattle fairs since ancient times.

Joseph and Sarah Conquest set up home in Little Bowden, and their nine children were to make up a substantial number of its few inhabitants. The male Conquests produced by this union, and by every generation in the following centuries, were almost invariably given one of six Christian names, a muddling business. Rice was now added to the canon, but always there would be a John, a George, a Thomas, a Joseph, a James, then an Alfred when all the other names had been used up. Of Joseph and Sarah's two daughters, only Charlotte survived; Harriet and Alfred joined that army of babies for whom was coined the tombstone inscription: 'So soon it was that I was done for, I wonder what I was begun for.' Six of their seven sons survived. John Conquest, the third of that name in Market Harborough, was born in 1804, George in 1806, Rice in 1808, Thomas in 1810, Joseph in 1813, and James in 1815. In due course most of them moved from Market Harborough, some to Leicester, and some emigrated – today the name Conquest is more common in the USA and Australia than in England.

By 1811, with four children born, Joseph *père* was working in the brewery of Joseph Timms in Kettering. Men of his class in those times left almost no traces of their daily lives, but what there is to find out about Joseph and his offspring emits a substantial odour of alcohol. Whether drinking too much of it or simple love of villainy led to his first disgrace is not known; what is certain is that in 1811, at Northampton assizes,

> Joseph Conquest, for stealing a quantity of malt, the property of Joseph Timms, maltster, of Kettering; and Richard Alsop, convicted of being an accomplice with Conquest, were both fined 1s and ordered to be imprisoned and kept to hard labour in the House of Correction for one year and until the said fine be paid.

Twelve months in such a place was no small matter. Branding was outlawed that same year, and prison reform was on the way, but most of the horrors of English prison life were on display in Market Harborough in 1811. Joseph was imprisoned in the airless guardhouse in the centre of town, where 'the poor unhappy wretches draw the noxious air' from the piles of dung left gracing the nearby stocks. Prisoners were put to hard labour, mostly beating hemp, particularly true in Market Harborough where flax was grown in the nineteenth century. Correction was provided by whipping, which was much advocated for Joseph's crime of theft. The jails were known as dens of iniquity, corruption, disease, overcrowding and hunger – prisoners had to pay their jailers for everything, buy their own food, and even pay a discharge fee. A year in such a place was a calamity. The birth of Joseph junior in 1813 suggests he found the necessary fee at the end of his sentence in 1812.

There are other signs of his considerable fall from grace. The couple's first four sons, John, George, Rice and Thomas, were all baptised in the Independent chapel, but after his year in jail, the Church of England received the family's patronage. It was the Nichols, rather than the Conquests, who were old Harborough dissenters: the hapless George Gill, whose powers were of such 'a low order', was Independent minister when Joseph senior was sent to the House of Correction, and any hope of a return to the fold was out of the question in the stormy Chapel years that followed. Thus the zone of comfort supplied by the Independent community of Market Harborough was removed from the Conquest family.

Market Harborough vociferously celebrated the defeat of Napoleon. The town's Peace Festival included a public dinner with riotous toasts, while 500 refined ladies took a most elegant tea. There were rural sports and fireworks. Bells, music, flags, and a band playing 'The Roast beef of Old England' accompanied a procession through the illuminated town, beginning at Mr Clarke's carpet factory. Three thousand spectators hurrahed; 228 plum puddings and ten hundredweight of fine English beef were consumed.

In the post-war years the landed gentry and aristocracy entered a period of swaggering high life, very noticeable in Market Harborough as 'fashionables' arrived at the inns of the town and lodges of the vicinity for the hunting season. There were assembly balls, charity balls, music festivals and concerts by foreign musicians, a reading society and lectures on astronomy. There were also many thousands of tramps. For the labouring classes, reduced rates and wages, the influx of returned soldiers and sailors and spiralling inflation brought about the decline of families such as the Conquests. Joseph and Sarah had not begun their lives at the very bottom of the Market Harborough barrel, in which position most of their children were to pass their lives, but any financial support from the Nichols family, modest though it might have been, was now quite gone. As the Allen family in Thurmaston had passed from their traditional lives as cottage framework knitters to the harsh paraphernalia of early industrialisation, so the Conquest men grabbed what they could, and got away with as much as they could.

The canals came to some kind of rescue, as so many of the Conquest boys worked on them. The heavy clay of Little Bowden made brickmaking a prosperous trade in the early years of the century, and bricks were an essential part of canal construction. Canal brickwork, most particularly the tunnels and the locks, needed constant maintenance, and brickmaking, their father's trade, became his sons' fall-back employment.

> The work, which was sometimes undertaken by family groups or gangs . . . was dirty and laborious, and involved a whole series of exhausting tasks. Stones were picked from the clay by hand and the puddling or tempering . . . depended on bodily weight, the clay being turned over repeatedly by the spade, mixed with water, and then trodden underfoot: the labourers who did this (sometimes horses, sometimes men, sometimes children) were said to develop 'puggers feet' from the sensitivity with which they could detect the slightest intrusive pebble . . . and 'wrist up' or 'lack of joint oil', according to a Chesham brickmaker, was an occupational hazard 'if you started off too rash'.

Anthony Trollope recorded this beautifully in *The Last Chronicle of Barset* (1867) as Mr Crawley, the impoverished and humiliated curate of Hogglestock, seeks out those unhappier than himself, and finds them

two miles distant from his house, through which was carried a
canal, affording communication in some intricate way both to
London and Bristol. And on the brink of this canal had sprung up
a colony of brickmakers, the nature of the earth in those parts
combining with the canal to make brickmaking a suitable trade.
The workmen there assembled were . . . in all appearance and
manners nearer akin to the race of navvies than to ordinary rural
labourers. They had a bad name in the country . . . They got drunk
occasionally . . . They fought amongst themselves sometimes, but
they forgave each other freely, and seemed to have no objection to
black eyes. I fear they were not always good to their wives, nor were
their wives always good to them; but it should be remembered that
among the poor, especially when they live in clusters, such
misfortunes cannot be hidden as they may be amidst the decent
belongings of more wealthy people. That they worked very hard
was certain . . .

'Are you here, Dan?' he said, knocking at the door of a cottage
which stood alone, close to the towing-path of the canal, and close
also to a forlorn corner of a muddy, watery, ugly, disordered
brickfield.

This describes the lives of the Conquest men at that time. In Market Harborough crime flourished, and its lower orders made frequent
appearances at both county and petty sessions. They indulged in
being drunk and disorderly, using foul language, committing assault
and wilful damage, non-payment of all rates, dangerous driving, and
theft. They poached and stole anything, from horses and sheep to
fish and chickens and fruit. Being a coaching town, robbery and highway robbery were extremely popular. The Conquest boys participated
in most of these pursuits.

The canals were owned by the companies who built them. Private
operators owned and ran most of the boats and fleets on the canals.
These were often wealthy merchants and colliery owners, gentry and
aristocracy, many of whom who had been involved in creating the canals
for their own business purposes. In the Midlands, such boats were
mostly 'narrow' boats, under seven feet wide and less than seventy-two
feet long. The company founded by the Pickford family, already wagon

carriers by road, began to transport goods by canal in 1770. They had fifty wagons, 400 horses and twenty-eight barges; by 1800 they had eight canal depots. Without mooring, their flyboats travelled day and night with four men aboard – two men on, two resting, using relays of horses.

By the early nineteenth century, life along the canals had become a world of its own, as flyboats competed with slow boats carrying coal or iron, competition becoming so fierce that god was mocked as the sabbath ceased to be respected. Cottages, stabling, inns and pubs, brothels (not so named) and boatbuilding yards grew up alongside the wharves and locks, tunnels and bridges studded the waterways. Beside the canals were towpaths for the horses (and sometimes children) that pulled the boats. The language of the canals was particular, and child labour well to the fore. Professional men – solicitors, engineers and treasurers – were among those employed at the top of the ferrying pyramid. At the labouring end came the horses – all too often horribly beaten – and men like the Conquests, working as labourers, brickmakers and inland boatmen. They came and went, often to jail, and often to look for work on dry land, but when Joseph senior came out of the House of Correction in 1812, work on and around the canals was there for the taking: in time his sons John, George, Rice and Joseph would all work as narrowboat men.

As the distances the boatmen travelled became greater, and the numbers working on the canals increased, the pay – good when labour was needed to get the waterways built – declined, and so, crime increased. There was much competition between the men on the flyboats and those on the narrowboats. Fisticuffs solved many a problem. Pilfering coal or 'disappearing' bottles of wine or liquor and poaching were added to any other inventive crimes these men fancied. Town and city wharves seethed with wharfingers, agents and clerks. Lock- and toll-keepers were at constant war with the boatmen – the former struggling to administer the bewildering array of pernickety charges which kept boats jostling alongside each other as they hustled to get through the locks. Winter brought ice and frost, summer water shortages that closed down the whole system. The labour was casual, two or three days on the boats, an odd job on land. Time wasted loitering around the wharves waiting for a captain to hire them; time always to spend money earned in a drinking or whoring den.

This is not young Joseph Conquest speaking, but it could be:

> I spent my time . . . lurking in fields where game lay, sometimes in
> beer-shops, public houses, and bawdy houses. When not in honest
> employ I was maintained by poaching and stealing.

How to describe the base reputation of these narrowboat men?
They were accused of 'drunkenness, dishonesty, violence, immorality,
ill-treatment of children'; of pilfering, buggery, illiteracy, cruelty,
rootlessness; of being a 'vile set of rogues' of 'decided wickedness',
having 'neither fear of God nor of man'. Incest was another accusation, as was murder. But the main begetter of all these sins was
drunkenness due to the string of beerhouses and inns that lined the
waterways. Contemporary denunciations paid little attention to the
excruciating boredom of canal work in the early years, the endless
hours when work there was; the primitive machinery on the boats
and locks, with human and animal toil doing most of the labour; the
irregular employment and the loneliness of it on the longer hauls. All
in all it was a frustrating and laborious means of transportation and
drudgery, soon to be replaced by the railways. Their lives were much
as the stockingers. Time off they did not want, and when they found
work, the hours were long and punishing. It was an itinerant life, for
men and boys only, their families installed along the banks or left at
home. Later, some families joined their men, particularly on the slow
boats, but it seems the Conquest wives remained in Market Harborough, Leicester, Little Bowden or other villages along the canals,
giving birth, watching many babies die, and then giving birth again.
The Conquest boys worked the canals in the first decades of the
nineteenth century, knowledge of this presenting itself through contemporary newspaper accounts of their peccadilloes. Trade on the
canals was at its most lucrative in the decade from 1828. The canal
companies made money, and so did their boatmen. The Conquest
boys seem to have spent most of it on alcohol.

  In 1828 the eldest son John, a boatman, and his canal mate William Sprigg assaulted the landlord of the Green Dragon Inn in Market
Harborough. It was half past ten on a Saturday night when they
'knocked violently at his door demanding to be served with liquor'.

Refused entry, they kicked the door down, and John gave the land-lord a blow to the ear, with Sprigg adding more abuse as the man lay prostrate; they then proceeded to attack others there, and to kick over a table laden with glasses and jugs. For this they were each fined a shilling and sent to the House of Correction for a month. By 1841 John was in the workhouse with his wife and their two daughters, Ann and Sarah. Ann, aged three, did not survive it.

In 1841 John's younger brother, Rice, a boatman who, like the other Conquest boys, reverted to their father's brickmaking labour when work on the canals was scarce, was charged with assault on his lodger, Thomas Newham, who had failed to pay his rent. Rice was fined five shillings, and spent a month in the House of Correction. Thomas, the next brother, only a year old when his father went inside for a year, was the exception to the family rule: he escaped to Bed-ford, where he passed his life safely as a hotel porter and waiter. The fifth brother, Joseph junior, took what passed for villainy in those days to a high art, the list of his misdemeanours regularly livening up gossip in the town and eliciting a choleric response from those above. Named after his father, he took on all his father's activities. He was a brickmaker, labourer, boatman and energetic snook cocker. Drink and women were his roads to ruin.

By 1832, Market Harborough had grown to a population of 2,500, and had twenty-four hotels, taverns, inns and beerhouses. In 1834 the Select Committee on Drunkenness bewailed the substantial increase in the number of inebriates among the labouring class. There was, they estimated, one drinking den for every twenty families in the country. The elder Conquest sons lived in tenement yards near Bowden or Pudding Bag Lane. In 1834 Joseph was twenty-one, living in one such dwelling and working as a brickmaker, when he was con-victed of assaulting a married woman, Elizabeth Wakelin, at Fleckney, a brickmaking village ten miles along the Grand Union Canal, which was to become home to some of the Conquest children in due course. His fine was a hefty £1 15s, or a month in prison.

Joseph had married when he was only eighteen, not unusual for the time as a way of avoiding imprisonment under the bastardy laws, and even less so for a boatman, as they had no prospects to wait for. Thomas Malthus could have used Joseph and his bride Mary as exemplars of his

theory that parish relief encouraged the poor to marry early and to
breed in droves. They already had a daughter, and another baby was on
the way: Joseph was out just in time for Christmas. Over the coming
years, almost every time Mary became pregnant – six of their children
survived – Joseph ended up either involved in some imbroglio with
another woman, or in the workhouse.

In 1836, a boatman by this time, Joseph was charged at Leicester
with setting his master's dog upon a boy. According to Joseph's
account, he had repeatedly told a pestiferous gaggle of boys not to play
on the boat, and had finally set the dog on them 'for they had *insulted*
the animal, by throwing stones at him'. 'Hey boy, fetch him out, bite
him,' said Joseph, choosing a particularly malevolent eleven-year-old
whose hands were then badly mauled. Joseph defended himself by
arguing that he was 'surprised parents did not keep their children at
home on the Sunday'. The mayor of Leicester, who was presiding in
court, ordered him to pay the boy's father fifty shillings, probably as
much as Joseph would have earned from a six-week trip (less the cost
of a horse and hand, for which the boatman had to pay). 'You men
who keep boats,' said the mayor, 'are a set of the most low and brutal
people *imaginable*.'

In April 1837, his wife Mary at home with three children of five,
three and one, Joseph's taste for wine and women brought him to
court again: 'Margaret Bryan, 24, charged with stealing a purse containing twenty-three shillings and sixpence, the property of Joseph
Conquest.' Joseph, in the Black Lion in Leicester with Margaret one
night, 'had some drink and pulled his purse out to pay for it and fell
asleep with the purse in his hand'. He woke up, and moved on to the
Red Cow with Margaret in tow, and there he realised his purse was
gone. He accused her, she denied it; he slapped her face and knocked
her down. She threw the purse on the table; it was empty. She defended
herself by saying that

> she was on terms of intimacy with the prosecutor, and had merely
> taken it to preserve it for him, when accusations were made
> against each other of the most disgusting description; indeed the
> whole of the witnesses in this case were characters of the lowest
> description.

5

The Journeymen

A stagecoach and coaching inn before the coming of the railways

O N 20 JUNE 1837, Victoria became Queen of the United Kingdom of Great Britain and Ireland, and two months previously, the new white settlement on the south coast of the Australian colony had been named after the prime minister of the time, Lord Melbourne. Despite his tumultuous marital arrangements, and his fondness for the flagellation of women and children, Melbourne was to become the young queen's trusted and honoured advisor, when not otherwise occupied persecuting the Chartists and other troubling members of the body politic. The 1834 New Poor Law had already set in train the punitive system that was to make life so exceptionally wretched for the poor. Almost in sympathy, in

October the Houses of Parliament in London had burned down. In 1837 Sary was in Thurmaston with the Allen family and her one-year-old son John, working the frames.

In December, Mary Ann Winsall, a twenty-year-old member of the Independent chapel in Market Harborough, married John Brooks, a twenty-four-year-old watchmaker, from the Lincolnshire town of Stamford, thirty miles to the north and connected to Market Harborough by the River Welland. Brooks lied about both his age and his achievements: he was only seventeen, and an apprentice to a clock- and watchmaker, but this was typical of the wayward behaviour this man was to favour during his life.

Mary Ann's mother, Mary Edens, and her father John Winsall, were both members of the Independent chapel in Bowden Lane in Market Harborough, where Mary Ann was baptised in 1817. John Winsall came from the nearby village of Desborough in Northamptonshire, a member of a family scattered around the Midlands counties – pub landlords, tradesmen and shop owners. Through her mother Mary Edens, however, Mary Ann was descended from an old Harborough Independent family, the Edens/Eadins/Edins – spelling only came gradually to this family over the centuries. By the 1830s the name had stabilised to Edens, and the family were firmly entrenched in the town. In general the men of the family were called Thomas or John or Joel, and were saddlers, collar makers and landlords, belonging to that class of artisans and tradespeople who so well serviced the coaching market town. They could be seen as being a rung or two above Sary or George Conquest, but theirs was a tenuous hold, many of them slithering down to the very bottom of the ladder at the whisk of a cat's tail.

In the decade of Mary Ann's marriage to John Brooks, Edens, Winsalls and Conquests lived and worked in the warren of tightly packed yards behind Market Harborough's Church Square, Church Street and the Sheep Market, between Adam & Eve Street, Tag Lane and Tripe Alley. Industrious artisans such as the Winsalls lived in the workshops, warehouses, stables, cottages and gardens of these yards, alongside the usual pigsties, tenements and malodorous privies. Until the very late nineteenth century Harborough did little about its sewerage, its stinking wells and polluted drinking water, nor about the overcrowded dwellings and yards in the centre of town. Mud cottages, damp and overcrowding exacerbated outbreaks of scarlet fever, typhoid, diphtheria, smallpox. The Edens, Conquests and Winsalls spawned by them took early death, so habitual in the town, to new heights. Life expectancy was only thirty-four years, and each generation lost babies and children to constantly recurring diseases and sudden epidemics.

From at least 1694, when George Conquest's ancestor John Nichols was a founding member of the Independent chapel, generations of Nichols, Edens and Winsalls mixed and mingled at the meeting house in Bowden Lane. Buckled shoes, waistcoats, hose, plain or decorated, three-quarter jackets, powdered wigs, top hats and evening dress were the garments of the favoured classes, rich colours abundantly displayed. Families of the Independent persuasion adopted more modest attire: breeches and hose for the men, bonnets and long dresses for the women, and whatever they could lay their hands on for labourers and paupers, the accent of Harborough perfectly comprehensible throughout the Midlands counties, despite many oddities of pronunciation particular to the town.

Mary Ann's father John Winsall had married his landlord's daughter, and ran his carpentry business on Adam & Eve Street, in Sulley's Yard. Nearby, by the 1830s, the eldest Conquest son John was labouring in Chapel Yard, and his brother Joseph junior was doing the same in Stiles Yard, living with his family in a tenement near the Meeting House and drinking his way through the inns and dens of Harborough, preparatory to the incarceration of both in the workhouse a few years later – not the old workhouse on the corner of Adam & Eve Street and Sheep Market, but a repellent new one in Great Bowden, brought into being by the Poor Law Act of 1834. Their parents Joseph senior and Sarah Conquest were living in Wheat Street, Leicester, he labouring as a brickmaker.

In the same small parcel of streets and yards in which Edens, Conquests and Winsalls worked, lived, prayed, procreated and misbehaved, Harborough's clock- and watchmakers were to be found. There were many notable Leicestershire and Lincolnshire makers, and Harborough was a centre of the trade in the late eighteenth and early nineteenth centuries. With the coming of the Industrial Revolution, clocks and watches were needed to keep factory hours and for travel timetables – first for stagecoaches, and then the railways. But by the mid-nineteenth century the craft was coming to an end as mechanisation and factory production gradually began to replace the village or town clockmaker.

Thus the young John Brooks had entered a dying trade when he went as an apprentice to a watch and clockmaker in Harborough, although it was to keep him gently upright until the 1860s. Apprenticed to one of the clockmakers clustered around Church Square and Church Street, he worked a step or two away from Sulley's Yard and Adam & Eve Street. From 1754 to 1837, all marriages in England had to take place in the established Church, so although Mary Ann Winsall was a member of the Independent chapel, she and John married in the parochial Chapel of St Dionysius, by special licence. Both could sign their names well – no crosses for them. The Independent meeting house in Bowden Lane taught the children of its adherents to read and write and to know their Bible: the more respectable Edens family made use of it for all of their children.

The marriage between Mary Ann Winsall and John Brooks took place as the glory days of Market Harborough were coming to an end. 1840 saw the opening of a railway from Birmingham to London by way of Rugby, twenty miles away, and the London–Manchester coaches ceased to travel through Harborough, bringing ruin to the numerous bodies that had depended on them. In 1843 the Harborough Bank failed, and the carpet factory in Tag Lane, which employed so many, went bankrupt. In 1849 a railway was built from Rugby to Stamford. Although it passed through Harborough, the station was half a mile outside town and required none of the food, drink and services which, during the coaching years, had brought some small prosperity to families like the Edens and Winsalls.

DWELLING-HOUSE, brick built, sash fronted, and slated, Adam and Eve Street in MARKET HARBOROUGH, consisting of a large parlour, convenient kitchen, pantry and cellar, three sleeping rooms and two attics. A very extensive YARD adjoining with commodious CARPENTER'S SHOP, saw pit, sheds, and every other convenience.

This was the house in which Mary Ann Winsall was brought up, the shop and yard in which her father worked. It was put up for sale in 1845, and by 1855 the Winsall and Edens families had all but disappeared from the town. Many of them died young including Mary's parents: the few remaining moved on, to more chequered careers elsewhere.

John Brooks came from an old Stamford family. In 1837 it was a town full of churches and fine Georgian buildings, many of them roofed in the local Collyweston limestone slate by John's grandfather William, a master slater. Stamford lies in Lincolnshire, at the junction of Leicestershire, Northampton and Rutland, and is traversed by the Great North Road, which was for centuries the main highway connecting the south and the north of England. Not for the county of Lincoln the industrial transformation of its Midlands neighbours: Lincolnshire remained more agricultural than industrial.

In the sixteen years John Brooks lived there, Stamford was a prosperous market town. The great turnpike roads built in the eighteenth century, like the canals and railways, opened up the country to travel, and Stamford became a major staging post for coaches and mails along the Great North Road, replete with inns and hostelries. It was not unlike Market Harborough in that regard but more populous, and certainly more feudal: its near 6,000 souls lived and died entirely under the thumb of the Cecil family who ruined life for the lower orders of Stamford for nigh on four centuries. Their influence was so strong that the industrial development of nearby Leicestershire and other Midlands counties affected the town hardly at all. Stamford was built to impress, and its beautiful stone buildings, commanding church towers and antique ways preserved it, as did the heavy hand of each succeeding Cecil.

William Cecil came from Bourne, twelve miles to the north of Stamford, in 1520. By 1558, through fair means and foul, he had become Secretary of State to Queen Elizabeth I. Among his myriad of services to her he oversaw the execution of Mary Queen of Scots in nearby Fotheringay. His rewards included the title of Lord Burghley, the position of Lord High Treasurer, and enrichment through the acquisition of most of the monastic land in and around Stamford, liberated by Elizabeth's father Henry VIII into the waiting pockets of men such as Cecil. He made Stamford his personal fiefdom, and passed it on to his descendants so that despite a slight hiccup in the seventeenth century, when the only available heir was female, Cecils inhabited the splendid Burghley House, just outside the town, throughout the centuries, negotiating national crises so adroitly that although Stamford was fought over by both parties in the English Civil War, its heart remained Royalist.

Over the years, succeeding generations of Cecils were rewarded by the Crown with a ladder of additional titles, ranging through earls, lords, barons and marquesses. Descendants of the first Lord Burghley established noble lines of their own, notably the progeny of his half-brother Robert Cecil, whose branch was also decorated with a plethora of names and titles – Marquesses of Salisbury, viscounts, barons, earls, mutating into Gascoyne-Cecils and providing the nation with prime ministers, bishops, Conservative political leaders and other men of substance and dignity who ran Britain and its empire.

Burghley House, Stamford

Stamford in the early nineteenth century is vividly described in the novels of Georgette Heyer, though Jane Austen provides a more satirical understanding of its way of life. Cards and dancing, the race track and concerts at the assembly rooms (both under the patronage of the Marquess of Exeter) were its most celebrated amusements as were its exhibitions, theatre, bowling green, the vast cockpit at the George Inn, its libraries and its endless charity balls. Prestigious visitors were constant, ranging from Madame Tussaud to Richard Cobden, with the regular arrival of various militias and regiments. Some thirty stagecoaches and forty mail coaches traversed Stamford each day, bringing profit to all the stables and coaching inns and the ever-growing number of public houses such journeys required.

Bull-running, which took place every winter, was as much a hallmark of the town as its heavy traffic, its fairs, its market days and its Cecils. 13 November was celebrated each year, beginning with the ringing of the bells of St Mary's Church – a duty performed for some years by John Brooks' brother Charles – announcing the beginning of the torture of the beast. The day continued with cheering human beings and barking dogs chasing the tormented bull up and down the blocked off streets and lanes of the town until it reached Town Bridge, where it was pitched into the river, and then of course, slaughtered. Booze and laughter accompanied the spectacle, the Cecils' vassals bathed in the happiness that comes from watching a creature in much more pain than oneself.

Stamford was not like Leicester or Market Harborough. If Leicester was radical, and Market Harborough mostly provided with an influx of nobility and gentry *en passant* or during the hunting season, Stamford belonged to king, queen and country. But the poorer parts of Stamford in the 1830s were the same as those of every other town and city: disease, early mortality and bastardy were the norm, as were the inventive crimes of every kind vigorously undertaken by Stamford's indigent classes, amidst its ancient, and permanent, squalor. The town's workhouse and almshouses lurked nearby – but who merited charity there, or a place in the free grammar school, was decided by the Cecils' minions. Some 1,500 convicts were despatched from Lincolnshire to various penal colonies in Australia, and Stamford provided its due share of them. John Brooks, a wise and an unwise man throughout his life, wisely left the town at the age of sixteen.

With the valuable trade brought by the coaching traffic, and by attending to the needs of both visitors and its aristocracy, in the first half of the nineteenth century Stamford was, like Market Harborough, a thriving town of artisans and tradespeople, with flourishing markets and fairs, a centre of business for prosperous merchants serving the towns and farmers surrounding it. The name Brooks was a common one in Stamford – some were bakers, some were printers, some worked in leather, a major trade in the town. John Brooks' father Richard was a cordwainer, a maker of fine leather shoes, placing him further up the ranks than a bootmaker as, like his father the master slater, he had served an apprenticeship in his trade. Richard could not read or write, but he was one rung above the industrial and labouring poor such as the Allen family, although this was a class such men often married into – John Brooks' mother, Sarah Figgen, being a case in point. She produced a baby every two years and lost the usual number – five of her seven children reached adulthood. She could neither read nor write and the family she came from appears to have been similarly untutored, as the name Figgen appears in scores of different spellings throughout the county.

Stamford's artisans and craftsmen clustered in shops around the centre of the town, in particular the horseshoe triangle of High Street, St John's Street and St Mary's Street, the last two on the trajectory of the Great North Road. A dangerous curve on the famous course swept sharply from the end of the narrow St John's Street into St Mary's Street. There, in view of the church spires and towers of Stamford, Richard Brooks lived and worked, facing the pinnacle tower and solid edifice of St John's Church across the road. The Brooks family of this generation benefitted from their connections to Stamford's churches and Sunday schools, and from the benevolent aspects of patronage, arranged by those inhabitants of Stamford who 'desire to see the labouring classes imbued with sentiments of love and reverence for true religion and virtue'. St John's was the church of the Stamford artisans, merchants and professional men who lived and worked around it. John Brooks was taught to read and write well. He gloried in a fine signature, with a bold and much scrolled 'B', which he used as often as he could.

The tombstone of Richard Brooks, Cordwainer,
St John's churchyard, Stamford, 1829

Cholera was rampant in the town between 1825 and 1832 and
Richard merited a tombstone in its churchyard when he died in 1829
at the age of forty-five. John Brooks was nine. His two older brothers
took over his upbringing, and the younger of them, Charles, would
play an important part in whatever prosperity he managed to achieve.

John's years in Stamford, 1820–36, were studded with royal celebrations. He was born as George IV became king, an event marked
in Stamford with proclamations, processions, cheering crowds, gun
volleys and barrels of ale, in a manner 'worthy of the rank of the town
for ancient consequence and present respectability'. A year later the
new king's coronation was marked by even more enthusiastic celebrations in the town. George IV lived only ten more years, so John was
ten when William IV ascended the throne in 1830, requiring yet more
proclamations and festivity, with volleys of musketry all over the
town accompanied by the melody of 'a new version of "God save the
King"'. And many hogsheads of ale.

The death of a monarch required an election at this time, which in Stamford in the summer of 1830 was contested – an entirely new occurrence. These were the years of turmoil leading to the Great Reform Act of 1832. The constituency was permitted to elect two Members of Parliament. Hitherto they had always been nominated by, or more commonly were members of, the Cecil families. Davids, Thomases, Williams, Richards and Henrys of the family had all performed the role over the centuries, often accompanied either by relatives or by other acceptable patricians. In 1830 the nominees of the marquess were the two sitting members: his brother Lord Thomas Cecil, and a relative, Thomas Chaplin, whose brother Charles had preceded him as the Cecils' other parliamentary representative. But then the 'gentlemen' of the town invited Charles Tennyson, the Whig uncle of the poet Alfred, to stand against the incumbents.

Never had the inns and taverns of Stamford seen such a flow of alcohol or such crowds as those which greeted Tennyson as he approached the town to begin his campaign. Some mounted on horseback, some on foot, they cheered Tennyson, hailing him as their 'emancipator'. They led him to the George and Angel Inn, where he was awaited by some 10,000 people, which considering the voting population of Stamford at the time – only about 700 – implies that every inhabitant of the town and its environs was there.

They would have included all the Brooks family, with Charles and John being fourteen and ten years old respectively. Houses, tenements and shops were festooned with blue (the Radical colour) flags and bunting, the town band played, the church bells pealed, tar barrels and torches lit up the beautiful churches and buildings of the grander parts of Stamford. In his address to the crowd, given from an upper window of the George and Angel Inn, Tennyson declared:

> I see before me a noble-minded population, panting for freedom,
> and if efforts of mine can accomplish your object, free you shall
> be, henceforth, and forever . . . You sought for a leader to conduct
> you into the sunshine of liberty, out of the darkness of the house
> of bondage.

Such an extraordinary event in a town whose feudal allegiance was to continue almost seamlessly until the present day, is a testament to the extraordinary hopes attached to the Great Reform Act and the turmoil throughout the country in 1830, the year of the Swing Riots. Hopes were not dashed when Tennyson failed to gain one of Stamford's seats, because he came in only twenty votes behind Chaplin, and the new Tory government led by the intransigent Duke of Wellington, hostile to all demands for parliamentary reform, lasted only two and a half months. Two weeks after Charles Tennyson's impudent near-victory, the agent of the Marquess of Exeter delivered an order

> to all persons renting any property under His Lordship, and who at the late election of representatives for the borough voted for Mr Tennyson: even those who gave one vote for the brother of the marquess, were not by that act redeemed from the consequence of voting against other nominees (Mr Chaplin) – all alike were served with notices to quit their messuages or tenements, farms, lands, hereditaments, and premises with their respective rights, members, and appurtenance before the 25th day of March next ensuing.

Two months later the resignation of Wellington's government in November was greeted in Stamford by the pealing of church bells and the burning of effigies, but all this popular activity in support of what was finally passed as the Great Reform Bill, celebrated again with much joyful bell ringing, was Stamford's last gasp of rebellion. Tennyson won a seat in the 1831 election, but the boundary changes of the Reform Bill gave more power to the Cecils, and a typical Stamford voter would lament to Lord Langford who attempted to stand against the Cecil interest in 1837, 'My heart is with you, but you know how I am situated, I live under Burghley [Cecil]. I wish you success, but dare not vote for you.' Cecil strengthened his hold over his Burghley tenants in the coming years, using 'the most unfair and tyrannous means' to 'prevent the humbler class of voters from exercising their franchise in favour of the Liberal candidates'. It was a rare Liberal, Whig or Radical politician who dared to show his face in Stamford thereafter, and a rare subject who dared to murmur the word 'reform' as Cecil's intimidation and bribery took effect on the town.

The voters of Stamford seldom opened their mouths again, and in return the Cecils preserved a town which changed little over the coming centuries. In 1846 the Cecils ensured that the Great Northern Railway did not make a diversion to Stamford, to the great disappointment, not to say despair, of the inhabitants of the town, for, as with Market Harborough, the coming of the railways brought Stamford's coaching prosperity to an end. Pickled in aspic by the Cecil family, today Stamford remains one of the finest and best-preserved stone towns in England, in constant use for television costume dramas. By 1836 Lord Exeter could assure the Duke of Wellington that 'whatever changes had taken place in other municipalities, the Corporation of Stamford were still subservient'. Such a town was of little use to a sixteen-year-old artisan adventurer, who left Stamford in that year, and never returned.

John Brooks' escape came about because of where he was born and raised – in one of a little cluster of shops in St John's Street, Stamford, which from 1819 to 1835 included that of William Hickman, a watch and clockmaker. In 1831, two years after Richard Brooks' death, his widow Sarah was married again – to a carpenter who signed his name with a cross at their wedding at St John's. The couple continued to live in St John's Street for some years thereafter, and it may be that the arrival of this stepfather enticed the two boys into the company of the childless clockmaker William Hickman, who trained Charles in his craft. In time Charles took over his shop, and sent his younger brother to Market Harborough to learn the trade.

With this piece of tremendous good fortune, the Brooks brothers entered into some decades of near-respectability. In August 1844, not without the malign influence of the Cecils, hostile as ever to change and reform, it was decided that the route of the London–Edinburgh railway line should pass through Grantham and Peterborough. Those two neighbouring towns sprang into prosperity while Stamford settled back into decorous decline as its coaching trade and attendant services collapsed, and the George and Angel Inn and many others closed down. Before then, however, Charles flourished, becoming an Overseer of the Poor in Stamford and the regulator and repairer of St Mary's spire clock.

With its religious and monastic past, silversmiths, goldsmiths and clockmakers were ancient trades in Stamford, and the town's artisans produced much work of great beauty. Charles Brooks' approach to his trade, however, tended towards enthusiasm for its financial prospects rather than to the finer points of intricate workmanship. Only one 'Longcase painted dial clock with automata swan extant' can be found as a possible relic of Charles's work. It is doubtful whether he made it himself, because not all clock- and watchmakers of the period were artisans of great skill: many were no more than retailers or repairers, very often making ends meet by providing other services such as spectacle making and, in particular, dentistry, as 'the increasing demand for artificial teeth opens a rich field for the enterprise and encouragement of ingenious mechanics, particularly clock- and watchmakers'.

Many mechanical advances were made in the world of clockmaking in these years, and the advice given an apprentice such as the young John Brooks was that:

> a boy the age of twelve years . . . should be placed in a clockmaker's shop till the age of seventeen . . . From the age of seventeen to nineteen or twenty he should be employed at watch work either repairing or finishing, in order to 'fine down his hand' . . . Having now, it is presumed, acquired mechanical knowledge and manual dexterity, he may commence the making of artificial teeth.

Mary Ann Winsall was three years older than John Brooks when they married. This habit of marrying women older than themselves, often practised by the Brooks males – their father had done the same – had the benefits not only of sometimes bringing money to the marriage bed, but also of making the production of an excess of children less likely. Alas, it was an insufficient age gap, and they shortly began the production of a quiverful of children. But not in Stamford or Market Harborough. Good fortune propelled John into the more colourful waters of Boston on the south Lincolnshire coast, which offers its subjects something denied to the other counties in the Midlands: the sea. More populous than Stamford at this time, and much jollier, Boston sits on the Wash and the River Witham, surrounded in times past by desolate fens and marshes, the draining of which in the eighteenth and early nineteenth centuries brought new life to the ancient town, so that by the time John and Mary Ann arrived there in 1838, Boston had blossomed and expanded to become the largest town in Lincolnshire.

As it grew, so did its Nonconformity, quite overtaking its Anglican community in these prosperous years. River, harbour and market dominated Boston life. It had bankers and merchants, busy shipyards with crowded wharves and quays, warehouses and windmills, breweries and foundries, and a population of over 12,000. Surrounding it was over 100,000 acres of reclaimed and fertile arable land. Seaward, its flourishing coastal shipping sailed north towards Lincoln and beyond, south to London, and across the North Sea to the Continent. And, by canal and waterway, inland towards Stamford and the other Midlands counties.

Boston sits on a tidal river, the Haven, into which flows the River Witham. The straightening of this river in the eighteenth century was one of the marvels of the canal age, capped by the engineering genius to be seen in Boston's Great Sluice, built in the mid-1760s, which protected the town from flooding by sea, river and fen, and diverted waters to secure river navigation. All these creations of the early industrial age meant that John and Mary Ann Brooks started their family in what was to remain a boom town for the next decade, connected to the outside world by wagon and coach, by road and navigable canal, by ship, boat and steam packet.

Lincolnshire had its great landowners, but in the nineteenth century the county tended to be more Whig than Tory, although, being largely rural, support for the Corn Laws – always seen as a conservative policy – was popular. Its people were ruled, in general, more by the county's landed gentry than by its noble families. Boston was run by a corporation made up of the usual oligarchs, but it was not in thrall to the divine right of kings as exemplified by the Cecils, and was also a trading town. Its huge sheep market was dominated by the enormous fourteenth-century cathedral, St Botolph's, commonly known as 'The Stump', with its stout tower rising to the skies, almost swaying, high, high above the town and port, seen from afar for many miles around.

The May Sheep Fair, Boston, with
St Botolph's Church tower, 'The Stump', soaring above, c. 1840

Boston had a long history of dissent and Nonconformity. Parliamentarian in the English Civil War, a source of many of those Separatists and Puritans who colonised New England in the seventeenth century, by the end of the eighteenth century it had begun to develop into that rarity in the county of Lincoln – an industrial town – as well as being a shipping, banking and engineering centre. Reformers were a vociferous presence in Boston, with Radicals, Whigs and Tories slogging it out in the years before and after the Great Reform Act, the violence of political disputation on the town's streets exceeding anything seen in Stamford by many a measure. Apart from riots, attacks on Tory houses and the placing of the tricolour on the steps of the police station, the battle was between Boston's corporation and its radical and Nonconformist middle classes, with a vigorous mob, unfettered by aristocratic control, 'venting their fury and indignation on them all'. In the election of 1831 Whigs won both Boston seats. When the Great Reform Act finally passed in June 1832, free ale was distributed, but the disconsolate corporation called in the dragoons, who prevented the celebrations which erupted elsewhere in the country.

In 1835 the new Municipal Corporation Act extended the franchise, which meant that, as in Leicester, Reformers took over the corporation. Many of those newly elected were dissenters. They got rid of the old guard, sold off the civic regalia of their Tory predecessors, and set about town improvements and expansion of a more democratic nature. Queen Victoria's marriage to Prince Albert in February 1840 was celebrated, of course, with due quantities of alcohol and conviviality as 'The spirited landlord of the Dog and Duck Inn gave away two hogsheads of ale'.

In 1838, when the Brookses went to live in Boston, Mary Ann was seventy miles away from her family in Market Harborough, the intractable Fens formerly surrounding the town now conquered by drainage and enclosure, turnpike road and canal. In these years Methodism flourished in Lincolnshire, a transformative force throughout the county. In Boston it presented its numerous forms ranging through Wesleyan to Primitive, from Reformed to New Connexion, and there were also thriving communities of General Baptists, Particular Baptists, Unitarians and Quakers. Mary Ann was thus in a town much more suited to an Independent chapelgoer from Market Harborough than Stamford could ever have been. A Boston banker had supported the construction of the Independent chapel in Boston's Grove Street in 1819, and it prospered just as Methodism did, its Good Friday tea festivals well attended, and a schoolroom with the capacity to educate up to 400 children, of whom John and Mary Ann Brooks were to supply four – a piece of good fortune for their daughters, because fifty per cent of women in Lincolnshire were still illiterate in the 1840s.

As well as these benefits, John Brooks had apprenticed himself to the most prosperous craftsman of the town, Benjamin Bothamley, whose shop was in Market Place, within praying distance of St Botolph's, at the very centre of Boston's universe and its roistering annual May sheep fair, the highlight of the year. Among the shop's neighbours in the teeming nearby streets were chandlers and druggists, blacksmiths and labourers, printing and clothing workshops, saddlers and furniture makers, as well as an overabundance of chapels, inns and taverns. Answering the following advertisement, John went to work there as a journeyman watch and clockmaker in spring 1838, only a few months after his marriage:

BOTHAMLEY, Watch and Clockmaker, Silversmith and
Jeweller, <u>Market-Place</u>, Boston, is in immediate want of a
Journeyman, a good hand: none else need apply.

Whatever he learned during his six years as an apprentice to the Bothamley family, John did not, alas, take their fine workmanship with
him. Though he was a master watchmaker, and would keep a silversmith, clock and watch shop on and off for most of his life in Boston,
there is nothing with his mark in the honourable list of the clock- and
watchmakers of Lincolnshire.

John and Mary Ann's first home in Boston was in Liquorpond
Street, named after the pond of a nearby brewery and undergoing
development after the new corporation made its presence felt. The
street was newly paved, houses and shops could be rented, and they
lived amongst ships' captains and a variety of Baptist chapels and
Temperance followers. John Brooks was to prove a repetitive impreg-
nator of the women in his life, but unless she had early miscarriages

Benjamin Bothamley's
shop in Market Place,
Boston, where John Brooks
went to train as a jeweller
and silversmith in 1838

or stillbirths, it was almost two years before Mary Ann had her first child, though the delay may also have been due to the death of both her parents and her younger sister in the months after her marriage. Their first child, Charles Hickman Brooks, named after his father's early patron, was born in 1840, Emily followed in 1842, and by the time their third child was expected, John had completed his apprenticeship. He opened his own shop in Bridge Street – number 3/5a, a step or two away from Bothamley's – and all too near one of the foulest smelling of Boston's five featherbed factories, for which reason the family did not live above the shop but moved to cheaper lodgings in nearby West Street, where alas the featherbed factory followed them. West Street boasted a Zion chapel, four inns and taverns, shops and small businesses of every description, and most unsatisfactory drainage and sanitary arrangements. This is where John and Mary Ann's third child, my great-grandmother, yet another Mary Ann, was born in 1844. Their last child, a girl, Sarah Jane, was born in 1846.

It was Lincolnshire's role during the Industrial Revolution to feed much of the nation. The fine land around Boston produced prodigious amounts of grain, brought to the town's granaries, quays and thriving Corn Market for despatch throughout the country. Boston also transported by water (and also by road) much of the Midlands' coal, shipping timber, agricultural produce, manure and cattle, passengers and much else – but by 1840, its shipping trade and inland navigation needed further investment. After years of debate and argument amongst the corporation and Boston's shippers, bankers and investors, the decision was taken to divert capital instead to the construction of railways. By 1848 they had not only reached Boston, but Great Northern Railway chose Boston for its headquarters. Rail could transport goods more quickly than coastal shipping, and the water transport Boston offered was taken over by Lincolnshire's numerous railways. No branch line was built to the port or the Haven, and nothing could replace the varied work available to the men who had poured into Boston's warehouses, market, docks and port. Silence fell upon its long-distance stage, mail and passenger coaches which centred around the Peacock Inn, the most celebrated of Boston's inns in the Market Place.

The birth of John and Mary Ann Brooks' four children also coincided with the onslaught of the Hungry '40s. The economic slump of 1839, followed by two years of bad harvests, led to depression, unemployment and bitter suffering for the working and labouring classes of Boston and its surrounds, as it did for the Allens in Leicester and the Conquests in Market Harborough. Skilled and unskilled workers alike scrambled for work, and so wages fell. The potato blight began in England and Scotland and had spread to Ireland by 1845, with murderous results, and by that year there was also 'great distress in the town' of Boston. The very cold weather prevented many from working on the land, exacerbating the poverty in Lincolnshire, as there was so little alternative work. In Boston itself, bankers and merchants, shipowners and principal traders, benevolent ladies and the quantity of friendly societies and flourishing chapels and churches offered soup kitchens and 'most seasonable relief to many industrious mechanics and labourers, who have been for many weeks deprived of employment'.

The very worst years of this decade in Boston were 1843 and 1844, just as John Brooks opened his shop, at a time when the town's prosperity was evaporating. This is probably the reason John did not become a manufacturer himself, like his former employer Benjamin Bothamley. Then in 1848, John Brooks' life changed entirely. In that year in England and Wales over 50,000 people died in the cholera epidemic. Sewage from Boston's open cesspools flowed down its drains and putrid streets, and the town's slums were exceptionally overcrowded with the influx of itinerant workers who came to look for work on the land and the railways. The Brooks family lived but four minutes' walk from Lincoln Lane, the Boston slum most affected by cholera, and in April 1848 it claimed the life of Mary Ann Brooks. She was thirty-one. She was buried in St Botolph's in an unmarked grave, leaving John with four children under the age of eight. He was only twenty-eight.

In December of that year John's shop in Bridge Street was broken into, and £200 of goods were stolen, worth over £23,000 today. By mid-century the popularity of the longcase or grandfather clock was in decline; the trade was becoming mechanised: ready-made cheap and foreign dials, workings and cases flooded the market. Already, by

1847, John was advertising himself as a repairer, rather than a maker of beautiful instruments, and as the seller of 'New and Second hand Watches, Eight-Day clocks, German Clocks, American clocks, Alarums, and a great variety of Jewellery.'

He was to bounce back, but uppery and downery were to mark his adventurous life henceforth. In its boom years, Boston had as many pubs and inns as any town in the Midlands. But it was also the centre of another poison, much more special to itself, and one as good as, if not better than, alcohol as an antidote to failure: opium, the 'insidious poison [more] consumed in the towns of Louth, Spilsby, and Boston, than in all the rest of the towns of the county'.

6

◄◉►

Bone Dust

A workhouse designed by Samuel Kempthorne, the architect who specialised
in their design and construction for the Poor Law Commission after 1834

T HE NEW POOR LAW of 1834 brought misery to the poor and
unemployed of Market Harborough, just as it did elsewhere.
Those above them bemoaned the new state of affairs:

The *Catalogue of Offences* committed in and near Harborough since
our last report is painfully long. Robberies and crimes appear to
be universally prevalent. We cannot resist the impression that the
operation of the New Poor Law is one great cause of the numerous
depredations committed.

In 1836 a new Union Workhouse was built at 33 Leicester Road in Harborough, and with the onset of the Hungry '40s both John Conquest and his younger brother Joseph entered its dismal portals. The coming of the railways had already clearly sounded the departing knell both for boatmen and their canal masters, and for Market Harborough's coaching trade. Sampson Kempthorne, one of the architects working for the Poor Law Commissioners, designed the new Harborough workhouse as a model establishment for the new law. Inmates were separated by age, sex and infirmity. An imposing maintenance block housing master, matron, staff and boardroom opened on to four wings for the inmates. There was a women's yard, a men's yard, a girls' yard and a boys' yard. Wives, husbands and children could only glimpse each other in the communal dining hall or chapel. They slept either on a narrow straw mattress on an iron or wooden frame, on a wooden box or platform, or on the floor. Other amenities included a much-shared privy, or a cesspit or chamber pot, with a bath (and for men, a shave) once a week. These new institutions were constructed to allow constant supervision, to be punitive and to encourage psychological suffering. The Market Harborough workhouse achieved all this very well. It was one of ten square workhouses Sampson Kempthorne oversaw during his career. As he was also responsible for sixteen hexagonal workhouses, and various pauper ones, in 1842 he sensibly emigrated to New Zealand, where his constructions were found to be most unsatisfactory.

In early 1841 John Conquest was in the workhouse with his wife Elizabeth and their two daughters, three-year-old Ann, and Sarah, born in April of that year. Their stay was not a long one, but Ann did not survive its rigours, dying in July in Leicester, where John had gone to join his brother Rice and his father Joseph, both working there as bricklayers and living with his mother Sarah in Wheat Street. Eaton Street, where Sary would live when she first married William Grundy in 1843, and Metcalf Street, to which she and her son Alfred later moved, were but two small streets away.

Misery, harsh work and half-starvation was the lot of every pauper in the workhouse: they were monuments to the inhumanity of man to man, although much depended on the character of the administrator. The inmates of the Harborough workhouse were exceptionally unfortunate:

> much ill-feeling has for a considerable time existed between
> Warburton, master of the workhouse and some of the unfortunates
> whom stern necessity has compelled to place themselves under his
> jurisdiction.

Joseph Conquest, not yet thirty, stripped, searched, his hair cropped, in the workhouse uniform of striped shirt and hobnailed boots, was put to work stone-breaking, sack-making, oakum picking, or walking the treadwheel of a corn mill. Nine hours' work a day in winter, ten hours in the summer. His wife Mary had by then given birth to four children and was pregnant with their fifth. Thomas, their two-year-old, had been sent to Leicester to live with his grand-parents; one can but hope that some Conquest siblings took in the other three children. At least all of Joseph and Mary's children sur-vived, unlike their poor little cousin Ann.

Mary would have been given a long, shapeless striped dress and a poke bonnet, and put to scrubbing floors and all other drudgeries that could be dreamed up for female members of the undeserving poor. Meals, which had to be eaten in silence, were another punish-ment. Mary's was bread and gruel, and some weak tea with perhaps a drop of milk; men had the same, but with meat, broth and more milk added. One day just before Christmas 1841, after dinner, Joseph pushed past the master to try to give Mary an apple. Warburton claimed that the apple was unlikely to be Joseph's and called him 'a thief and a rogue'. Joseph called Warburton a liar.

On the first day of the New Year 1842

> a pauper named Conquest charged Warburton with treating him
> with undue severity and harshness and exercising an arbitrary
> power in the discharge of his duty.

The case was taken to Harborough petty sessions. Hatred of War-burton and his workhouse was such, and Joseph's connections with the labourers of the town so strong, that a subscription was raised to

pay for his defence, and the inmates of the workhouse supported
him vociferously. If Dickens had written the court report of the session and those that followed, as the war between Warburton and
Joseph raged on, it would have made a masterpiece of English workhouse history.

Before a packed crowd which filled the hall and spilled out onto
the staircase, Warburton was accused of

> withholding a part of the oatmeal in making their gruel . . . of
> intruding himself into the women's bed-rooms . . . of compelling
> a woman to get up and dress herself in his presence, a day or two
> after she had given birth to a child.

One of Joseph's fellow inmates who was there 'kicked up a shindy . . .
he would rather be transported than live any longer with such an old
d---l [devil]'. His reward was twenty-one days' hard labour in the
House of Correction.

Later in January, Harborough petty sessions assembled again to
hear 'a continuation of the contentions at the Union Workhouse'. The
court heard that on Christmas Eve:

> after leaving the dining room on that day, Conquest . . . waited in
> the passage to inform his wife how he got on in Leicester, where
> he had been in search of employment [with his father and
> brothers]. As he did not quit the passage at the command of
> the porter, he was seized by the collar, shook very much,
> and ejected.

Men in the Harborough workhouse had not been allowed to
speak to their wives until the commissioner had advised more leniency, but John Hughes, the porter, mourned his previous instructions.
He protested that the master had said:

> The men go out first, and the women after, and it is the duty
> of the Porter to clear the room, and lock the doors, and he
> had often complained that the men staid behind and obliged
> him to go and turn them out. He had refused a man speaking

to his wife but had been ordered by the Board [of Guardians]
to do so. Since the Commissioner said, he could see no wrong
in it, we have allowed them, but that has occasioned much
disorder . . .

Joseph charged Hughes with assault. Once again Market Harborough's hoi polloi came out to support Joseph and object to the 'violent
manner of the porter', but the case was dismissed.

Warburton could not come to terms with Joseph's vigorous will.
He proceeded to charge him and his brother-in-law Thomas Swingler, also in the workhouse, 'with gross misconduct and riotous
behaviour on the third and fourth of January'.

Mr Warburton, the Master, laid information against Joseph
Conquest for disorderly conduct and a breach of the peace, and
against Thomas Swingler for disorderly conduct . . . On Monday,
the 3rd inst, the Master read an order at dinner time, made by
the Board, that Conquest should have no meat that week, and the
following being meat day Conquest was provoked at his having
no portion allowed him, which gave rise to the charge made
against him. The Porter said on Tuesday the 4th January at dinner
time Conquest said to the Master: 'Are you a man?' and held up
his knife to the Master, and told him to take it, his breast was
open to receive it. Swingler said he [Warburton] was an old rogue
and would rob any man. Conquest said he was a perjured villain;
he would do him. Joseph said if they had been at Leicester, his
wife said they would have killed him and eaten his bones. Some of
them were frightened there was such an uproar.

Joseph's lawyer protested that:

it all had the appearance of a trumped-up charge against the men,
in retaliation for the former proceedings, there being no one of
the poor in the House that could be brought to give evidence to it,
and surely there were good ones out of the number (118) as they
had been represented to be, but not one would come to speak on
behalf of the Master, as it appeared they were all against him.

Some of Joseph's fellow inmates appeared as witnesses in his defence:

> William Collins . . . has been in the house five years. Never saw
> Conquest disorderly, he reads the Hymns, and Psalms, and
> conducts himself very well.
> William Riddington . . . never saw Conquest misbehave himself, he
> never said any such words . . . the Master said he would shew him no
> favour if he came to tell tales, but he would come to tell the truth.
> Samuel Watkins . . . Conquest wanted to know why his meat was
> stopt. The Master said he did not know.

Five other inmates also testified on his behalf:

> Some of the witnesses who could not read, felt under great
> obligations to Conquest, who, at their leisure hours, would read
> the Bible and other good books to them.

(Joseph had not learned to read and write at the Independent Sunday
school as had some of his older brothers, but his mother, coming
from a long line of Harborough Independents, would have considered
the Bible a primer for all her children.)

The case was dismissed, but Joseph was bound over to keep the
peace for twelve months, and fined £20. Sureties from two others for
£10 each were immediately offered. Within a month seven men from
the workhouse were charged again with disorderly behaviour. Joseph
and Thomas Swingler were among them. Mary had been pregnant
throughout her time in the workhouse, and her fifth child, yet another
Joseph Conquest, was born a month later, in March 1842.

In the following spring of 1843, by which time Joseph and Mary
were out of the workhouse, 'one of the most heartless and wicked acts
of sacrilege' took place in Market Harborough. The Harborough Bank
failed that year, as did Clarke's carpet factory, throwing its 500 employees out of work. Joseph and other workmen who were reflooring the
ruined Church of St Mary in Arden in Great Bowden broke into the
coffins in the vault and stole the lead, carting it off to be melted down
and sold. Three of the men – Thomas Garlic, William Garlic and
George Cooke – were sons or relatives of men who had volunteered for

the army with Joseph's father in 1803, and some of them were already notorious in Market Harborough for their participation in the riots of 1838, when the town's Anti-Teetotallers took on its Temperance Society, whose leading light was Thomas Cook, the total abstainer who invented the idea of modern travel. Among the rioters in favour of drink had been Thomas Garlic and other associates of Joseph Conquest – probably paid, or at least encouraged, by the owners of the town's taverns and hotels to pursue Cook and smash his shop windows. Which is presumably why Thomas Cook moved to Leicester shortly thereafter.

In May 1843 the Garlic brothers, George Cooke and two others were arrested and sentenced to twelve months' hard labour, but Joseph scarpered, finding refuge in Chiswick, then on the outskirts of London, where his sixth and last child was born in 1848. When he thought it safe, he returned to his brothers in Leicester, but was tracked down in 1850 and sentenced to six months' hard labour. He was lucky, however, because in the same list of returns for 25 March 1850, one James Felstead was tried for buggery and sentenced to death (commuted to transportation for life), while the clerk of courts was also required to note, under the column headed 'Imprisonment': '(State if also whipped or fined)'.

The convulsion propelling the Conquest brothers into frequent conflict with the law had come in the midst of these decades of family misconduct. 1828 had been a bad year for the Conquests, and 1829 was to be much worse. The second son, George, was arrested in that year, at a time when savage physical punishment for the most trivial crimes was the order of the day, and transportation to Australia well underway. Early in the year, while George's older brother John was spending his month in the House of Correction for assaulting the landlord of the Green Dragon, cattle sales and prices at Harborough market began to fall. Then one of those phenomenal downpours, an eternal feature of the English summer, descended in July and ruined the harvest. There were severe floods, making work on the canals both difficult and sporadic.

On 9 October 1828 the Michaelmas session of Leicestershire

County Quarter Sessions issued a bastardy indictment naming George Conquest as the father of Sary Lacey's illegitimate daughter Eliza – 'Allin, Eliza, ill/e Dr. of Sarah Lacey', born in Thurmaston on 12 August 1827. Shortly thereafter George was arrested for stealing hemp from a 'flat' – the crude square-ended workboats developed for the upkeep of the canals – at the hamlet of Newton, in Cheshire. Newton is an adjunct to the salt-mining town of Middlewich, and the salt-works chimneys stood by the canal, together with a coal yard, pubs, inns, stables, warehouses and other necessaries of canal life. There were three rope factories and three boatbuilders in Middlewich: hemp was needed for rope.

Middlewich could be reached from Market Harborough by narrowboat, but it was not on the habitual run of the Conquest boys, who usually worked on the slow-trade, hauling heavy raw materials to Loughborough. George could have worked his way up the canal network to Middlewich, presumably in search of work and better pay, for after the bastardy indictment he had to find money to pay for his child. In the autumn of 1828, George was working as a maintenance man on the boats at Middlewich. Poor George: he was accused, with a mate called John Hall, of trying to sell the hemp he had stolen, to Thomas Goodwin, a Newton ropemaker, the very man from whom they had stolen it. Only a desperate man could have attempted such a thing, and by this time George was a desperate man.

Leicester Navigation Canal curved in and out of the River Soar, stopping on the way at the locks and weirs and three busy wharves of Thurmaston. Garden Street, where Sary and the Allen family lived, was one street away from Canal Street and Boatyard Lane, which led to the wharves. Thurmaston's canal life bustled there, providing supplies for the boats, stables for the horses, food and beer for the boatmen at the Boat Inn and True Blue Inn, and cottages for the toll- and lock-keepers. 1827 was the rowdy year in Thurmaston so noted by the Justices of the Peace in Leicester. Sary was known to gallivant with her brothers in the lanes and alleys of the village after dark. In 1827 she was nineteen, and George Conquest twenty-one. Exactly where and when he impregnated her remains unknown, but what is evident is that he moored his narrowboat at Thurmaston locks; that they had their way with each other; and that Eliza was the result.

Before the New Poor Law Act of 1834, under the Bastardy Act of 1732, a man accused by a woman of the paternity of her illegitimate child had three choices: marriage to the woman in question, payment of maintenance for his child, or imprisonment for refusal to pay. Many putative fathers absconded, and lists of names were published in newspapers: 'The following persons have left their families chargeable to St Mary's Parish [in Leicester] . . . a reward and reasonable expenses will be paid for the apprehension of the above persons by applying to the Overseers of the above parish.' Parishes were required to provide support for unmarried mothers if the father could not be found. Another reason that Church, squire, overseers and the affluent so fretted about illegitimate children and so harried their parents – they had to pay for them. Much energy went into identifying the father of any illegitimate child, and this they succeeded in doing with George Conquest.

That baby Eliza had already been baptised – as was often the case with illegitimate children – suggests some churchwarden involvement in Sary's life. A parish overseer would have brought her before the local magistrate, and there she would have had to name George. Sary's mother Dorothy had given birth to her eighth child, Benjamin, shortly before Sary gave birth to Eliza – Sary had to get relief. Thurmaston Parish then pursued George by way of the overseer of the parish of Market Harborough, who in turn pursued him to Middlewich. A modern historian best describes it: 'The practices and litigation of settlement and removal survived to blight the lives of the poor throughout the nineteenth century', and humiliation was the name of the game. Relations between those in places of 'settlement' and their overseers were rarely friendly, and correspondence relating to their battles reveals the low view the overseers took of paupers such as Sary and George, and the miseries they imposed upon them. A Leicester overseer wrote to his equivalent in Market Harborough on 25 February 1823:

Sir,

In answer to your communication of the nineteenth Inst relative to Widow Stringer I have to inform you no such Person has ever applied to St Mary's for relif [*sic*] consequently the rest of her tale is a fabrication of removal and I take pleasure in exposing her, this is one of many impositions I have exposed of Paupers endeavouring to impose on Parishes to which they belong.

I am Sir,
Your Ob/d serv/t
J. Deakins
Overseer

The bastardy indictment was later discharged by order of the court, probably because George was then in Chester jail, awaiting trial for the theft of the hemp. Or perhaps Eliza was already dead, which would have cancelled the indictment. Had he not stolen the hemp, George could well have accepted a 'knobstick' wedding.* More, had they married, as George's wife, Sary would have taken on her husband's place of settlement, so she and her baby would have been chargeable to Market Harborough and not to Thurmaston. In later life George proved to be the sort of man who would have accepted the paternity suit, so it is more than likely that he stole the hemp to pay a legal order for the usual weekly maintenance of a shilling.

He was tried at Chester Easter Quarter Sessions 1829 by Trafford Trafford, Esq., chairman of a bench of magistrates full of similar Esqs, and a jury comprising farmers, innkeepers, salt merchants and one or two gentlemen. The indictment was:

> George Conquest Late of Newton Laborer & John Hall Late of the same place Laborer for Larceny and stealing the goods and chattels of Thomas Goodwin.

George maintained that he was innocent, but the jury found him guilty. His co-defendant John Hall was acquitted on the grounds of insufficient evidence. George's sentence read in full:

> TRANSPORTED 7 YEARS – George Conquest (22), for stealing a quantity of hemp from a flat on the canal, the

---

* Named so because the church wardens who urged and attended marriages of the parents of illegitimate children carried such an object as their magic wand of office.

property of Thomas Goodwin of Newton. George Conquest of
the township of Newton in the said County Laborer Transportation
Order hath at this present session been indicted and Convicted of
Larceny.

Now it is ordered by this Court that the said George Conquest
shall be transported to such ports beyond the Seas as His Majesty
with the advice of His Privy Council shall direct for the term of
Seven years to be computed from this time. And it is further
ordered by this Court that the Constable of the Castle of Chester
and Keeper of His Majesty's Gaol or Prison there do receive into
his custody the body of the said George Conquest and him safely
keep and to hard Labour in this said Gaol or Prison in the
meantime until he shall be transported as aforesaid.

Over 16,000 subjects from the Midlands were transported to Australia between 1788 and 1852 and George Conquest was one of them.
The words of the crime reporters for the Chester newspapers, describing a week in the criminal justice system of a typical early Victorian
English town, need no decoration:

The Quarter Sessions terminated yesterday after an arduous
sitting of almost seven days. The calendar was very heavy, a true
indication of the melancholy state of trade, and consequent
distress of the working classes. Many of the prisoners were
sentenced to banishment for seven and fourteen years; but in
those cases they were generally incorrigible offenders who have
been convicted several times before, and who were fit objects for
severe punishments. We are inclined to attribute the great increase
of crime, as manifested at the late Assizes and at these Sessions,
not to any degeneracy on the part of the working classes, but to
their unfortunate and disconsolate condition, growing out of the
situation of the country; and should the depression we are now
suffering under continue or increase, we may confidently expect
a very heavy calendar at the next Assizes. We must say that several
of the indictments were founded on evidence extremely frivolous,
and in our humble opinion, the county might as well in several
instances have been saved the expense of prosecuting.

The state of the nation becomes quite clear in the words of the chairman of the magistrates, Trafford Trafford, Esq.:

> The Chairman, in charging the Grand Jury, expressed his regret
> that he could not congratulate them upon any diminution of
> crime since the last Sessions, which he had hoped he should be
> able to do, in consequence of the very great number of prisoners
> for trial on that occasion. – The learned gentleman then adverted
> to the extraordinary increase of crime of late years, as indicated
> by the expence to the county for the prosecution of felons. In the
> year 1797, the total disbursements under this head was only £239,
> while for the year 1827, it amounted to the enormous sum of
> £7,822 and some odd shillings; and the expense of prosecutions,
> at the assizes alone, for the year and quarter ending at the last
> assizes, amounted to upwards of £2,800 or more than one-third
> of the whole County Expenditure . . . The Chairman then went
> on to state the beneficial effects of associations of the respectable
> inhabitants, such as existed in the neighbourhood of Middlewich,
> in consequence of the discovery of a desperate gang of burglars
> and robbers in that part of the county, and recommended the
> formation of similar associations throughout the county. The
> learned gentleman, in conclusion said, he was happy to state for
> the information of the County, that the New Lunatic Asylum
> would be ready for the reception of the pauper lunatics in the
> course of a few months. The Grand Jury then retired, and the
> Magistrates were occupied during the greater part of the day in
> their private room.

The state of the nation and the lives of the lowest of the low are clearly revealed in the list of those tried with George Conquest at Chester Easter Sessions, 1829:

> John Gibson, 70, and Ralph Meigh, 19, for stealing a quantity of
> bone dust. Both sentenced to transportation for seven years. Value
> of the bone dust £300.
> Samuel Needham, 57, the prisoner was old in crime as in years,
> twice before convicted and once transported for seven years.

His house was searched and they found the following stolen items: a bunch of skeleton keys, several nets, wires & c. for the destruction of game. His sentence was one week's hard labour in Chester Castle, 7 years' transportation, and a second seven years to be computed from the expiration of the first.

Thomas Dudley, 29, a noted receiver of stolen goods, lots of same found in his house, sentenced to 14 years' transportation.

These were the serious offences the Chairman mentioned above. Then followed the list of others transported for seven years:

Joseph Hancock, 20, an old offender, for stealing from the property of James Lowndes, of Macclesfield.
George Conquest, 22, for stealing a quantity of hemp from a flat on the canal, the property of Thomas Goodwin, of Newton.
William Waring, 73, a notorious fowl-stealer for stealing a goose.
Joseph Price, 21, for stealing from his master.
Isaac Hanables, 24, for stealing a wheelbarrow.
Ann Charlton, 40, an old offender, for stealing a topcoat.
John Rowbotham, 20, a practised thief, for stealing fowls.

Sentenced to eighteen months' imprisonment:

Robert Brough, 29, for stealing a hat and a looking glass.
John Kitchen, 37, and William Jones, 20, for stealing a quantity of potatoes.

Sentenced to twelve months' imprisonment:

Mary Ann Simpson, 45, for stealing a watch, shirt and other articles, with hard labour, the last month solitary.
Henry Morris, 23, for stealing a cotton waistcoat, shawl and other articles, the last month solitary.
Abraham Brown, 24, for stealing a pair of bedsocks and a quantity of potatoes.
Richard Jepson, 30, for stealing a quantity of boards, the 6th and 12th months solitary.

Joseph Yates 18, for stealing 50 lb of lead, the 6th and 12th months
solitary.
Sarah Turner, 27, for stealing a cloth cloak, a shift and a flannel
waistcoat, the 6th and 12th months solitary.
William Jones, 19, for stealing a silver watch, the 6th and 12th
months solitary.
John Wells, 42, for stealing a topcoat.
Thos Dungan, 20, for stealing a quantity of potatoes.
Richard Leigh, 18, for stealing from the person of Wm. Robinson.
John Acton, 24, for stealing poultry.

Imprisonment for six months:

Thos Jackson, 32, for stealing a quantity of brass steps and other
brass.
William Steins, 33, for stealing 6 stone chisels, the last month
solitary.
William Worrall, 30, for stealing a piece of ash timber.
John Woolley, 43, for stealing two ale glasses – to hard labour and
the last month solitary.
John Smith, 18, for stealing out of a boat upon the Trent and Mersey
Canal, a quantity of wearing apparel, the last month solitary.
Jane Winstanley, 38, for stealing silver tea spoons and tea tongs.
James Platt, 31, for stealing a twelve-inch ivory rule, compasses,
and drawing pen. Hard labour and the last two months solitary.
Kitty Duffy, 20, for stealing a cotton gown.

Three months' imprisonment:

Alice Ashton, 29, for stealing one cap, the last month solitary.
George Jones, 17, and Jonas Jackson, 19, for stealing a loaf of
bread.

Two months' imprisonment:

Jane Winlock, 19, and Jemima Waller, 17, for stealing a pound and
a half of bacon and a loaf of bread.

One month's imprisonment:

William Stafford, 30, for stealing six bags.
Margaret Coffey, 18, for stealing a shawl and basket.
Samuel Hambleton, 42, for stealing a watch.
Betty Davison, 45, for stealing a piece of beef. (This poor
woman was proved to be in great distress at the time she took
the beef.)
Wm Symonds, 39, for stealing a pewter pint.

Fourteen days' imprisonment:

Fanny Oldfield, 18, for stealing a quantity of silk.
James Scott, 18, for stealing a spade.
Martha Worrall, for stealing a piece of ash timber.
Peggy Webb, 43, for stealing a quantity of coals.
Saml. Parker, 14, and Job Hulme, 13, for stealing a loaf of bread
(to be privately whipped in addition to their imprisonment).

Seven days' solitary confinement:

Sarah Bennion, 15, and Owen Bennion, 13, for stealing a quantity
of coal from the saltworks.

————————⚬⌇⚬————————

There are many oddities about the crime, trial and sentence of George
Conquest. Not the least of them is the dismissal of all charges against
his mate John Hall and the severe sentence imposed on George.
There is something even stranger about George stealing the hemp
from Thomas Goodwin, and then trying to sell it back to him. Stu-
pidity wasn't something George seems to have been generally prone
to. Criminal trials in the nineteenth century were not as they are
today: it would have been Thomas Goodwin himself who brought
George and John Hall before the magistrates, and Goodwin himself
would have been the prosecutor in the case and paid the cost of the
trial, with George defending himself as best he could. Witnesses were

permitted: did Goodwin use Hall in some way to incriminate George, with Hall's own acquittal as reward for doing so?

Those judging a criminal in the early nineteenth century were much less fettered than they would be today by laws of evidence, and much more given to airing their own prejudices and opinions; prosecutors and jurors were equally unconstrained. The tenor of the day was a pervasive fear of the loss of property and possessions which meant that the theft of a shirt or a hen was seen as a mortal blow, rather than a peccadillo brought about because of hunger, cold or want of money. Thus the severity, indeed barbarity of punishment, and the sense of desperation to control the labouring poor and the paupers who lurked beneath them. They were the refugees and immigrants of our own times, the objects of that so oft-repeated fear, expressed over the centuries and in so many countries, that 'they breed like flies'. Religion, as it was practised and agonised over at the time, had much to do with it. 'Crime was thought to be caused predominantly by sinfulness; lack of religion; immorality and vice; bad parenting and neglect; and alcohol.' Reforms began in the 1820s, most particularly with Robert Peel's reorganisation of the penal system after 1827. But magistrates such as Trafford Trafford, Esq. luxuriated in the old ways, and benefitted the miserable souls presented before him with an avalanche of animadversions, instructions and cries to heaven.

After 1822 magistrates could grant bail to the accused, but who could provide this for George Conquest? He had spent some months in Chester jail, probably in solitary confinement, before his trial. The jail, completed in 1792, was considered a model new establishment, but that was a judgement of its construction, not of its treatment of prisoners. After trial, convicts sentenced to transportation returned to jail, again in solitary confinement, to wait for the arrival from the Secretary of State of so-called caption papers, listing all the details of his or her crime and its punishment. They were then delivered to convict 'hulks' – rotting decommissioned ships – before assignation to a particular convict ship. George's period of solitary confinement was mercifully short. His order came almost immediately:

> To be removed, with all convenient Speed after the Receipt of this
> Order, on board the *Ganymede* Hulk at Woolwich on the River

Thames, and there delivered to the Superintendent of Convicts, or to the Overseer of the said Hulk, if the said Convicts, upon being examined by an experienced Surgeon or Apothecary, shall be found free from any putrid or infectious Distemper, and fit to be removed from the Gaol. The Superintendent or Overseer will give you a Receipt for your Discharge. You will at the same Time deliver him a true Copy, attested by you or by the Gaoler having the Custody of the said Convicts, of the Caption and Order of the Court by which each of the said Offenders was sentenced or ordered for Transportation, containing the Sentence or Order of Transportation of each, and also a Certificate specifying concisely the Description of each Prisoner's Crime, his Age, whether married or unmarried, his Trade or Profession, and an Account of his Behaviour in Prison before and after his Trial, and the Gaoler's Observations on his Temper and Disposition, and such Information concerning his Connections and former Course of Life as may have come to the Gaoler's Knowledge.

George was marched in chains from Chester jail four days later, on 4 May 1829. Ten days later he arrived at the appointed hulk, the *Ganymede*, with thirteen others, three of whom – Joseph Price ('21, for stealing from his master'), John Rowbotham ('20, a practised thief, for stealing fowls') and Ralph Meigh ('19, for stealing a quantity of bone dust') – had been tried with him at Chester Easter Quarter Sessions. After boarding, their money (what money, one asks?) was taken by the captain, and they were sent shackled below deck, where the convicts already there would pounce on the new arrivals. A wonderfully named actor, Mansfield Silverthorpe, had stolen a trunk and, sentenced to seven years' transportation, was also sent to the *Ganymede*:

> my long hair underwent the operation of clipping by the Barbarous Barber, I was then soaked in a cold bath and afterwards was arrayed in the Uniform of the Hulks.

One benefit of George Conquest's criminal record is that it provides some sense of what the Conquest boys might have looked like – that is, if George resembled his siblings in any way.

He was five foot seven and a quarter inches tall, not too small for a man of his time. He could read, but not write.

He was listed as being a member of the Church of England (which he was not, although it was sensible of him to say so).

He had hazel-coloured eyes and the ruddy complexion of a bargeman.

He had freckles, and a scar along the outer part of his right eyebrow.

III

BENIGNANT TORTURE

The end of all punishment, legitimately considered, is torture . . . the latter is the Russian and Chinese practice and is to be reprobated by all civilized nations. Never let us lose sight of the ends of punishment. Those ends are benignant . . . A modern author has undertaken to vindicate scourging, as being more effectual, and less calculated to raise vindictive feelings and not more degrading than the divers substitutes for it invented in modern times. But he guards his subject by one condition. He insists, that the punishment be inflicted with every mark of solemnity, and even pomp. We agree with him in this respect. And we think that, not only should the proper officers all be in attendance, and the ceremony performed with solemnity . . .

Extract from the *Sydney Monitor*, 28 September 1833

7

'Floating Dungeons'

Convicts being rowed out to a prison hulk on the Thames, 1826

I N 1776 THE CENTURY-OLD practice of shipping Britain's criminals to its North American colonies was brought to an abrupt
halt, with the start of the American War of Independence. When
the war ended in 1783, Australia became the prison farm of choice.
Until the new system was up and running, disused, captured or unsea-
worthy old ships were moored in rivers and estuaries and turned into
floating prisons. The parliamentary Act of 1776 setting this in motion
decreed that any criminal sentenced to 'transportation to any of His
Majesty's colonies or plantations in America' would first be set to
hard labour, for the 'cleansing of the River Thames, or any other

service for the benefit of the said river'. Once Parliament had passed
the necessary Act, the justices of Middlesex outsourced the management to overseers, government contractors with strong connections
to the navy and shipping, not to mention the slave trade, who ran the
operation as a business. It was intended that the new system should
last only until the end of the American War, but it survived for more
than seventy years after its end.

The hulks themselves, which decorated the Thames from 1776
until 1857, were the residue of England's naval service over the decades
of war in America and Europe. The first prison hulk was named – not
ironically – *Justitia*, and in time they were moored all over the empire –
Bermuda, Gibraltar, New York, Sydney, Hobart, Cork, Northern
Ireland. In England they studded the ports and dockyards of Kent and
Hampshire, while on the Thames, the centre of their terrors was at
Deptford and, above all, at Woolwich. Female convicts were rarely
interred on the hulks, although some were held on the *Narcissus*, the
Heroine and the *Dunkirk*. HMS *Ganymede*, on which George Conquest
was a prisoner, was the former French frigate *Hébé*, captured in 1809
and converted to a prison hulk in 1819. George Conquest spent seven
months on this hulk, moored at the Royal Arsenal Docks at Woolwich. Sometimes the hulks were towed to the north shore of the river,
alongside the desolate and feared Essex Marshes, but usually they were
moored off the south shore, facing the Woolwich Warren, as it was
called, a labyrinthine melange of 'workshops, warehouses, wood-
yards, barracks, foundries and firing ranges'.

The Warren manufactured arms and explosives for the British
state and its armed forces. Here were the Royal Engineers, Sappers
and Miners, the Royal Military Academy, the Royal Military Deposi-
tory, Royal Carriage Factory, Royal Gun Factories, Royal Carriage
Department, storehouses for all the tools of war, and much more. By
the time George Conquest came to Woolwich, his royal namesake
King George III had instructed that the entire complex should be
named the Royal Arsenal, thus saving a great deal of printer's ink.

For this military and armament centre, convicts held on the hulks
built a boundary wall two and a half miles long enclosing the site, a
massive new wharf, and dug its defence and transport canal. They
worked at the dockyards, carting coal and timber, breaking stones; they

worked in the Warren digging roads, cleaning out drains, sewers and sheds and shot and shell, loading and unloading ships . . . and more. They were ferried or led to work attached to a single chain, with 'fetters on each leg, with a chain between that ties variously, some round their middle, others upright to the throat'. Lesser criminals were chained in pairs; the fetters of serious criminals were painfully heavier.

Attended by guards bearing cutlasses or pistols, these shackled convicts trudging to work, clanking like evil church bells as they dredged the river and built the docks and yards and walls at the Arsenal, became, like the public hangings at Tyburn – which were still going strong and amusing the English public until 1868 – a spectacle so popular with sightseers that a brick wall had to be constructed so that 'Spectators will soon . . . be barred the sight of these miserable wretches'. In all accounts of what they did, how they worked, and above all how (and how often) they attempted to escape, the words most commonly associated with the convicts on these hulks were 'flogging' and 'heavy irons'. They were flogged for what they did, for what they did not do, and for what they did not do correctly, which is no doubt why they so often tried to escape, risking yet more of the same: 'the villains were dragged from their lurking places . . . and they were marched back to Woolwich'. On board the hulks the words 'they were severely flogged' were so common a comment it could have been embroidered on a sampler.

In 1776 the government paid the hulks' first manager, Duncan Campbell, £32 per convict per year, later lowered to £28. Campbell was a sugar plantation and slave owner in Jamaica, and his niece married Captain William Bligh, which was how that unappealing man was appointed captain of the *Bounty*, of mutiny fame. The business of the hulks was closely connected with British shipping merchants who had lost income and profits with the ending of their trade in slaves, and the transportation of convicts to America. Slavery was not actually abolished until 1833, but it was becoming a shaky business for decades before then. Campbell, the son of a Scottish clergyman, started out in the navy, and subsequently became a wealthy shipping merchant, one of those British businessmen – many of whom congregated around Blackheath and its golf club – who had been running slaves and shipping convicts to America since 1758 – though the

British slave trade had been a flourishing source of British wealth since the early seventeenth century. With the appropriation of Australia and the settlement of Botany Bay these men moved seamlessly into the transportation of British convicts to Australia.

Campbell was a remarkable example of these unsavoury men, and now he turned his attention to the hulks. He made more money by overcrowding his hulks. At night, six men were chained together and packed on to platforms, so closely that contemporary witnesses of this portion of convict life could hardly bear to describe what they saw, and mostly did not:

> at night, these men were fastened in their dens – a single warder
> being left on board, in charge of them! The state of morality
> under such circumstances may be easily conceived – crimes
> impossible to be mentioned were commonly perpetrated.

It was Campbell who extended the travails of the convicts on the hulks to include servicing the Royal Arsenal. Once described as 'a man whose one remembered comment on his inmates was their "Universal Depression of spirits"', he was further surprised to note that the convicts' misery seemed to cause more deaths than 'any fever or other disorder'. Although he appointed a deputy, Stewart Erskine, who was to show some signs of compassion, Campbell treated the convict establishment as a business, a family business, and he placed his brother Neil in charge of it and gave him the rich bounty of supplying everything required.

The diet for their prisoners consisted of wormy biscuits and bread, boiled ox cheek – often high – and salt pork once a week, small beer – a watered potion, not beer as we know it – pease, or barley made into a gruel; sometimes oatmeal and cheese. Not all of this allotment reached the convicts' stomachs: 'first the steward took his cut, then the cook, then the inspectors, then the boat's crew who rowed the food ashore, and lastly the dock overseer'. Of course the convicts returned villainy with villainy; and every ingenious attempt to escape led to more floggings, heavier irons, solitary confinement – also habitual – and death. In these early years there was no medical officer, no chaplain: one prisoner in three died. 'A foul odour infested the vessels from end to end' – notably, as one doctor remarked, 'near the necessary'. The prisoners were regularly ravaged by disease and epidemics: gangrene, dysentery, venereal disease, scrofula, tuberculosis, scurvy, cholera – so many caused by contaminated water, the stagnant marshes and the wretched diet – and a species of typhus, spread by the vermin on board and encouraged by the lack of ventilation and the packed platforms on which the prisoners slept.

From the earliest years of the hulks, prison reformers such as John Howard, who published his *State of the Prisons* in 1777, and his followers, including Elizabeth Fry and many others over the coming decades, pleaded and campaigned to reform or abolish them. They were the refugee camps of their time, and like those which were, until recently, outside Calais, a blot on English history. 'Blot' is perhaps too mild a word, for learning of the tortures of convict life on the hulks in the early years was, for me, like the first time I read about the German death and labour camps – knowledge that blights the mind and heart for ever. The very worst years preceded George Conquest's imprisonment on the *Ganymede*, but the last of the hulks was not burnt until 1857. So although the appalling early years were over by the beginning of the nineteenth century, horrors sufficient to chill the blood continued well after George Conquest's transportation in 1830.

In 1802, with the appointment of a new governor, Aaron Graham, a man whose primary interest was not merely the feathering of his own nest, hell was replaced with purgatory. Hospital ships were introduced early, but no description of them includes anything that might gladden the heart of a prison reformer. Hammocks replaced wooden platforms, rations were improved, a chapel, a voluntary evening school was set up, and surgeons consulted. But clambering into a hammock while chained was not easy, and the nature of such services and the overseers, officers and guards scarcely changed. The transportation of convicts to Australia – the First Fleet set sail from Portsmouth in May 1787 – had at least eased the overcrowding.

George Conquest had a better chance of survival by 1829, but the hulks remained 'floating dungeons', flying lines of bedding and ragged clothes between their masts. They were still a world of sodomy, bribery and brutality – always vermin, always fetters, always flogging. Even the insane were flogged to keep them quiet. In addition to the usual, the hulks continued to be ravaged by scurvy and tuberculosis, and epidemics of jail fever – commonly known as Hulk Fever – in 1821, inflammation of the lungs in 1826, cholera in 1832. By George's time, however, the earlier death rate of one in three had gradually ameliorated.

Still, the convict burial ground on the Plumstead Marshes provided many a corpse for body snatchers, and few were the corpses that reached the ground intact, for 'robbery of the dead was habitual, open, and vulturine'. 'Resurrection Men', as they were called, did a good business supplying corpses to surgeons and anatomy schools. Bones, still encased in their irons, were found in the Arsenal grounds in the years to come.

There were ten hulks in use in England by 1829, and George was one of nearly 5,000 men incarcerated in them. Many convicts served their full sentences on board. Chronicles of life on the hulks are overabundant perhaps because historians and journalists could, and can, scarcely credit that such horrors were a part of British life in the midst of its flourishing century of empire. A hulk at Woolwich was described in 1849, twenty years after George Conquest left the *Ganymede*:

> In the hospital ship . . . the great majority of the patients were
> infested with vermin, and their persons, in many instances,
> particularly their feet, begrimed with dirt. No regular supply of
> body-linen had been issued; so much so, that many men had
> been five weeks without a change; and all record had been lost
> of the time when the blankets had been washed, and the number
> of sheets was so insufficient, that the expedient had been resorted
> to of only one sheet at a time, to save appearances. Neither
> towels nor combs were provided for the prisoners' use, and the
> unwholesome odour from the imperfect and neglected state of
> the water-closets was almost insupportable . . .

John Henry Capper, a Home Office functionary, was appointed Superintendent of the Hulks in 1815. He continued in that role until 1847, lessening the prisoners' sufferings almost not at all. Like Campbell before him he appointed a relative, his nephew Robert, to oversee the day-to-day running of the ships; both led comfortable lives salting away fees and allowances, muffling the true state of affairs. Robert Capper was also a grocer in the Strand, a useful and profitable connection for supply of the hulks; in due course he took over the entire running of the convict establishment from his uncle.

By this time an attempt to reduce the 'general depravity' below decks, noted and abhorred but always officially denied– although Jeremy Bentham insisted that homosexual rape had become an initiation ceremony on the hulks – had been made by dividing the prisoners amongst three decks. The unventilated lower deck housed new arrivals and the worst criminals, good behaviour could merit the middle deck, and finally the upper deck – where more air reached lungs already destroyed by life at the lower levels.

George was one of 350 men packed closely on board the *Ganymede*, their hammocks in tiers. The prisoners were locked in at 9 p.m. and let out at 5.30 a.m. Ten hours' hard labour each day in summer, seven in winter. They were dressed in convict 'slops': a coarse grey jacket, a shirt and canvas breeches, shoes, handkerchief and stockings (did they come from the framework knitting machines of Leicester?). These slops were usually not new, and were all too rarely replaced. Under Capper's regime convict labour was less chaotic, but still hard: 'loading and unloading vessels . . . constructing or repairing public works . . . excavating, stacking or carrying timber, painting ships, cleaning cables . . . scraping shot.'

Mustered on the quarterdeck and given breakfast at 5.45, by 6.45 they had scrubbed the decks and stowed their hammocks. Searched, irons checked, they were then sorted into sections for the day's hard labour in the dockyard or the Arsenal. Dinner at noon, either in a shed on land, or eaten locked into their wards back on the ship. Searched and irons checked again, by 1.20 they were back at work. At 5.45 they returned to the ship, to be searched and examined yet again before school at 6.30. (This may well be where George added writing to his reading capacities, because he could do both well in later life.) At 7.30 they went to the chapel for prayers, were mustered again and locked back in their wards at 9 p.m., lights out. Washing and shaving were for Saturday evenings or Sunday morning. Divine service every Sunday morning. Always in chains.

Many were the variations to this ritual, many the specified breaks

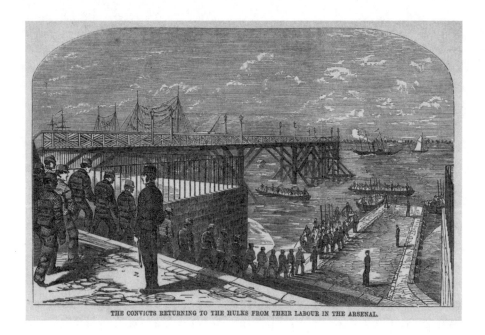

THE CONVICTS RETURNING TO THE HULKS FROM THEIR LABOUR IN THE ARSENAL.

missed; many the bribes paid to warders or guards for 'easement of irons' and much else. Irons were now lighter than in earlier times, made heavier if punishment was due. To prevent accusations of slavery, convicts were paid for their work on shore, with the government adding a penny for each shilling earned, although the money for their labour was held for them by their masters. They were permitted the purchase of an occasional treat – tobacco mostly, before the rigorous reforms which were attempted following the Parliamentary report of the Select Committee on Secondary Punishment in 1832. This, and the shorter hours they worked, caused resentment among the free labourers in the Arsenal, who nevertheless often helped the convicts with smuggled goods, and in their attempts to escape.

In the English world outside the confines of the hulks, things were not much better for the likes of Sary or the Conquest family. Indeed, many a pauper would have had less to eat than the prisoners on the hulks. 1829 was 'a disastrous year for labourers – cold, hungry, unemployed. Crime increased'. Sary was in Thurmaston, framework knitting and recovering from the loss of her baby Eliza and the departure of George, while the other Conquest boys were raising their fists to it all throughout Leicestershire.

The Anglican chaplains on the hulks proved themselves to be typical men of their class and calling – there is little evidence of Nonconformist interest in the plight of the lost souls in the hulks. Like their fellow administrators, they viewed the prisoners as the dregs of the earth, scarcely human: vermin, like the insects which crawled over them. In due course libraries were set up for the convicts, and it is a measure of the chaplains' lack of comprehension that the titles on offer included such works as *Conversations on Natural Philosophy*, *The Rites and Worship of the Jews*, *Short Stories from the History of Spain*, *First Steps in Scottish History*. Dickens' weekly magazine *Household Words* was often banned. The Rev. William Quartermain, who served as chaplain on the *Ganymede* at the time George was on board, appeared before a parliamentary inquiry into the hulks in 1835. His testimony provides information as to how George learned to write, because although a laggard in his religious attentions, Quartermain took an interest in the ship's evening school – which was pretty much all he did for his annual fee of £100.

These chaplains, generally speaking, were businessmen of the cloth, satisfied if the convicts met the requirement to 'repeat once a month the Church Catechism . . . memoriter [memorise] the Thirty-Nine Articles of Religion [and] a Homily against the fears of death'. In 1821 one unfortunate group of inmates memorised 'two hundred and eighty Chapters of the Holy Writ containing 7750 verses'. Two years after George was transported, the cholera epidemic of 1832 struck the *Ganymede*: the chaplain reported that the convicts 'evinced a becoming fortitude and resignation under the fatal disease with which it has pleased the Almighty so lately to afflict them'.

Divine service did not diminish attempted murders, smuggling and constant attempts to escape; bribery was rife, discipline chaotic. After lights out at 9 p.m. it was mayhem below decks. A blind eye continued to be cast on rampant sexual activity; convicts were left to themselves to sort out constant eruptions of violence as the strong persecuted the weak below decks, just as they did above. Parliamentary inquiries were launched into the condition of the convict establishment many times between 1828 and 1856. Thomas Knight, who had also been held on the *Ganymede*, gave a description of the life George would have lived there in 1829, when he appeared as a witness before the 1832 Parliamentary Select Committee: 'all sorts of iniquity was carried on, robbing each other, quarrelling and fighting, cursing and swearing, and singing of bawdy songs; the language was most horrid to listen to'. There was much 'scuffling and knocking about. Gambling was common and pilfering incessant . . . as to cleanliness, if a man did not want to wash himself he need not wash himself except on Sundays', when 'if found dirty', he would be scrubbed.

Tobacco, strictly limited, was nevertheless widely available until 1832. The 1832 committee heard accounts of life on other hulks on which music was played on clarinet and fiddle, beer was available as well as tobacco, and women visitors – sisters and wives were permitted only every three months or so – slipped a shilling to the guards to have a quiet moment or two with their man in a cabin, while captains, officers and guards stole the convicts' allowances and clothes. Of all the hulks at that time, the *Ganymede* appears to have been the worst. Generally order was kept on each deck at night by watchmen or wardsmen, but the *Ganymede* had none:

> a lantern, supposed to be left burning, was often blown out, so
> that prisoners could the more easily rob each other. The *Ganymede*
> appears to have been Pandemonium, and we are not surprised
> when one witness speaks of it as 'hell upon earth'.

Thus it was for boys as young as six, youths in their teens, and men a great deal older than George's twenty-three years; thus it was for the feeble and insane, the elderly and infirm – though for the last, it was, of course, much worse. After 1824, children of seven upwards were confined to hulks of their own, where they continued to mimic the habits and horrors of their elders. Pardons could be granted: in that same year, 500 of the 3,000 convicts on the hulks were reprieved. George Conquest was not to be one of them: he raises his head above the parapet only once, in the reports for the June quarter of 1829: 'Bodily State: Healthy. Behaviour: Orderly.'

In 1847 a parliamentary inquiry was finally set up to investigate the management of the hulks. The Cappers, uncle and nephew, received – not their just deserts, which never came – but at least some public scrutiny of their brutality and profiteering. Perhaps the most astounding revelation in the report's long and dismal litany was the truly remarkable amount of unauthorised flogging, lashing and birching of convicts – with particular delight being taken in the cat-o'-nine-tails – that went on in the hulks under the Capper regime. Vermin, disease, filth, malnutrition, abuse of the sick and mentally ill are there too, to read and wonder at in the Report of the Inquiry of 1847, which reveals the above, and more, but the delight in flogging tops all. By that time conditions had improved to such an extent that only one in fourteen prisoners died. The report describes the inmates of the hulks during the reign of the Cappers:

> In 1841, the gross number of convicts received on board the
> hulks in England during the year was 3,625, and these were
> natives of the following countries, in the following proportion:
> 3,108 were born in England
> 80 were born in Wales
> 229 were born in Scotland
> 180 were born in Ireland
> 13 were born in British Colonies
> 15 were born in Foreign States
>
> Their occupations had been as follows:
> 304 had been Agriculturists
> 1,176 had been Mechanics and persons instructed in manufactures
> 1,986 had been Labourers and persons not instructed in manufactures
> 82 had been Domestic servants
> 69 had been Clerks, shopmen, and persons employed confidentially
> 8 had been Superior class, or men of education

As regards the religion of these same 3,625 convicts, the subjoined are the statistics:

2,934 belong to the Established Church
269 belong to the Roman Catholic ditto
167 belonged to the Scotch ditto
245 were Dissenters
9 were Jews
1 was of 'another denomination'

Concerning their prison 'antecedents':
1,451 were first-offence men
487 had been in prison before
1625 had been convicted before
10 had been in penitentiary
52 had been transported before

Their ages were as follows:
3 were under 10 years old
213 were from 10 to 15 years old
958 were from 15 to 20 years old
1,612 were from 20 to 30 years old
839 were above 30 years old

Lastly:
1,103 were married

In *Great Expectations*, which opens in 1812, the escaped convict Abel Magwitch presents himself to young Pip in the graveyard on the Thames marshes. No historian, writer or poet described those dreadful expanses, the hulks, and the lives of the convicts of that time as Dickens did in this novel. This is Pip describing the recaptured Magwitch being shipped back to his hulk:

> No one seemed surprised to see him, or interested in seeing him, or glad to see him, or sorry to see him, or spoke a word, except that somebody in the boat growled as if to dogs, 'Give way, you!' which was the signal for the dip of the oars. By the light of the

torches, we saw the black Hulk lying out a little way from the mud of the shore, like a wicked Noah's ark. Cribbed and barred and moored by massive rusty chains, the prison-ship seemed in my young eyes to be ironed like the prisoners. We saw the boat go alongside, and we saw him taken up the side and disappear. Then, the ends of the torches were flung hissing into the water, and went out, as if it were all over with him.

8

Scarred Backs

View of Port Jackson and part of the town of Sydney by
Richard Read Senior, the convict artist, c. 1820s

EORGE CONQUEST HAD TO wait for luck to come his way,
but the first faint whisper of it was his transportation in 1830.
New South Wales remained a penal colony, in many ways a
stricter one than in its traumatic first years, but by 1830 British laws
and practices, albeit including gruesome brutality, also offered whatever justice was inherent in British domination of the lands it invaded
or appropriated to form its empire. He arrived in a colony ruled by the
more fortunate men on the British social pyramid. They had two
classes of human beings to control, one of which – to which George
belonged – they despised and feared; the other whom they treated as
primitive savages, and whom they also came to fear. In principle they
were willing to treat the latter well as long as they behaved like good
savages. As they did not, British settlement brought disaster to the
First People, the traditional owners of the continent which was to be
called Australia after 1770.

Transportation of criminals was not a new aspect of the British legal system. It had been in use since the early seventeenth century – mostly, but not exclusively, to its American colonies – as an alternative to branding, whipping or hanging. There were also penal colonies in the Caribbean islands, Bermuda, India, and more. Transportation was permitted from the age of ten, and about one per cent of convicts were under fourteen years old. The majority, both men and women, were between fifteen and thirty years of age, and about three per cent were older. No colony was as distant from the motherland as the remote and almost unknown continent of Australia, and between 1787, with the sailing of the First Fleet, until the departure of the last convict ship in 1868, the British government despatched to its strange shores some 160,000 of its undesirables. About three-quarters of them came from Britain, almost a quarter from Ireland, with a number from various British possessions. The 40,000 Irish convicts included not only petty criminals, but a substantial number of political rebels – the product of the miseries of British rule in Ireland, the empire's first colony.

And so the island continent was taken over by Britons and Celts – mostly English, Scots, Welsh and Irish in the very early days. They brought desolation and disease to the human beings whose 60,000-year-old civilisation was impenetrable to them, providing at the same time a much better life for the dregs of their own society, and for their descendants. Over the next decades the Indigenous Australians who already lived there were dispossessed as white settlements spread up and down the east coast, across the southern coast, and later to Western Australia.

A reverence for the sanctity of property was a major cause of the British view of their criminal, destitute and pauper classes, and the desire to banish them to the ends of the earth. This near-religious fervour was not extended to the Indigenous Australians, whose land they considered British territory from the moment Captain James Cook ceremoniously raised the flag for the British Crown at Botany Bay in April 1770. This fear of their own lower classes was exacerbated by the rise in population – from 6 million in 1700 to 18 million by 1851 – and by the influx of returned soldiers after the end of the Napoleonic Wars in 1815. Unemployment, repeated poor harvests, rising prices, the widespread hunger and pauperdom of so many: all this led to Britain's crowded prisons and hulks. The fear that the nation

was being engulfed by a crime wave suffused the words and actions
of governments, officials and the public at large.

This belief strengthened an already obsessional desire to manage
and regulate these rapidly expanding 'perishing classes' by a maze of
laws, and do's and don'ts which increased in number more than sixfold between 1805 and 1848, and which corralled both criminals and
the products of industrialisation and its consequences into prisons,
houses of correction, workhouses and hulks. Over 200 crimes were
punishable by death, with an inundation of lesser penalties such as
the pillory, the stocks, branding, public whipping, the treadmill, the
crank, chains and irons, solitary confinement, semi-starvation and
transportation.

A body of reformers in pursuit of moral salvation for evildoers
represented a third impulse towards transportation – though not all
of this ilk believed transportation could rehabilitate, including the
evangelical prison reformer Jeremy Bentham. These men and
women were influenced by a different interpretation of the word of
the Christian god, connected to the fight against slavery and to
that radical and humanitarian aspect of British thought, always
there, often defeated, trailing back in time through revolutions,
civil wars, Nonconformist preachers, writers and artists, rebels and
revolutionaries.

Uncomfortably sharing some of their views were the remarkable
men and women of the Enlightenment – European, English,
Scottish – who replaced religious faith with a belief in the powers of
Reason, and whose embrace of science, philosophy and much else
led to an independence of thought which heralded modernity. A
major element of their thought was rejection of the concept that
men and women were born evil, and a conviction that they could be
improved by education, secularisation, liberty, and freedom from
hunger. The American War and the desperate conditions in prisons
and on the hulks were the main impetus for transportation, but the
settlement of Australia also bears marks of this philosophy.

Enlightened thinkers hoped that transportation would bring
about redemption for the wretched creatures they sent in chains to
the other side of the world. Disillusionment impelled such thinkers to
work towards the ending of transportation in 1868, their contribution

as valuable as that of Christian reformers, driven not only by human concern, but also by their abhorrence of the moral laxity, drunkenness and irreligion they observed in the convict colony. The politician and anti-slave-trade campaigner William Wilberforce, an excellent and pious example of a Christian reformer, nevertheless managed to provide New South Wales with such chaplains as the flogging parson Samuel Marsden, whose use of religion in the pursuit of personal wealth and the infliction of suffering on the ungodly, even Dickens would find it hard to give words to. Liberal Reform was in the air in Britain: the battle for the Great Reform Act of 1832, however limited its parameters, was one of the great causes of the day, and the ideas of the Enlightenment, though limited by British imperial ambitions, nevertheless permeated the body politic and the moral imperatives of empire. As George Conquest was transported, the agitation to end slavery was entering its final stages.

There are today some 24 million Australians, speaking 200 languages, the result of 'epic migrations from Auschwitz, Somalia, Italy, Vietnam, Beirut, Tiananmen Square' and many another corner of the world. However, Australians were a motley crew well before the White Australia policy – practised since the mid-nineteenth century but only formally adopted into law by the newly federated Commonwealth of Australia in 1901– was dreamed up by those determined to defend white Anglo-Saxon racial purity and in fear of the millions of Asian peoples hovering dangerously to the north. This perhaps also had much to do with those British free settlers who could not bear to be associated with the 'convict stain', a label they and their countrymen back home imposed as an extra burden on the prisoners they despatched to Australia. Many non-whites arrived before settlers from the British Isles settled upon such exclusions. But the White Australia policy insisted on only European, and preferably British, additions to its population. After the Second World War the policy was gradually softened, and eventually abandoned, allowing the arrival of the legions of nationalities that would lead to the remarkable racial mix in Australia today.

From the very beginning there were hundreds of black convicts – from the Americas, the West Indies, and Britain itself. Before the White Australia policy was introduced, a Noah's Ark of nationalities made their way to Australia from all parts of Europe, from Asia, from the Levant, from the crews of the transport ships ... There were American and Caribbean former slaves, Maoris, Chinese, Russians and Spaniards well before the flood of humanity that poured in during the gold rushes of the 1850s. 'Black Caesar', one of the earliest convicts to take to the bush and become a bushranger, was African, the convict 'Black' John Goff was either West Indian or African, while the convict lawyer George Barrow came from Guyana. 'The vineyard ... was put in charge of Greeks who had been transported from the Ionian islands for piracy ... Offenders against the law in India were sent to New South Wales.'

But generally speaking, until the end of the Second World War Australia was a land settled by the lower reaches of the British class pyramid, and it was they, together with the injection of a significant number of rebels and protesters, who provided the pearls in the oyster – or the flies in the ointment – of what was to become an Australian human being. Though most of the early English immigrants and settlers brought with them an acceptance that inequalities of every kind were among the laws of nature, many of those who came from elsewhere, and many an Irish and British convict, free settler and immigrant were social or political protesters, an attitude that they passed on to their descendants.

A Sample of Protesters sent to NSW
or Van Diemen's land

Irish
Defenders of Ireland and rural protesters before 1798
Rebels of 1798, 1803
Transported under the Insurrection Acts of 1814–1815
Armed rebels, Whiteboys, Ribbonmen, etc.
Young Ireland Movement of 1848
Fenians ... 1868
Marginal Protesters ... Arsonists, 'Houghers' and
maimers of cattle
Destroyers of trees

British

Scots Jacobins, 1793, 1798
Naval mutineers, 1797
Luddites, 1812–13, 1817
Agricultural labourers (Isle of Ely)
Pentrich Rebellion, 1817
Scots radical weavers of Glasgow and Bonnymuir, 1820
Cato Street Conspiracy, 1820
Yorkshire radical weavers, 1821
'Swing' rioters, machine-breakers and arsonists (inc. 2 women)
Bristol riots, 1831
Welsh industrial riots, 1831, 1835
Tolpuddle Martyrs, 1834
Battle of Bossenden Wood, 1838
Welsh Rebecca Riots, 1842–3
Chartists, 1839, 1842, 1848
Marginal Protesters: arsonists, poachers, cattle-maimers
Destroyers of fences, trees, etc . . .
Machine breakers, riots, Wages Movements, assaulting
peace officers, miscellaneous protest

Canadians

Anglo-Canadians, Americans, 1838
French Canadians, 1838

Lord Sydney, Home Secretary to Pitt the Younger from 1783 to 1789, was charged with the establishment of the convict settlement in New South Wales. Other lands 'beyond the seas' were considered as possibilities. At the time those in charge of hulks, prisons and workhouses all over Britain were bewailing their gross overcrowding, and pleading for transportation to be resumed after its suspension during the American War. The decision to settle upon New South Wales was primarily its suitability as a penal colony, though the government which formed the plan tacked on defence, trade and supply considerations and the establishment of a strategic outpost to protect trade routes in the South Seas – to be built with cheap convict labour. Tangential benefits such as the provision of flax and hemp, spices, timber and so forth from the new colony, drift in and out of disputations about the reasons for the settlement of the distant continent.

All these considerations are what one would expect from an imperial government, and were of little importance beside Lord Sydney's key clause in his 'Heads of a Plan' for:

> effectually disposing of convicts, and rendering their transportation
> reciprocally beneficial both to themselves and to the State, by the
> establishment of a colony in New South Wales, a country which,
> by the fertility and salubrity of the climate, connected with the
> remoteness of its situation (from whence it is hardly possible for
> persons to return without permission) seems peculiarly adapted
> to answer the views of Government with respect to providing a
> remedy for the evils likely to result from the late alarming and
> numerous increase of felons in this country, and more particularly
> in the metropolis.

A penal colony is what British Australia began as, and for many years remained; that and the dispossessor of the Indigenous inhabitants it found living there.

That extraordinary finagler Duncan Campbell provided information as to probable costs as and when required. The final decision on Botany Bay was much influenced by the voyages of discovery of Captain Cook, particularly that of the *Endeavour* from 1768 to 1771, when the great Lincolnshire naturalist Joseph Banks accompanied him. Their reports, and their description of the existing inhabitants as both passive and few and far between, meant that the immense continent was considered an empty land. What was different about this latest British imperial project was that these convicts were not to be sent out for others to support and control, as had been the case with the Americas. This time the British government would control the sentences, treatment, rights and futures of the convicts it transported, through a governor, officers and men sent out to do that specific job.

Once the decision was taken in August 1786, the Admiralty supervised its implementation, but the Navy Board deputed most of its fulfilment to private contractors, many of them those merchants and shipowners who had shipped and sold slaves in America and Africa.

Some also had whaling interests in the Pacific or had considerable experience in supplying ships to the forces when Britain was at war, and the transportation of convicts to America – a valuable source of income that had been lost when the American Revolution broke out in 1765. It was these men who would supply the necessary ships, victuals and crews required by Lord Sydney's 'Heads of a Plan'. The only exception was the First Fleet, which the Navy Commissioners oversaw themselves.

From then on, transported prisoners were at the mercy of private business contractors whose primary interest was to use convict shipping as a means of back-door entry into the East India Company's monopoly of trade in the South Seas, and, officially at least, its exclusive control over all trading in the new colony until 1813. That murky and monstrous company was well aware of the threat to its interests represented by such a penal settlement, referring to it as 'the serpent we are nursing at Botany Bay'. As Superintendent of Overseers of the hulks, Duncan Campbell supplied the convicts for the first three fleets. His approach to this task would provide Captain Arthur Phillip, in charge of the First Fleet, with constant cause for complaint. Phillip could not discern the 'deeply Christian outlook' Campbell professed to bring to the management of the convicts under his control.

The first transports were undersupplied, overcrowded death traps, and many of the convicts they carried were unfit for the voyage from their time on the hulks. Instructions for cleaning and fumigating the ships were often ignored, as was access to exercise and fresh air. Much worse are the descriptions of the chaining and shackling of prisoners below decks, 'chilled to the bone on soaked bedding, unexercised, crusted with salt, shit and vomit, festering with scurvy and boils'. The lack of antiscorbutics – citrus fruit, green vegetables, any food or drink containing Vitamin C – on voyages that took six to eight months meant that many died of scurvy; some pitiful convicts arrived at Port Jackson in the last stages of the disease, flesh swollen, gums bleeding, teeth fallen out or blackened, joints in agony.

Cheated by masters, stewards and guards, their rations pilfered or sold, these early convicts had no resistance to disease. The clothes they were provided with in England failed to take the weather into account; one blanket only did not help, and bitter cold exacerbated scurvy. The bedding was rarely aired on deck and the sleeping quarters were hot as Hades as they passed through the equatorial tropics, freezing when they reached the Roaring Forties.

Cooped up on this long voyage, crew, officers, convicts and free settlers regularly set upon each other like rats in a sack. The merchant seamen who crewed the ships caused as much, if not more, trouble than the convicts, the most probable reason being that only a sliver of circumstance divided such men from the prisoners with whom they travelled. Men and women who were drunk and disorderly, unruly and unmanageable, mutinous on occasion; plots, hunger strikes, shipwreck, arson, sadistic masters, general villainy and terrible human suffering were the stuff of these early ships. As to fornication, there was plenty of that, as seamen, officers and guards were much at play with the female convicts, the results of which were the firstborn white Australians, free ones at that.

Sodomy flourished as it had on the hulks, muttered over by those above, not much fussed about at convict level. This was to continue on land, in the chain gangs and in the infamous secondary penal colonies such as Norfolk Island, Moreton Bay, Port Arthur and Port Macquarie, where the hardest, most troublesome convicts were sent for exceptional punishment. Violence and barbarity jostled with British concepts of justice and law in the occupation of the continent of Australia. Soldiers and sailors in the British armed forces were still flogged, and the flogging of criminals did not cease until the 1860s.

The Britons sent out to govern Australia were members of the officer caste. Many had fought in the American Revolutionary Wars. There is a whiff of salt air about the early settler colony: the first governors were all navy men, accompanied by corps of soldiers; army men were appointed only later. There was also a considerable number of seamen and watermen among the early convicts, and many marines and sailors from the transport ships settled in the colony. Some governors were good, some were bad, some were very, very bad; some were worse – much, much worse – than horrid.

Captain Arthur Phillip, a Londoner and an experienced naval captain who commanded the First Fleet, was certainly one of the best of them. The eleven ships in his charge sailed from Portsmouth on 13 May 1787 with 1,500 human beings on board, including 770 convicts. They sailed down to the Canaries, then across the Atlantic to Rio, where they stayed for a month, then south to Cape Town, where seeds, plants and 500 animals were taken on board. Among them were sheep, which were to establish the wealth and prosperity of the new colony, while bullocks and horses, and later camels from India and Afghanistan, would, with the convicts, provide the labour required.

From there, through thunderstorms, gales and the sighting of splendid sea animals, they ploughed across the Indian and Southern oceans. The first of the fleet to arrive, the *Supply*, sailed into Botany Bay on 18 January 1788, eight months after the departure from England. Finding Botany Bay unsuitable for settlement, Phillip sailed his flagship *Sirius* and the rest of the fleet a short distance northward to Port Jackson, entering what is now known as Sydney Harbour on 26 January, depositing convicts male and female, ranging in age from a nine-year-old chimney sweep to a female convict of eighty-two. Forty-eight people had died en route. That same day Phillip hoisted

Captain Arthur Phillip,
first Governor of
New South Wales

the Union Jack and took possession of the continent on behalf of His Majesty King George III, as Captain Cook had done for the same king in 1770.

Arthur Phillip was governor from 1788 to 1792, establishing the town of Sydney and the penal colony in extraordinary and extraordinarily difficult circumstances. Phillip had many of the attributes of a man of the Enlightenment. He envisaged a colony in which convicts would be reformed and make new lives for themselves. He insisted on members of the military force and convicts receiving the same rations, which thoroughly offended the former. The British government had instructed him that these convicts should never return home; distance from Britain was a major factor in the choice of Botany Bay. Once they had served their terms, the government foresaw the opportunity of a new life for the felons. Convicts had rights in the penal colony – they could petition governors – and a future before them, if they behaved, which would never have been given them in the motherland. And children born to them were free.

Phillip was also instructed to provide women from the Pacific Islands for the male convicts – an idea he sensibly abandoned. Nearly 25,000 female convicts were transported to Australia from Britain and Ireland, and it is a testament to their sex that they were considered the most difficult, the most troublesome and the most intransigent of all – but that is another, and a very good, story. The most exceptional story, however, lies in the encounters between Phillip, his officers, men and convicts, and the Indigenous Australians whose land they had invaded. During the early days of the colony, happily described as a 'springtime of trust', the natives could not yet have any concept of the mighty assumptions of European civilisation; their lives ultimately transformed into haunting sadness by years of violence, brutality and indifference to the wonders and sophistication of *their* civilisation. From the beginning London had instructed that the Indigenous peoples should be treated with 'amity and kindness'. At best benevolence and interest alternated with ignorance and indifference – and brutality.

Much of this failure stemmed from a view that the Indigenous tribes of Australia were savages or mystical wanderers, but this they were not. Much of it stemmed from the belief in Christian and

European civilisation as the highest form of human development, to be forced on all unbelievers – at gunpoint if necessary. Much of it was connected to a collective lack of intelligence, in that so many of the British invaders, explorers, officials, settlers and convicts simply could not see what was before them. This imperial ignorance was fatal for the people who had lived on the continent for millennia, and whose 500–600 tribes knew its every secret, whose cultures connected them to every leaf, animal, waterway and desert in their land.

All that was hoped for is described by Captain Lieutenant Watkin Tench, a man of sensibility with an enquiring and compassionate mind, whose enchanting chronicles of the first four years of the British settlement of the continent were published in 1789 and 1793. Born in Chester in 1758, Tench fought in the American War of Independence, after which he volunteered for a tour of service and sailed with the First Fleet. His accounts of what he saw say all that needs to be said about what might have been, for Aboriginals and convicts and settlers, in this new world. Tench called the Indigenous Australians 'Indians'.

> I went with a party to the south side of the harbour and had scarcely landed five minutes when we were met by a dozen Indians, naked as at the moment of their birth, walking along the beach. Eager to come to a conference, and yet afraid of giving offence, we advanced with caution towards them. Nor would they, at first, approach nearer to us . . .
>
> I had at this time a little boy, of not more than seven years of age, in my hand. The child seemed to attract their attention very much . . . and as he was not frightened I advanced with him towards them, at the same time baring his bosom and showing the whiteness of his skin . . . The Indian, with great gentleness, laid his hand on the child's hat and afterwards felt his clothes, muttering to himself all the while.

Such gentle encounters did not continue. Property was the rock that broke any hope of accommodation between Indigenous Australians and their invaders.

For convicts, the floggings Phillip authorised were conducted in

The pomp and ceremony of British flogging, George Cruikshank, 1825

public, to ensure the maximum humiliation. They horrified the watching Indigenous Australians – those left after the European gifts of
smallpox, typhus and other new infections had cut a swathe through the
tribes. Their first view of convicts introduced them also to chains, as for
many years intractable convicts were chained together to work in road
gangs numbering seventy or eighty men. Shackles were added after 1791,
with iron collars linking the chain to a belt. Treadmills later provided
seven to fourteen days' additional punishment, another being that,
except on Sundays, the convicts worked in chains and irons all the hours
of daylight.

Phillip had the hardest task, and did the best job, battling against
a government in Britain and its contractors who between them despatched a Second and Third Fleet, the horrific deaths on which, and
the half-alive humans who survived them, bring one to tears. This is
not surprising, as the fleets were supplied and fitted out by the London slave-trading firm of Camden, Calvert & King. The Second
Fleet, despatched in 1789, was the worst. The convicts on its six ships
were starved and kept in irons below deck. Scurvy was rampant. Of

its 1,026 convicts, a quarter died at sea, and the rest arrived at Port Jackson little more than skeletons, and those unable to walk or crawl 'were slung over the side'.

Reports of the horrors of the Second Fleet caused a furore in London. An inquiry was held, but neither the most sadistic of its captains, Donald Trail, a former slave-ship captain for Camden, Calvert & King, nor the company itself, was prosecuted. Camden, Calvert & King went on to assemble the Third Fleet sent in 1791. Of the 2,041 who sailed, 182 convicts died, and nearly 600 of those who disembarked at Sydney Cove were 'so emaciated, so worn away by long confinement, or want of food' that 'many of them will never recover'. It took months for furious reports of such disasters to get back to England, and the same for instructions to travel back. But the government in London now took note, for above all the colony was intended to be self-supporting, and living convicts were needed to work.

1788 and 1789 were years of near starvation. In principle, convict, soldier or seaman received the same punishment for pilfering food: 'a convict found guilty of pilfering potatoes from a garden was sentenced to 300 lashes. The shredded wreck was then to be chained for six months ... to two other felons serving out their sentences.' For the first years, convicts worked only for the government of the colony, their needs supplied by the government store. Then free colonists took them on, still at government expense. By 1800 convicts could be assigned to work for free settlers, the first of whom arrived in 1793. This forced labour, a 'modified form of slavery', both enabled the survival of the first settlers, and established their wealth. A number of the guards and seamen on convict transports stayed on and settled in New South Wales. After the end of the Napoleonic Wars commissioned officers, naval and military, were available to serve in the colony, and convict transportation began in earnest. The New South Wales Corps was formed in 1789 to guard convicts: due to the unsavoury nature of the posting, they were men often no better those they guarded.

Arthur Phillip left New South Wales in 1792, but not before he had seen to it that the settlement could now be almost self-supporting. There were over 4,000 convicts, and over 1,700 acres had been cleared for, or were under, cultivation. He also left behind a new breed: the emancipist. These were convicts who had served their terms, and had received either a conditional or absolute pardon, as set out in the original instructions for the colony. Rules and conditions changed under each governor, but settled into a system which allowed a first stage of freedom for a convict, the ticket of leave, granted after four years of a seven-year sentence, longer for convicts transported for fourteen years or for life, allowing limited freedom within a stipulated area. For those with long sentences there could be conditional pardons, which meant that they could never return to England, and absolute pardons, which meant that they could.

After 1810, Certificates of Freedom were issued at the end of a sentence. Convicts who were well educated, or with useful talents – such as forgers, architects, carpenters or, happily for George, brickmakers or stonemasons – achieved these freedoms speedily. Exceptional talents or good behaviour were the *sine qua non* for these blessings and this system meant that within a very few years of first settlement, former convicts were free to become butchers, bakers, small landholders, domestic servants, clerks – anything the colony or the ships needed.

Convicts whose sentences ended shortly after arrival in the colony – having served much of their sentences on the hulks before departure – became free. From the beginning governors were instructed to offer them land – at least thirty acres – and provisions with which to begin a new life. By 1794 there were seventy-eight such individuals. Much the same was offered to guards and seamen who had come over on the first ships and had settled in the colony. This land was free of rents and taxes for ten years, with the proviso that its new owner stayed on the land and developed it. Besides land grants, free passages, other assistance and concessions were offered to settlers. Women were needed, domestic and farm servants were needed. Sometimes the wives and children of convicts were granted free passage to the colony. Convicts were allowed to petition for such benefits as permission to marry, to have a day off, to be given a ticket of leave, and suchlike. These 'humble petitions' became a small business for the literate – convicts and non-convicts – who could write the letters or fill in the necessary forms.

There were fortunes to be made: some emancipists became wealthy landowners or traders in Sydney, as did many free settlers. In

Great Expectations, Abel Magwitch earned only a conditional pardon. He flirted with a death sentence or transportation to one of the terrifying secondary penal stations by returning to England in 1829 to see what his emancipist wealth has made of Pip. In the surge to acquire pastoral land outside Sydney, land was settled without legal grant. Often such men were ticket-of-leave convicts or emancipists, but by 1830 large landowners had moved in, the process was legalised and land was formally leased from the Crown, thus creating a new and wealthy colonial class, the Squattocracy. As these successful men rose in status there still remained that class of British settler who insisted that as 'free untainted colonists' they would not mix with emancipists, however free, skilled or wealthy. The entrenched British class system was to transmute into a far less hierarchical form in Australia, but with these early settlers it was still on the rampage.

Captains John Hunter and Philip King followed Phillip as governors: both had served under him on the First Fleet, and both struggled endlessly with the New South Wales Corps, whose officers grabbed land and became rich men – not that there was any currency: its currency was rum, and they controlled the traffic in it. In the 1800s Sydney was awash with alcohol, with tobacco, sugar and tea trailing behind as lesser means of both addiction and barter. Matters came to a head under the next governor, William Bligh of *Bounty* fame, a most odd appointment to the troubled colony – he was still known in irreverent circles as 'That *Bounty* Bastard'. By this time Sydney was a small, fortified port town, dominated by the buildings and military barracks that housed the governor and his officers and men, with the convicts lodged where they could, in

> an unplanned straggle of shacks 'in most ruinous decay' perched on the rim of the shining, amethyst, many-lobed harbour. The judge-advocate's residence was a 'perfect pigstye', and the convict barracks . . . beyond mere disgust. There was no proper hospital. The churches were huts . . . the town streets were dusty tracks in summer and ditches after a rain, and no sewers existed.

There were shops, a guardhouse, a church, a garrison, courts, whitewashed brick houses for the governing fraternity and the free, pubs and rum shops for everyone, and newspapers – the *Sydney Gazette and New South Wales Advertiser*, the *Australian*, the *Monitor*. Convicts started the newspapers, convicts and ex-convicts built the buildings, oiled the wheels of the town and served the officials and military and settlers who ruled them. And always there were the original local inhabitants, the Gadigal clan of the coastal Eora people. Always, in these early years, relations with the human beings whose lands the British had taken included attempts at understanding, and co-habitation. Always they failed.

As well as the activities of the New South Wales Corps and the growing prosperity of the land-owning settlers and freed men, the pursuit of seals and sea elephants and boatbuilding were making emancipists and others wealthy men – navigating both the Pacific waters and attempting to avoid the pouncing glances of the East India Company. Later, British whalers moved in, and the slaughter of these great beasts became a major source of income for the port town, until the land and its produce took over, and wool and gold brought new wealth to the colony. When he arrived in Sydney in August 1806, Governor Bligh described it as a 'sink of iniquity'. The evangelical flogger the Rev. Samuel Marsden agreed, bewailing the sexual licence, drunkenness, villainy and Catholics he observed and pursued every-where in the convict town. Bligh's performance was predictably disastrous, and the New South Wales Corps instigated the 'Rum Rebellion' of 1808, imprisoning Bligh, the second time in the colony's short history that the New South Wales Corps had seen off a gov-ernor and taken charge of the colony themselves – the first being Governor King, worn down by constant conflict with the military.

This chaos was remedied by Bligh's successor Lachlan Mac-quarie, the longest-serving governor. A Scot from the Hebridean island of Ulva, he took up the post in January 1810, the first army man to hold the position. He brought his own regiment with him, and despatched the New South Wales Corps back to England, not before time. Macquarie was a conservative man, a despot but with a better heart than most – 'a man of great physical presence. Broad-shouldered and ebullient, his voice was impressive'. A formidable explorer himself, he encouraged others to find ways over the moun-tains to the interior, opening up new land with rich plains and

Major General Lachlan
Macquarie, fifth Governor
of New South Wales

pastures: the starvation years were over. Members of the New South
Wales Corps and free settlers had already taken over land for pasture, so the demand for convict labour became insatiable. Macquarie
introduced proper currency to replace rum; he forbade goats, pigs
and dogs the freedom of Sydney's gathering spots, and was in favour
of as much marriage as possible. He straightened streets, oversaw the
building of schools, barracks and public buildings, and much else.
He was opposed to drunkenness and the excessive flogging he
found in the colony – several hundred lashes were not unusual. The
flogging of women ceased in 1817, and Macquarie lowered magistrates' sentencing power to a hundred lashes, with fifty being the
expected limit.

Macquarie had plans to allot land to Indigenous people, which
came to nothing – for how could they comprehend being allotted
plots of land that were already theirs? His reprisals against Aboriginal
resistance or attacks on settlers or their livestock were swift and brutal. They were whipped and flogged as convicts were, they were
poisoned, shot and massacred. Macquarie had other battles to fight
too, for he was happy to invite emancipists to his table, appointing

them as magistrates and permitting them to work in previously pro-
scribed professions, thus mortally offending those free emigrants and
men of capital who remained tremulous with fear of the 'convict
stain'. This row became so ferocious, both in print and in person, that
it could well be one of the reasons for the lack of deference favoured
by Australians ever since. Time, however, eventually caused the fret-
ting about the 'convict stain' to drift into the ether, never to reach its
source back in Britain.

Macquarie left office in 1821. Today his name is commemorated in
lakes, streets, rivers, mountains and community centres in every part
of Australia. The penal colony that gave such opportunity to men like
George Conquest owes most to him. Macquarie's tricky relationship
with John Macarthur – the father of Australia's wool industry (though
the flogging parson Samuel Marsden was also a contributor to this
future wealth) and the man who had led the rum rebellion against
Bligh – together with complaints from other 'gentlemen settlers'
about his patronage of ex-convicts, caused trouble for Macquarie in
England. Stories of convict success, of convict wealth, became cou-
pled with a view that the lax control of convicts, required in the
colony's early years when the need for survival was paramount, now
threatened the deterrent effect of transportation.

This led the British government to set up an investigation in 1819
into conditions in New South Wales, to be carried out by an English
judge, John Bigge. Macquarie and Bigge shaped the years George
Conquest would serve as a convict in Australia, as did Governor
Richard Bourke, an Irish Whig and a liberal Anglican, during whose
time as governor George served most of his sentence. In 1822 and
1823, John Bigge published his report for the Commission of Inquiry
into New South Wales, based on a two-year sojourn in the colony
from 1819 to 1821. He disapproved entirely of the immoral drinking
den he found Sydney to be, and his report demanded that the system
be made more rigorous, that the rules of convict assignment in the
iron gangs and at the extreme penal settlements such as Norfolk
Island and Van Diemen's Land should inflict punishments that could
be seen to be severe by a British public charmed by tales of convict
wealth and success. When George Conquest arrived in New South
Wales in 1830, most convicts were assigned to free immigrants who

now took on the responsibility of feeding, clothing and housing them, in a successful attempt to save the British government and its taxpayers money by reducing the cost to the Exchequer of each transported convict from £24 to £10.

After the Bigge report, severe punishments for non-compliance in specified convict work replaced the limited laissez-faire system that had previously allowed them rights over their hours of work, extra work in their free time and other indulgences. Bigge was particularly hostile to convicts working for ex-convicts, and as a result of his report more land was opened up to free settlers, particularly in the southwest of New South Wales, around Bathurst to the west of Sydney, and in the Hunter Valley to the north, where George was to begin his sentence. Thus land appropriation increased. Bigge advised that convicts should be sent inland, beyond the temptations of Sydney, to be used as cheap labour for the agricultural development of the colony. He particularly favoured the chain gang. Shackled in chains or ankle irons, these convicts did the back-breaking work of building colonial Australia, including the three great roads that opened up the interior: the Great South Road, the Great Western Road – which by 1823 cut through and over the Blue Mountains to the rich grasslands beyond – and the Great North Road to Maitland in the Hunter Valley, built between 1826 and 1836.

George could not have failed to see these gangs – he was assigned to settlers near two of the new roads during their construction. Nor could he have avoided seeing the Indigenous Australians summoned into service for every British settlement, their knowledge so essential to the exploration and opening up of the interior. He, like his fellows, was thus in an unusual position, inasmuch as he, and they, witnessed two versions of human ferocity: the British treatment of their own people – their convicts and their poor – and the British treatment of the Indigenous 'savages'.

Assignment could still hold terrors for convicts, but it also had advantages. Convicts could complain to the magistrate should their master or mistress not provide proper rations and clothing, or permit adequate rest hours. A settler could not physically punish his convicts; only the magistrates' courts could authorise that. All too many masters ignored this and flogged away, especially in rural districts where many of them were magistrates themselves. However, in principle at least, convicts lived under a British system of law by which they had certain rights that had never been available to them in the mother country. Skilled convicts could do well in such circumstances, for the governors who followed Macquarie could never realise John Bigge's vision of a rigorously controlled penal dreamland. Without convict labour, the colony could achieve nothing. 1830 was the peak year for this privatised enterprise, George Conquest being one of the 5,000 men who arrived in New South Wales in that year.

Conditions on board the convict ships had improved by the time George sailed on the *Nithsdale*, which he boarded on 9 December 1829, one of sixty men from the Woolwich hulks *Justitia* and *Ganymede*, who were later joined by sixty-four from the *Retribution* at Sheerness and another sixty from the *Dolphin* at Chatham. Carrying these 184 convicts, fifty of them with life sentences, the *Nithsdale* sailed from Sheerness on Friday 1 January 1830, one of eighteen such ships to be sent off in that year. It was George's good fortune that he had not been sentenced to transportation before 1815, when safeguards began to be put into place to protect the convict cargo from the worst contractors.

By then, surgeon superintendents had been installed to supervise the health of the transported men, over whom they had more power than the ship's captain. The impetus was for convicts to survive the journey, as disease-free bodies who could work, and not infect the colonists and convicts already there. Now private contractors were paid for the number of living convicts they delivered to the colony, not by how many boarded the ships in England. Nevertheless, trouble was always in the offing from the seamen who manned the ships – ill-paid, ill-treated, often rebellious or mutinous. And the biggest killer on the long journey to New South Wales remained acute infectious disease – typhus and dysentery caused the most deaths, though storms and shipwrecks, mutinies and malefactions of both crew and convict also claimed many.

As so many died en route in the early years, surgeons were instructed not to allow any men unfit for the voyage to board. Before embarkation, George, like his fellows, was inspected by the *Nithsdale*'s surgeon superintendent, Robert Malcolm, was washed and shaved, and recorded as good to go. In charge of the military personnel on the ship was Robert Moffatt, captain of the guard of the 17th Regiment, who was to settle in New South Wales. Four women were on board, one of them Mrs Moffatt; another suffered a miscarriage at Sheerness. There were two free passengers and four children. Rations, antiscorbutics and clothing suitable for the voyage were provided: 'jackets and waistcoats of blue cloth or kersey, duck trousers, check or coarse linen shirts, yarn stockings, and woollen caps'. George missed the addition of warmer clothes for winter, which were not added until the 1830s.

Irons and chains were removed once the ship was properly out to sea – though kept ready to be used at the slightest sign of refractory behaviour. Vinegar, lime juice and sugar were doled out against scurvy, and exercising, handcuffed and chained on deck, was part of the routine. On an adequately run convict ship, of which the *Nithsdale* appears to have been one, convicts could be given occupations which ranged from the eternal chore of picking oakum to carving, fishing, singing and learning to read or write, with, as ever, the provision of improving literature. There are accounts of convicts who danced 'and (when in irons) managed a clinking beat with their chains'. Wine, provided as another precaution against scurvy, was always cheering. Sometimes they could earn a bit of money, tobacco, clothing or rum by doing chores on the journey. Below decks, they gambled like fiends, and drank and smoked whatever they could lay their hands on.

The *Nithsdale* sailed by the direct route, via the Canary Islands and then down the western coast of Africa, stopping at Cape Town for repairs and supplies, before embarking on the long eastward trawl across the Indian and Southern oceans. The voyage took 131 days, a good twenty days longer than most transport ships of the time. Stays in ports along the way before attacking the great Southern Ocean could enable all sorts of goodies to be smuggled aboard: tobacco, coffee, sugar, booze, and much else, and as the *Nithsdale* seems to have had a relatively untroubled voyage it is likely the convicts did well with these. Bedding arrangements had improved by now, though they still seem little better than those in German Stalag huts in a Second World War movie: 'Two rows of sleeping-berths, one above the other extend on each side of the between-decks, each berth being 6 feet square, and

calculated to hold four convicts, every one thus possessing 18 inches'
space to sleep in.'

As the ship's human cargo consisted of men only, carnal activity
was confined to the usual practices. Acute attacks of diarrhoea were
noted, as well as fevers, seizures and ophthalmia, but only one convict
died during the voyage, all others arriving in Port Jackson on Wednesday 12 May 1830, almost winter in Australia. George and his fellow
convicts had spent five months cooped up on the *Nithsdale*. Two days
later they were ashore in Sydney. Convicts could bring some possessions, and George arrived with £1 15s 10d from his earnings on the
hulks. Put into the hands of the captain when the convict boarded
ship, on arrival in New South Wales it was deposited in a savings bank
until the end of the convict's sentence. That the *Nithsdale*'s voyage had
been marked by at least some of the disturbances habitual at the time
is suggested by the fact that the ship's steward sued the captain,
Thomas Christian, for his wages in court in Sydney, Captain Christian
responding by accusing the steward of drunkenness and desertion.

George first set foot on Australian soil when the town of Sydney
was forty-two years old, and he himself just twenty-four. By 1830
50,000 people lived there, nearly half of whom were convicts. With
perhaps twice as many grog shops as twenty years before, still oozing rum and breathing tobacco, still dominated by barracks and the
military, the coaches, drays and carts of settlers filled the streets.
Now the waterside town had a flourishing trade in wool, wheat and
maize, and rum was replaced by a sterling currency in pounds, shillings and pence. Time had gone by: 'In 1828, the *Sydney Gazette*
announced the death of the colony's first great-grandmother, with
100 descendants.' As omnipresent as the remarkable birds, flying
jewellery in the skies, the Aboriginals who remained observed the
convicts in their slops or uniforms or chains, their garments adorned
with the ubiquitous convict arrow. And still there was the flogging:
'I have seen young children practising on a tree, as children in England play at horses.'

On arrival, convicts known to be incorrigible were sent on to the
secondary penal colonies or prisons. The rest were assigned to settlers,
labour gangs or government work under overseers – often former
convicts themselves – or military supervision. George had a piece of

good fortune. After mustering, convicts were meant to be chained and put to public works – or to road gangs for the most recalcitrant – for a short period only, to prepare them for the joys of assignment. But by the time George arrived there was such a demand for convict work on the land that he was sent directly to the new settlements north of Sydney. Accompanying him was an array of fellow criminals, many of whom were being sent to work for the men of substance who, after the Bigge Report, had acquired large tracts of fertile land, with the extra bonuses of coal and timber, in the Hunter River district.

The outpost of Newcastle, at the mouth of the Hunter River, is sixty miles north of Sydney by sea and a hundred miles by land. It was set up as a secondary penal colony in 1801, and served as a repository for the residue of some 200 of the Irish rebels of the Castle Hill convict rebellion of 1804, also called the Second Battle of Vinegar Hill after that of the same name in Ireland in 1798. Many of the convicts who organised the Sydney uprising were graduates of the first in Ireland, and used the words 'Vinegar Hill' as a code word. Nine of the ringleaders were executed and two were gibbeted; the rest went in chains to Newcastle. Newcastle was opened for settlement in 1813: small farmers moved in first, then the Squattocracy, and in 1822 the penal colony was moved further north to Port Macquarie and the Hunter Valley was opened to full-scale settlement. The settlers did not see the cultivation of the region as practised by the Indigenous Australians of the Valley lands. They saw only the fertile plains, the abundant water, the magnificent bush – though not as magnificent as the great red-gold cedars, soon sawn down, chopped up and shipped away. In a sense George Conquest was entering a rare Australian paradise. His new employer, Thomas Liscombe, was a free settler who had arrived from England the previous year, and had been promised a land grant just as the *Nithsdale* was setting sail from Sheerness. In March 1830 he was given 640 acres at Stockrington, near the town of Maitland, twenty miles inland from Newcastle. Liscombe's property, when it later came to be sold, was described as rich with 'Coal, which makes it very valuable'.

More than half a million acres of the Hunter Valley were appropriated, and the Indigenous people living there, the Wonnarua, the Awabakal and other tribes, were dispossessed. Disease and starvation attacked them first, then brutal reprisals for their resistance to the occupation of their land. The savagery of the destruction of these tribes was particular, perhaps because of the beauty of the valley: the settlers wanted it for themselves.

After 1824 Indigenous Australians were thought to have become more 'peaceable': they proved to be excellent stockmen, and some worked for the pastoralists and farmers, tracked for them, served them, some even became policemen, and many, of course, did none of these things. The early settlers and their convicts could have done little without their knowledge of, and ability to thrive in, the *terra nullius*, the 'land without inhabitants' that the British were taking from them. But they never ceased to fight for their territory, battles increasing as free settlers moved further from the original settlement at Sydney to take over rich food-bearing land. As just one example:

> 1834, October: Governor Stirling leads a party of men to a site near present-day Pinjarra, on the Murray River, and attacks 80 Aboriginal people. One of Stirling's men dies and many Aboriginal people are killed. Official reports say that 14 Aboriginal people were killed but Aboriginal accounts suggest a whole clan was decimated in the attack.

The early history of white settlement in Australia is a contested, politicised field. Those who acknowledge and record the frontier wars in which Indigenous people resisted and died in their thousands have been branded 'left wing' or 'black-armband intellectuals' by some politicians and historians. Dispossession, poverty and discrimination were not the only despoilers of Aboriginal lives: some historians have added verbal lashes to their plight. What is certain is that the Indigenous people of Australia did not give up their land without using every ounce of invention, skill and weaponry in their possession: they lost out to a radically different civilisation, superior weaponry and imperial manpower.

By the time George Conquest reached Maitland, Newcastle had ceased to be a secondary penal colony, and the Great North Road from Sydney was all but completed. But Newcastle was still most easily reached from Sydney by sail, and it is probable that many convicts were shipped to the Hunter Valley. They found a land sprinkled with large pastoral properties – needed for sheep and cattle – and homesteads, the wilderness already domesticated, echoing the mother country in its number of pubs and inns. Coal, convicts, cattle, sheep, mixed farming, horse studs, tobacco and squatters were the substance of the Hunter Valley then; today its wine industry, begun with convict labour in the early 1800s, is its claim to fame.

George was one of eighty convicts from the *Nithsdale* who travelled to the Hunter Valley. One of them, Joseph Bold, transported for seven years for picking pockets, was assigned with him to Thomas Liscombe. In the troubled waters of contemporary Australian history, certain historians have claimed that most of the convicts sent to New South Wales were guilty of serious crimes, and that their character defects were innumerable and irredeemable, the most common accusation being that 'they were too fond of drink'. Also proposed is that flogging was standard practice for the time, and that convicts either didn't mind it or became accustomed to it. Certainly if offered the choice, a convict might well choose fifty lashes over solitary confinement, the alternative which came to be favoured in the mother country after 1830. But in New South Wales, on they flogged. Flogging was easier and cheaper, and to such historians a necessary part of the system: 'The lash had to do the work of the walls, the warders, and the punishment cells.' Better still, British flogging was considered superior to the unregulated flogging of slaves in the United States, because its application was governed by British law. It is, however, impossible to find a document written by a convict expressing gratitude for a flogging.

These historians tend towards a certain emotional attachment to and idealisation of the British legal system and the great gift it was to Australia: 'the plain fact is that the majority of eighteenth-century convicts sentenced to transportation were convicted of crimes that we continue to consider serious'. The use of those lethal words 'the plain fact is . . .' illuminates a historian's pathway to perdition. George's companions in New South Wales give the lie to it, as do the misdemeanours of those convicted with him at Chester Easter Quarter Sessions in April 1829. Certainly there were many hardcore habitual criminals, but many thousands were like John Boyles, a Hampshire farmer transported for 'conspiring to raise wages'.

On arrival in the colony, each convict was assessed for the uses to which he might be put by each master. Those assigned with George from the *Nithsdale* were thoroughly recorded, and so we know the crimes for which they were found guilty and their good or bad behaviour during their sentence. Richard Babbington's crime was stealing bacon, for which he got seven years. A Lincolnshire man, he could shear, plough and reap, and any convict who could claim those skills, who could milk an animal or had been a domestic servant, was valuable to any settler and was swooped upon from the *Nithsdale* roster. John Callaghan, a waterman from Kent, got fourteen years for stealing an umbrella; Robert Furze, a London boatman, stole a hat (seven years). There were future bushrangers on board the *Nithsdale*: one of them, Andrew Hamilton, was a soldier and deserter from Lanarkshire (seven years). George travelled with weavers and ploughmen and watermen and shepherds and labourers, cloth workers and cooks and servants and shoemakers and cotton spinners, blacksmiths, deserters, sailors and tailors. They had stolen oats, fowl, a parcel, a coat, shoes, a hankey, a donkey, a horse; a few were shoplifters, house breakers, deserters, burglars, highwaymen.

9

Scarred Faces

A Government Jail Gang, outside Hyde Park Barracks,
Sydney, by Augustus Earle, 1830

T HE NEW WORLD IN which George found himself was warm
and sometimes very hot, with plummeting rains in summer, frequent floods, frequent droughts, rarely very cold,
but with chilly nights in winter. George arrived in the autumn
when it rained less, which was fortunate for him because Thomas
Liscombe had owned his land for only two months: it is very likely
that on arrival George laid his head down in an empty paddock.

Some Australian
birds – flying jewellery:
clockwise from top right:
two superb lyrebirds,
Major Mitchell's cockatoo,
a Victorian crowned
pigeon and a bird of
paradise

Being in the Hunter Valley, however, there was beautiful rolling
country, flanked by mountains, blessed with rivers and creeks,
huge trees and wilderness.

It is difficult not to romanticise the skies, so infinite and often of so
cerulean a blue, or the peculiar birds giving forth strange melodies and
chirrups. All torture and boredom could be ameliorated by the wom-
bats and platypuses, bell birds and cockatoos, kangaroos, possums,
koalas and emus, the leaf of each tree or bush never seen or even imagined before. Every spider (mostly pestiferous), snake (so often
poisonous) and insect – ants, fleas, mosquitoes and flies of every
variety – would be pesky for every minute of the day, but balanced
by the sounds of the bush – always a joy. George's arrival in the
Hunter Valley coincided with the lyrebirds' peak singing and mim-
icking season. English, Irish, Scots and Welsh accents and their
languages – there were many convicts from the British Isles who
spoke no English at all – could now be added to the birds' repertoire. The most modest claim would be to say that however much
he itched and scratched, what George now encountered had much
to recommend it to a boatman from the English canals or a convict
from the Woolwich hulks.

Christian missionaries of many persuasions were well to the fore from the earliest days, attempting to reform the convicts, but also setting up stations to bring Christianity, salvation and European civilisation to Indigenous Australians. George Bidmead, sentenced to fourteen years for stealing cloth, was with George Conquest on both the *Ganymede* hulk and the *Nithsdale*, and was also sent to the Hunter Valley. He was assigned to the Congregational missionary the Rev. Lancelot Threlkeld, an extreme example of English religious dissent at its most peculiar.

Threlkeld tended to the Indigenous peoples of the Hunter Valley at Lake Macquarie, and spent many years translating the New Testament into their Awabakal language. At one point in his chequered but worthy career he was permitted convicts on assignment, and George Bidmead was one of them. Threlkeld deplored the convict system, which he considered to be little better than slavery, and he regularly sent reports of military abuse of Aboriginals to the authorities. The group of convicts he was allotted tested his sanctity to the utmost. After many attempts to bring them to book, he was reduced to sending them to be flogged and put in jail. Nothing helped. Then:

> The breaking point came when the men refused to accept their ration of beef. They dumped it outside the door of the store and said it was too boney. It was a little boney, Threlkeld admitted, but they had been given extra weight to make it up, and his own family were eating the same. The men also said in a cocky and mysterious manner that they were making a present of their meat to Threlkeld as they could do without it. He soon learnt why. They picked the lock of the store and took away nearly all the pork. Threlkeld gave up. He sent the seven men back to the government and asked for better replacements. The men had got what they wanted – after a period on the roads, which if they were lucky would not be too arduous, they would be assigned somewhere else.

This, or something like it, may be how George Conquest managed to get himself moved on as often as he did, though by the 1830s masters could get permission to swap or transfer convicts. There were many reasons for a convict to be moved from an assignment – misbehaviour, redundancy, inadequacy or ill-suited skills. George was with Liscombe for barely three months before he was moved on to the township of Bathurst on the banks of the Macquarie River, 200 miles south-west of Maitland, and over a hundred miles west of Sydney. Opened up by explorers who found a route from Sydney over the Blue Mountains in 1815, Bathurst was well established by the time George went there, and had become a military and police post and a centre of British government.

The Wiradjuri tribe who lived there fought fiercely to keep their land, but the Bathurst Wars between them and the British were over by the time of George's arrival. The Wiradjuri tribe, despite being led by the great Aboriginal resistance leader Windradyne, were of course defeated.* In 1830 the greatest threat to white settlers in the isolated settlements inland came from bushrangers. In the 1830s they were usually convict runaways, 'bolters' from settlements or chain gangs who fled their assignments to form gangs in the bush, accosting travellers, settlers and coaches – anything they could lay their hands on to supply food, weapons and cash. Bushrangers were to become a major government problem and a major expression of convict desperation during the years of George's sentence and for many decades afterwards.

Ralph Entwistle, a young English brickmaker from Bolton, sentenced to life for stealing clothes, arrived in Australia on the *John* in 1827. He was assigned to Thomas Liscombe's brother, John, as a convict servant on his property Stowford in the Fitzgerald Valley, to the south of Bathurst. In November 1829, with another convict, Entwistle was sent to Sydney by bullock dray to deliver some goods for Liscombe. On the way back they made the mistake of stripping off and taking a dip in the Macquarie River. Ralph Darling, the governor at the time, was inspecting the new settlements at Bathurst with his retinue. As they were crossing the river, they spotted the naked men and arrested them. The Bathurst magistrate, who happened to be there, charged them with 'causing an affront to the governor'.

They were publicly flogged, with fifty lashes each, and Entwistle lost the right to his ticket of leave. There are many descriptions of the horror of the first flogging for a convict, and this was Entwistle's

* Further information on Windradyne of the Wiradjuri people can be found here: http://abd.anu.edu.au/biography/windradyne-13251

first. Injustice and the desire for revenge were not the only reasons that led Entwistle into the bush. Another grievance was the inadequacy of the food and clothing provided by Liscombe. Other convicts joined Entwistle and took to the bush in September 1830, including four more of Liscombe's men, though Entwistle forced some of them at gunpoint to join his gang. Many of its members were Irish, and Entwistle used the Irish rebel cry 'Death or liberty!', which added to the fear felt by the British settlers and officials, whose contempt for, and dread of, the Irish was endemic.

The Ribbon Gang, so called because Entwistle wore strips of white cloth on his hat like an Irish Ribbonman – the rebel movement of poor Catholics in Ireland – created a tempest of robbery, murder and general mayhem in Bathurst and the surrounding properties for two months. Twice they defeated forces sent after them until the 39th Regiment and mounted police joined Bathurst civilians and Aboriginal trackers, and fought it out in gun battles and sieges near the extensive Abercrombie Caves. Reinforcements had to be called in but by 2 November it was all over, and those who were still alive were sentenced to death and hanged in public on 30 November, in batches of six, from huge gallows put up in the centre of Bathurst. Nine of them were Catholics: a priest, Father John Joseph Therry, came up from Sydney to perform the last rites.

Convicts, white settlers and authorities may have considered Indigenous people as savages, but the last two made use of their tracking skills to hunt down escaped convicts – one of the reasons convicts' relations with Indigenous Australians could be as damaged as those with government and master. For their part, the Indigenous Australians were astonished and appalled by the way the British treated their own people, and fought desperately, and unsuccessfully, to avoid the same fate for themselves. 'Whenever the British were behaving despotically, there was almost always a liberal critique of that behaviour within British society' wrote the historian Niall Ferguson in defence of the British Empire – the drawback being that a liberal critique was of no help at all to a convict being whipped by a scourger, or to an Aboriginal losing land or life near Bathurst.

Fear stalked British settlers in Australia in these early years. Fear because they were so far from home; fear because they were in a

strange country about which they knew nothing; fear of dark bodies
lurking in the bush; fear of the creeping, flying and slithering animals
that everywhere surrounded them; fear of their own convict people.
They passed this fear on to the convicts, from the lonely shepherd in
his hut guarding the sheep and cattle his master had imported into
this unwelcoming continent, to the men on the chain gangs.

Besides Ralph Entwistle, four members of his gang had been
John Liscombe's convicts, so in September 1830 Liscombe needed
replacements and his brother Thomas provided at least one of them
in George Conquest. John Liscombe had arrived in Australia as a free
settler in 1825, and he had 2,500 acres, 200 acres of which was cleared,
and twenty cultivated. He had horses, over a hundred cattle and 600
sheep. Liscombe employed many convicts over the years, male and
female, and he was Bathurst's district auctioneer, clerk to the bench
and postmaster. He resigned the latter post in 1836. Settlers protected
their own, but there were plenty of convicts throughout the district to
give him the evil eye. It is easy to imagine the huts or shacks he provided as convict quarters, and doubtful that any convict at Stowford
had a good time of it. But again, George's stay was not long. By this
time he takes on heroic proportions as a representative of those thousands of convicts who put up with everything thrown at them, who
bided their time and survived to make a new life for themselves.
Scarred backs, scarred faces, but the last word was theirs.

George's next move was to the Argyle district, named by Governor
Macquarie after his native county in Scotland, south by some hundred
miles from Bathurst, south of Sydney, to the north of Australia's
present-day capital Canberra. He was moved to the small town of
Inverary, the land of the Gandangara and, to the south, the Ngun-
nawal, on the cusp of many other clans and that of the Wiradjuri nation.
There were ninety Indigenous Australians left there when he arrived.
Inverary was set in another stretch of excellent grazing and farming
land and by 1830 was a prosperous little place; there were plans for it to
become an important inland town. However, when the Great South
Road was built the nearby town of Goulburn was chosen as the
principal connection to Sydney, thus bypassing Inverary and ending
its aspirations. After which loss, in 1836 Inverary reinvented itself as
the new township of Bungonia, thought to be a corruption of the

Aboriginal term *bun-gunyah*, meaning 'good camp site' or 'camp on the creek'. But for most of George's time there – 1830 to 1837 – Inverary was the administrative and police centre of the penal system in the southern pastoral settlements, overseeing the road gangs and the stockades that housed the chained convicts.

White settlers had moved into the Argyle district from 1820 onwards, and by the time George arrived there were four or five large properties in the area, among them Reevesdale, the estate of a free settler, James Styles; Lumley Park, the estate of retired naval lieutenant Robert Futter; and Inverary Park, the homestead of David Reid, a naval surgeon who emigrated from Aberdeen in 1822 with his wife Agnes, and started their new life in a slab hut on their land. Futter and Reid were both magistrates. All the accoutrements of control were to be found in Inverary, its small white population consisting mostly of convicts and ticket-of-leave men. The surrounding plains supported cattle, sheep, wheat – and fleas, the latter crawling over all in the colony, no respecter of persons. As with the effluvia that coated the boots, shoes and clothes of pre-twentieth-century Britishers, early white Australians carried around clouds of fleas. There was plenty of work for a willing convict, whether on the land or building the settlers' new mansions and homesteads, and it seems that it was working for Dr David Reid, either at Inverary Park or on his other properties, that George served out his sentence.

By the time he reached Inverary Park, George had worked near all the provincial capitals of the rich settlement areas of New South Wales – Maitland in the Hunter Valley, Bathurst in the western district and now near Goulburn. The free landowners acquired multiple properties and runs, using convict labour to work them, producing large families to inherit them, establishing estates that brought them both status and influence, in many cases without having to bother about actually living on their land. Some English companies and landowners never saw the very considerable tracts of land they had invested in and controlled from 'home'. These landowners had arbitrary powers over the convicts in their service, a

> tyranny of the worst kind exercised to the full . . . Prisoners were often punished most severely for very trivial offences . . . If a

man approached his master . . . and did not take his hat off and
hold it in his hand whilst talking to him, it would be considered
insolence . . . it was more likely he would receive the sentence of
being flogged with 50 or 75 lashes by a cat-o'-nine-tails while tied
up to a gum-tree . . . or the corner-post of a fence.

David Reid was not one such. George's good fortune at this
point was to spend the rest of his sentence working for a doctor
and pastoralist who could have been invented by Dickens, as witnessed by this contemporary report of him as: 'one of the old
magistrates, an old medical gentleman, was very much beloved by
all classes'. Being a Briton of his time and class, however, the Aboriginals of the area could not say the same. Reid had served as a
naval surgeon at the Battle of Trafalgar, and was recalled by the
Admiralty in 1815 to combat the mortality rate on convict ships. He
accompanied several voyages, and his knowledge and humanity
delivered 'most extraordinary' results. In 1822 he was rewarded
with 2,000 acres of land in County Argyle, where he settled and
which he named Inverary Park; he was to receive more grants in
due course. As a magistrate, Reid held his sessions in a hut on his
land before a courthouse was built in the township in 1835. Despite
the crackdown on leniency of any kind towards convicts after the
Bigge Report, it seems that George's family trade enabled him to
have a favoured life, for stone and brick masons were valued above
all in the colony. Reid

sometimes had as many as forty assigned servants at one time,
of various trades and occupations, having very little trouble
with regard to the management of them.

With the help of four convicts . . . [he] built a magnificent
homestead with . . . fourteen rooms, flagstone verandahs, a
spiral staircase and cedar beams.

Reid signed George Conquest in and out of his time as a convict
in Bungonia. The homestead was built from rock quarried on the
property; the convict builders working under a convict overseer

completed it in 1837, the year in which Reid gave George his final Certificate of Freedom.

The pastures and creeks of this land look as ancient and lonely today as they must have looked when George first saw them, with, always, the ubiquitous gum trees shedding their beautiful streams of bark and making a carpet on the ground below. David Reid proved to be an accomplished man of the land. He bred cattle, kept horses – to which George was accustomed from his years in Market Harborough – and 3,000 sheep; he grew barley, hops and peach trees, made malt, beer, whisky and peach brandy. He feared the 'savages' but hated only one thing – the parrots that loved his peaches and at which he would aim his gun. Blue-eyed satin bowerbirds, native to the region, also loved peaches.

George's companions in these years would have been almost entirely fellow convicts or ticket-of-leave men or women, the women generally in service at or near the homestead where David and Agnes Reid raised their six children, the last of whom was born just after George was granted his freedom. Reid's convicts did more than build his homestead, they worked as stockmen, dairymen, shepherds, shearers, wool pressers, musterers or overseers.

> There were at times up to forty convict-assigned servants and Reid . . . had no trouble with them. He augmented the meagre government rations with an additional half-pound of tea, three pounds of sugar, and a 'fig' of tobacco a week.

Some were sent away to work as shepherds in the rough scrub or at Reid's more distant grazing lands, others worked in the house, or in the stables, woolsheds, yards and barns of Inverary Park. The estates of early settlers such as Reid were like medieval villages, with all the tradesmen needed on hand. Reid's property had 'blacksmiths, carpenters, shoemakers, wheelwrights and even tanners'. Convicts lived amongst dogs and horses, cattle and sheep. They tended to live and cook together, often building their slab or bark huts or sheds themselves at a distance from the homestead. Making a bed from straw and ticking, sometimes two, sometimes six, sometimes eight convicts shared the hut together, supplied with an iron pot, an axe, a billycan and a frying pan, mucking in amongst all the mosquitoes, blowflies, snakes, scorpions, spiders and rustling inhabitants of the Australian bush. Night sounds might be shots fired by marauding bushrangers – Inverary was plagued by them – or the roaring echoes of men at their drink, for dotting the area were grog shops and drinking shacks of one kind or another. Stockades nearby housed the convict chain gangs cutting the Great South Road.

Although there were rules concerning convict clothing, in practice they were often disregarded, especially in rural outposts. The regulation trousers were called 'punishment trousers' because they could be fitted over leg irons. This 'canary' suit of clothing was officially reserved for repeat offenders, so it is not what George would have worn during his years at Inverary, although, like the rattling convicts on the chain gangs, he would have seen plenty of them. Far away from prison barracks, Reid supplied his convicts with 'one light suit of duck (frock and trousers) for the summer and one warm suit . . . for the winter, plus two pairs of boots a year'. George would probably have looked like a character from one of the many works of artist and traveller Augustus Earle, who captured so much of early colonial life in Australia.

By 1831 George was better fed and probably better clothed than

A convict uniform for continuing offenders: black and canary yellow, with a grey cap and a brown leather cap, c. 1830s or 1840s

any of his family in Leicestershire, who were living through the year of riots and protestations that led to the passing of the Great Reform Act in 1832, on the way to making a life for himself that would be inconceivable to them. However, he lived with convicts who were destroyed by the system. Two convicts working on a neighbour's farm murdered their brutal overseer ('slaves make the most tyrannical masters' – convicts turned overseers had a reputation of excessive savagery towards the men whose lives they had once shared). The murderers were hanged and gibbeted at Goulburn, and remained dangling for some years, their chains and skeletons rattling in the wind until Governor Richard Bourke demanded that the bodies be removed and buried.

The increasing appropriation of rich inland territory meant that the 1830s were years of serious confrontations between settlers and the Indigenous inhabitants. Aboriginal tribes attacked settlers and were massacred in return in the so called 'frontier wars' – exacerbated by severe, recurrent droughts. George also lived safely through a period when the Bushranging Act meant that any doubtful-looking fellow could be taken into custody by country constables. He saw captured bushrangers brought to Dr Reid at Inverary Park to have bullets extracted; he saw a fellow convict known as Dick sentenced to nine months on the chain gang for stealing turnips from Reevesdale, the neighbouring property owned by the less merciful James Styles. Accounts of settlers without Reid's kindness are as numerous as Australian flies:

> The masters hereabout seem generally in very bad odour with their
> men . . . At one of the farms I went to they were almost starved:
> and indeed they looked so. What else can you expect under this
> system of white slavery? The master's interest is to get as much as
> possible for as little as possible . . . This leads to bitter, ineradicable
> animosity in the men, which year by year gets deeper and stronger;
> until at last the magistrate, himself a settler too, and equally a party
> in the iniquitous system, is appealed to by the master. Of course he
> orders the man a flogging, and I am sorry to say generally with as
> much nonchalance as the housewife sends for a pound of candles.
> Then comes bushranging – robbery – murder – and capture and
> execution.

In George's time Inverary had a school, a post office, a black-smith, a butcher and two inns, one of them the well named Hope Inn built by the convict stonemason Patrick Kelly – the township was built with convict labour. During George's years there, Inverary had sixteen houses, three police constables and a lock-up keeper under Constable John Jones. Troopers were stationed nearby for protection from, and the pursuit of, bushrangers, and also because many convicts on the way to trial in Sydney were confined in the town jail. Magistrates of uncertain temper frequently evaded Governor Bourke's order that no more than fifty lashes should be given for an offence by cleaving crimes into two, so that fifty lashes could be applied for each crime. By 1835 the township had a well-used flogging post, attended to by ex-convict Scourger Thomas Hyams. But under magistrates such as Reid, Bourke's law would have been followed to the letter.

Was George ever whipped? Who knows? His survival of every-thing thrown at him is a testament to his character, perhaps to the Independent chapel of his early childhood, but also to the happier possibilities of the system itself. Governor Bourke's humanitarian approach to convicts was in contrast to his authorisation in 1835 of the legal removal of land from Indigenous Australians. More than fifty years after the first invasion, without consultation with, or the consent of, its Indigenous people, he declared Australia *terra nullius*, which meant that this vast land and its numerous islands were empty and belonged to no one except the British Crown.

In David Reid, George Conquest found a master who provided both kindness and opportunity for a young Englishman used to harsh work and hunger at home. As a convict in Australia he had more rights, more food and more opportunity than would ever have been offered him in Leicestershire. In England, 1834 was the year of the New Poor Law which introduced the impoverished classes to the full persecution of the workhouse. On 31 March of that year George began the first stage of his freedom. He had completed four years of his sentence without a blemish on his record, and was issued with his ticket of leave, which permitted him to live and work in the district of Inverary on the condition that he reported to his magistrate, David Reid, once a month.

As a ticket-of-leave man, George could be self-employed, and acquire property. But he had to get permission to leave the area should he wish to do so, and church attendance was compulsory. The 1841 census for Bungonia includes a clutch of Irish names – Farran, Keeffe, Kelly, Lennon, Lynch, O'Brien, O'Donell, O'Neill, Cusack. Irish Catholics made up a substantial proportion of George's fellow convicts, and until 1839 they attended Mass in the Hope Inn, possibly preferable to the vestigial wooden Anglican chapel, St Luke's.

In one sense, after George embarked on the *Nithsdale* and his trajectory as a convict was duly recorded, he disappeared from history for a number of years. We know he went to the Liscombes, and that David Reid signed off both his ticket of leave and his Certificate of Freedom in Inverary. Because he was a model convict, he could be seen as a forgotten man. But certain facts emerge from the silence, and one of them is that his family in Leicestershire did not forget him. As George worked through his sentence, and in the years that followed, each of his brothers married, and each of them (except John, the eldest, who had only daughters) called their first son George. Joseph named his eldest George in 1834, and Rice was to do it twice: his first George, born in 1837, disappearing into the moat of dead babies in his family, to be replaced by a second George born in 1844. Thomas's George was born in 1839. The youngest brother, James, produced the final George with his eldest son, born in 1847.

George could write by this time, as could some of his brothers – and for those who could not, friends, parsons and charitable people who could were usually at hand. After 1825, letters to or from convicts were free of postal charges, and in Dr Reid, George had a master who would help him.

> Thousands of letters were written by literate convicts for themselves or for those who could not write, precious letters posted from British jails and hulks, as well as from distant Australia – reminders that loved ones were not dead, that they had not slipped over the horizon into the abyss. A few of these letters were passed down the generations, sometimes losing the story of who the convict was and how the letter came into a family's possession.

In Leicester, 1837 was another wretched year for the stockingers. Sary had just given birth to her second illegitimate child, John. On 2 February of that year George, prisoner number 30/897, received his Certificate of Freedom from the Inverary district, signed off by David Reid. This was an absolute pardon, which meant that should he wish to, he could leave Inverary and return to England.

George Conquest's Certificate of Freedom

CFNO37/00081
February 2 1837
Prisoner's number: 30/897
Name: George Conquest
Ship: *Nithsdale*
Master: Christian
Year: 1830
Native Place: Leicestershire
Trade or Calling: Bargeman
Offence: Stealing Hemp
Place of Trial: Chester QS
Date of Trial: 27 April 1829
Sentence: Seven Years
Year of Birth: 1806
Height: Five feet 7 and 1/4 inches
Complexion: Brown
Eyes: Hazel Grey
General Remarks: Scar outer part of right eyebrow – another on
     inner corner of left – scar on left side of forehead.

This certificate of freedom reveals that since he had been signed on to the *Ganymede* hulk in 1829, George's experience as a convict had added two more scars to his face, and his complexion had changed from 'ruddy' to 'brown'. There is no way of knowing what his back looked like. A conduct record maintained throughout a convict's sentence listed every misdemeanour. George's record lists none, whereas his former companions on the *Nithsdale* fill up many a register. He also now had returned to him the £1 15s 10d he had arrived with in Sydney in his convict's savings book to help start his new life. At home in Market Harborough, his brother Joseph, drunk in the Red Cow pub, was accusing Margaret Bryan of stealing his purse. In Leicester and its surrounding knitting villages the worst was yet to come.

———————⌁———————

HMS *Beagle* sailed into Sydney Cove in January 1836, while George was serving his last year as a convict in Inverary. Charles Darwin kept a diary of his month in New South Wales. There was much he disliked, including gum trees:

> To families there are some very serious drawbacks to their comforts, the chief of which being surrounded by convict servants, must be dreadful. How disgusting to be waited on by a man, who, the day before, was perhaps, by your representation flogged for some trifling misdemeanour? The female servants are of course, much worse . . . I am not aware that the tone of society has yet assumed any peculiar character: but with such habits & without intellectual pursuits, it must deteriorate & become like that of the people of the United States.

In 1837, in Australia, George Conquest set off to ensure that this did not happen. The convict system in New South Wales had just three more years to run. In England, the revelations of the Molesworth Committee's inquiry brought an end to transportation to New South Wales in 1840, though it continued to the hellish penal colonies of Van Diemen's Land and Norfolk Island until 1853. The last gasp of the system was in Western Australia, to which convicts were sent from 1849 until 1868, the last ship carrying sixty-two Fenian political prisoners, transported after the Irish rising of 1867. George Conquest became a free man three years before the Hungry '40s began in Britain, a decade which saw the emigration to Australia of well over 100,000 emigrants – labouring families on assisted passages and free settlers who paid for themselves.

George Conquest stands as a representative of the good things in the dark patchwork of British intentions in their invasion of Australia. Yet even so, he was never to have a family life until his last years; and he must have seen terrible things — who is to know how they marked him?

For a true understanding of British treatment of the convicts it transported to its Australian colonies — some guilty, some not — read the stories of the remote penal stations of Norfolk Island, of Moreton Bay and Newcastle, of Port Arthur and above all, of Point Puer in Van Diemen's Land, if you can stand them. I have confined this account to what George Conquest would have seen as a convict in Sydney, or safe inland on the pastures of New South Wales, in the 1830s. On the transport ships, the flogging of convicts and of offending crew and soldiers alike began well before they reached the unpromised land, and the surviving ships' journals and colonial correspondence tell a myriad of gruesome tales. Here are just two such documents.

Government House
Sydney
12th September 1817

My Lord,

I am under the painful necessity of reporting to Your Lordship that on board the Male Convict Ship, *Chapman*, which arrived here from Ireland on the 27th July last, such a series of cruelty and oppression towards the convicts took place during the passage hither, as has induced me to appoint a Court of Enquiry to investigate the circumstances . . .

The killing of twelve of these convicts and the wounding thirty others, together with the killing two of the seamen, and nearly starving and destroying two hundred men, have to be accounted for by those to whose charge they have been committed, and although a plea of mutiny with a purpose of seizing the Ship by the convicts has been alleged in justification of the severities adopted yet it does not at all appear to me that any such object was in view with them, or if it even had, that it would by any means have warranted the extraordinary cruelties and punishments inflicted . . .

I have the Honour to be
My Lord
Your Lordship's Most obedient and Humble Servant
[Governor] L. Macquarie

Governor Macquarie attached his secretary's report:

To The Right Honourable Earl of Bathurst
His Majesty's Principal Secretary of State for the Colonies
Copy of Report: Sydney, 1st August 1817

Yesterday in pursuance of Your Lordship's Commands conveyed to me in the Government and General Orders of 28th ult. I proceeded at nine o'clock yesterday morning on board the hired male convict Transport Ship *Chapman*, John Drake master lately arrived from Ireland, to muster the convicts on board and to make report thereon to Your Excellency . . .

I asked Cptn Drake why he kept the men in irons at the time contrary to all usage and to the instructions conveyed to him by the Superintendent of Convicts to which he answered in an insolent tone that he received them on board in irons and would land them in irons . . .

I find that the same person has been repeatedly flogged on the most frivolous if not unjust charges. 74 to 100 men were chained naked to the Iron Cable, the first set for nearly 24 hours and never fewer than 74. Sometimes 106 were thus nightly chained to the Cable. The system of terror was carried to such a cruel excess that when these poor creatures were on the Cable they were afraid to express having a call of nature least a brutal fellow, the 3rd Officer called Baxter should beat them with his fist or cut them down with a cutlass or bayonet and if they voided their excrement under them rather than being beaten by one or other of the Ship's Officers they were sure to be flogged for filthiness . . .

If a man's chains were heard to rattle he was flogged and if he muffled them to prevent noise he was likewise flogged for disobedience of orders. After the 17th April they were not allowed knives to cut their meat with and some of the convicts broke off the tin handles of their mugs to use as knives for this they were also flogged. Thus were these most unfortunate men so tyrannized.

Over that as many of them said on their examinations they would rather they had been hanged for their original offences than subjected to the hardships they endured. To aggravate their miseries they were nearly famished with hunger having been after the business of the 17th April deprived of one half their allowance in every thing and this severity was continued until the 10th or 11th of July last being a period of nearly three months. From the time of leaving Cork until they arrived in Sydney Cove they were never once allowed to be out of irons. Even those who were lame of Arms lost as Soldiers and Sailors in fighting the Battles of their Country at Copenhagen and Waterloo were thus starved, double ironed and chained to the Iron Cable. Many fainted from pure weakness on the Cable arising from hunger.

A hurried letter can but ill give an idea of these peoples' various miseries. Let a humane man figure to himself a fellow creature double Ironed Chained to an Iron Cable and handcuffed for 3 months except when taken off to be flogged. He will then be able to form some idea of the sufferings these men endured . . .

I have the honour to be

Your Excellency's most Obt Hble Servant

J. T. Campbell [Governor Macquarie's private secretary]

(John Thomas Campbell came with Macquarie as his private secretary; an inordinate number of Campbells made their presences felt in the white settlement of Australia.)

10

Scarred Albion

Flogging as a spectator sport, 1836

T HE SETTLEMENT OF AUSTRALIA was by no means the most
violent appropriation undertaken by the British Empire, nor
were its people the only native inhabitants to be ravaged by
British imperial invasion. India, Africa and the West Indies have
harsher stories to tell. India stands beside Australia, however, in the
'mixed blessings' school of history. British law, British civilisation,
British culture, liberal democracy and its representative Parliament,
the English language, and, always, railways, are mentioned as the
advantages which should be set against the sufferings perpetrated

by the British Empire and its merchant-adventurers, slave traders, politicians and military men. (Team sports and banking, although the latter is hardly a British invention, are also often added, the former being perhaps the superior of the two.) This is the 'lasting benefit' view of the British Empire, a view not shared by a good number of other nations or those on its receiving end. There is the further strange claim that by comparison with other empires, European and otherwise, the British can be judged favourably – the 'at least we were better than them' school of history.

Whatever the view of the historical balance sheet, although brutal corporal punishment was used by almost all nations at that time, the British indulgence in it remains startling and particular, obvious well before the establishment of the penal colonies and the hulks but reaching its apogee once the continent of Australia was added to its empire. Religious belief of a particular kind had a great deal to do with this. The behaviour of the denizens at the bottom of the British class pyramid was attributed to lack of belief in a Christian god, and the resulting indulgence in, and addiction to, vice, immorality, thieving and alcohol. How this Christian approach came to be connected with flagellation as a method of punishment and deterrence is all the more contradictory when one considers Christ and his crucifixion.

One explanation offered is that as god permitted his only son to be flagellated, its spiritual benefits were divinely authorised. In one sense, the labouring, pauper and criminal classes of the British Isles were seen as the refugees of their time, the eternal other, who could be put to suffering or death at whim. It was believed that ignoring the word of god produced these criminals and destitute wretches, not poverty, hunger or the cesspit that was life in early industrial Britain. It remains mysterious as to why the pious felt that torture would bring the wretched into the arms of a loving god. Perhaps it was this sort of thinking that enabled British men of business to transport almost a million Africans to Jamaica, half that number to Barbados, for its slave ports and ships to corner so much of the slave trade market, and for the British government, when slavery was finally abolished in 1833, to pay compensation to the former owners of the slaves for loss of 'property', and not to the slaves themselves.

There is a suggestion of vengeance in the violent beating of convicts in the early years of white Australian history. Also a sense of tremendous anxiety, a vulnerability almost, on the part of the British flagellators. This oozes through the British treatment of Indigenous Australians, and is evident on every page of the meticulous records they kept documenting the punishments administered to their own people. The passing centuries, and understanding that habits, beliefs and traditions were different in the eighteenth and nineteenth centuries, cannot obscure a feeling that such treatment has echoes in the systemic inequality that curdles the British body politic today. It is sometimes argued that these punishments were standard practice for the age, and thus, no acknowledgement, apology, restitution or pity is necessary. But blood spurting out of a back in the eighteenth century caused the same agony as it would now; human suffering remains the same, whenever it is inflicted; it is not ahistorical to understand this.

In 1835, the colony's convict population of 27,000 received 7,103 floggings. It was as much a part of the life of the colony as rum, tobacco, and in principle, church on Sundays. For the British, flogging was administered with the cat-o'-nine-tails, whipping with a whip, cane or a birch, though piano wire was used in Jamaica in 1865. It is for the devotion to this form of punishment, in public, in private, in prison, at school and presumably at home, that flagellation has long been known as 'the English vice'.

The eighteenth century was a barbarous one for the necessitous classes in Europe and beyond. Since ancient times, humankind has used corporal punishment to deal with miscreants, slaves, soldiers, sailors and domestic servants. It was how husbands controlled wives, how schools and parents controlled children. Many still do. Although flogging was abolished in France in the nineteenth century, it remained ubiquitous in the British Army and Royal Navy, being particularly harsh in the latter. Russia dealt with its serfs in this way; Turkey and Morocco were equally enthusiastic. American settlers took the practice with them to their new world: any history of black Americans bears witness to the avidity of their masters for physical abuse, their treatment of indigenous people having already habituated them to abusing those in their power.

The British social reformer and sexual researcher Henry Havelock Ellis stated that while Germans were extremely enthusiastic beaters, 'Flagellomania, while almost totally absent in France, Spain and Italy, was widespread in Britain, especially in England.' England and Wales used the lash in prison, Scotland and Ireland did not. In English prisons this continued until the 1960s and was finally abolished in 1967. The records and accounts of the nineteenth-century British Empire are devastating to read for the brutality they describe, a brutality repeated wherever the British supplied slaves, and in so many British colonies after slavery ended – in Africa, India, the Caribbean, Burma, Ceylon: all those possessions coloured so delicately in pink on maps.

The British in the Caribbean, the British as slave traders, and the British in India: there the accounts of flogging exceed all calm consideration. It became part of the penal law after the Indian Mutiny of 1857, and after the addition of a Whipping Act in 1864, became habitual. 'In 1878 alone 75,223 floggings were inflicted. These floggings were habitually administered with a rattan or cane to naked buttocks in public.' But then, India, by sheer weight of numbers and much else, could not be settled as the British occupied Australia. There was no way the inhabitants of that land could be magicked into disappearance. Nevertheless the parallels between India and Australia in the early years of settlement were considerable. Calcutta and Canton, so much nearer to Australia than any English port, could provide essential supplies. From India came 'chaplains, judges, bureaucrats, merchants and convicts' who moved between the two colonies, applying similar attitudes to both.

There were always, of course, sexual and religious aspects to flogging: religious flagellants wandered around Europe for many centuries. Is the English vice perhaps a hidden residue of the time when England was a Catholic country? Whatever the reasons, there remains a strange note in the accounts of floggings kept by the officials of New South Wales as their scourgers whipped their convicts into bloody shape. Even stranger tones appear in the accounts from the vicious penal colonies of Norfolk Island, Moreton Bay, Port Macquarie in New South

Wales and Macquarie Harbour and Port Arthur in Van Diemen's Land, where secondary offenders could receive anything from 200 to 2,000 lashes. Convicts could be punished for a myriad of transgressions: insolence, absconding, theft, smuggling, refusal to work, sodomy, being a difficult character generally, being found in a disorderly house, feigning sickness, absence without leave, gambling, drunkenness, petty crime, neglect of work, insolence, indolence . . . the seven deadly sins cannot compete with the list.

One convict, William Riley, incurred the following punishments:

100 lashes	For saying 'O My God' while on the Chain for Mutiny.
100 lashes	Smiling while on the Chain.
50 lashes	Getting a light to smoke.
200 lashes	Insolence to a soldier.
100 lashes	Striking an overseer who pushed him.
8 months' solitary confinement, on the chain	Refusing to work.
3 months ditto	Disobedience of orders.
3 months' Gaol	Being a short distance from the Settlement.
100 lashes before all hands in the Gaol	Insolence to the Sentry.
100 lashes	Singing a Song.
50 lashes	Asking a Gaoler for a Chew of Tobacco.
100 lashes	Neglect of work.

By the time George Conquest arrived in New South Wales in 1830, the laws and practices of scourging in the colony had been honed to a fine art. The convict would be firmly tied to a triangle, the body spread and displayed for maximum whipping efficiency. Care and attention was given to selecting the correct whipping instrument. Similar attention was paid by the convict as to the age of the whip, a much used one being preferable to one newly minted.

Each district magistrate was supported by a constable and two underlings, and also an official scourger whose job it was to flagellate. The scourgers – by 1836 there were twenty-five of them – were paid 1s 9d a day. Almost always convicts or ex-convicts, they were much hated by their fellows. Letitia, the wife of convict James Waddale/ Waddell, who was appointed a scourger in 1826, 'declined to join him at Newcastle . . . because of the peculiarity of his employment'. Details of every lashing inflicted were required to be noted down and reported to those in command. As a result there is documentation aplenty of this strange British ceremony, almost fetishistic in its minute detail, indicating perhaps unease in the flagellators as they set about beating to near-death their countrymen. The regulation of flogging in the British Isles continued until the last flogging of a prisoner in the 1960s, though for the hundred years before the final use of the birch, the law kept a careful eye, constantly curtailing, minimising, controlling who could be whipped and on which portion of their anatomy.

> The convict flagellator at this time felt a gratification in inflicting
> and witnessing human misery. There were many prisoners who
> would bear any punishment rather than complain; I am certain
> that they would have died at the Triangle rather than utter a groan.

The significant point about British flogging is that unlike the indiscriminate whipping and lynching of slaves in the United States, it was institutionalised, regulated, very well documented, and claimed to be carried out for reformative reasons. The following document does not record the 1,500-lashes-before-breakfast punishment of secondary penal settlements such as Norfolk Island, but the typical daily punishments which George Conquest would regularly have seen or heard, and possibly experienced, during the years of his sentence 1830 to 1837. Over that same seven-year period, 'a total of 268,013 lashes were distributed among a male convict population of 32,102'.

Parliamentary Papers, House of Commons and Command
RETURN of Corporal Punishments inflicted by Sentence of
the Hyde Park [Sydney] Barrack Bench, from the 4th to the 30th
September 1833, in the presence of E. A. Slade, JP Superintendent,
Hyde Park Barrack.

Following the name of the convict, the ship on which he sailed was always given. There are shorter, and longer such reports, but this one captures particularly well the meticulous attention to detail so favoured by the inflictors of punishment. This is but one of innumerable documents available for historical inspection.

William Leach, ship *Hooghly*, taken out of a disorderly house at the hour of 10 at night, 25 lashes. The 3rd lash drew forth groans, which were continued until he was cast loose; the skin was torn at the 11th, and blood effused slightly at the sixteenth lash. The skin of this convict was thick and hard, but I am of opinion that he felt his punishment sufficiently. He says he was flogged in the Barrack three years ago.

John Lenon, *Mangles*, absent one night from Barrack without leave, 25 lashes. The skin torn at the 8th, and a slight bleeding at the 10th lash; at the 15th lash the skin was decidedly flayed off, the blood flowing slightly; the flesh much swollen. The severity of this man's punishment was manifest. He says he was never flogged before; I could not discover any marks of punishment on his back.

James Jones, *Layton*, larceny, 50 lashes. He was punished with 50 lashes four months ago for the first time; the skin was lacerated at the 14th lash; he neither cried or spoke; no blood appeared. This man's skin was thick and hard, but if I am to judge by his countenance, he did not consider his punishment slightly.

Daniel Culnane, *Norfolk*, having a pair of stolen boots in his possession, 50 lashes over his breech [the buttocks]. The skin was lacerated at the 4th lash; he cried out at every lash; blood appeared at the 35th lash, he suffered much pain.

John Carroll, *Dunvegan Castle*, neglect of duty by feigning sickness, 25 lashes on the breech. This boy received 12 lashes about three weeks ago, and was flogged a short time before that; cried out loudly at the 1st lash; blood came at the 18th lash, and ran freely throughout the remaining part of the punishment. He must have felt much pain.

Daniel Coleman, *Waterloo*, neglect of duty by feigning sickness, 25 lashes on the breech. This prisoner, by his own statement, was never flogged before; he cried out loudly at every lash; skin lacerated at the 14th lash. He must have suffered much.

John Tree, *Asia*, neglect of duty by feigning sickness, 36 lashes on the breech. At the 11th stroke the blood appeared, and continued running; he cried out loudly at every lash; this was the first time of corporal punishment. This boy suffered most severely; and, in my opinion, 12 lashes would have been sufficient for him.

Thomas Jackson, *Camden*, neglect of duty by feigning sickness, 25 lashes on the breech. He received 12 lashes 7 months ago, 50 six months ago, and 25 six weeks ago; his breech was sore from last punishment; the blood came at every stroke; he complained bitterly of the treatment at Carters' Barrack.

Edward Scandrake, *Mangles*, neglect of duty by feigning sickness, 25 lashes. He received 50 lashes last Monday week, but was never flogged before; his breech was sore from the last punishment; blood came at the 1st stroke; he screamed dreadfully at every lash; the blood running freely from the old wounds; he lost much blood; complained bitterly of the treatment at Carters' Barrack, and wished someone would examine into it; indeed all the Carters' boys invariably make the same complaint.

James Corcoran, *Captain Cook*, neglect of duty by feigning sickness, 25 lashes on the breech. By this boy's own statement, he was flogged four months ago for the first time; cried out loudly at the first lash, and continued crying; the skin was lacerated at the 8th lash, and the blood ran. Twelve lashes would have been sufficient.

John O'Donnel, *Sophia*, absconding, 25 lashes. The back of this man was sore from a flogging he received up the country about a fortnight back; the skin was lacerated at the 20th lash, and blood appeared slightly; he never cried or spoke. This man had been for some years a flogger himself.

William Johnson, or Hawkes, *Guildford*, absconding from escort to the Hulk, 100 lashes. This man was flogged about 10 months ago; the skin was slightly lacerated at the 12th lash, he cried out several times; the blood appeared at the 35th lash, at the 90th lash he asked me 'to let him off the remaining ten lashes'.

Adam Ballatine, *Captain Cook*, disobedience of orders in going to the hospital, under pretence of sickness; a troublesome character, 25 lashes over the breech. This boy received 25 lashes on the 22nd of July; he cried out loudly at every lash; the blood ran freely from fresh and old sores; he was severely punished.

James Skiddy, *City of Edinburgh*, absconding and giving a false account of himself, 25 lashes. This man was never flogged before; he called out at the 2nd lash, and at each following lash repeated loud cries; he fainted at the 13th lash. He declared he would never come again.

James Bulerankle, *Portland*, breaking out of his cell, and releasing his fellow prisoners that were under punishment, 50 lashes. This man was never flogged here before; the skin was lacerated at the 10th lash, and blood at the 22nd lash, and increased in quantity at the 30th lash; this man was severely punished.

John Jones, *Royal George*, refusing to work, and mutinous and insolent language to overseers and constable, 75 lashes. This man was flogged about six weeks ago; the skin was lacerated at the 12th lash, and blood came at the 30th lash. This man did not call out; his skin appeared hard, I should say from former punishments.

William Hodder, *Burrell*, drunk and disorderly conduct, 25 lashes. This man was never flogged before, and the blood came at the 5th lash; he cried during the whole punishment.

James Burnett, *Florentia*, attempting to rob the till, in Barnes's public-house, the sign of 'St Patrick', in Clarence Street, 25 lashes, and sent to a distant road gang. This boy was never flogged before; he cried out at the 1st lash, and continued his cries; the skin was lacerated at the 13th lash; he seemed to feel much pain; 12 lashes would have been sufficient punishment.

John Dowlan, *Mermaid*, absconding, 50 lashes. This boy was flogged six months ago; he cried out at the 1st lash; the skin was lacerated at the 13th lash; the blood came at the 19th lash, and ran down at the 24th lash. Twelve lashes would have been sufficient punishment.

George Conquest and others like him stand in contrast both to his blood-soaked fellows and the hierarchical way of life he and they had left behind. Three years after he was granted his freedom, in Britain the Hungry '40s and very worst years for the stockingers of Leicestershire and the watchmakers of Lincolnshire were about to begin.

IV

PORT MIDDLEBAY

'What I chiefly hope, my dear Mr Copperfield,' said Mrs Micawber, 'is, that in some branches of our family we may live again in the old country. Do not frown, Micawber! I do not now refer to my own family, but to our children's children. However vigorous the sapling,' said Mrs Micawber, shaking her head, 'I cannot forget the parent-tree; and when our race attains to eminence and fortune, I own I should wish that fortune to flow into the coffers of Britannia.'

'My dear,' said Mr Micawber, 'Britannia must take her chance. I am bound to say that she has never done much for me, and that I have no particular wish upon the subject.'

'Micawber,' returned Mrs Micawber, 'there, you are wrong. You are going out, Micawber, to this distant clime, to strengthen, not to weaken, the connexion between yourself and Albion.'

'The connexion in question, my love,' rejoined Mr Micawber, 'has not laid me, I repeat, under that load of personal obligation, that I am at all sensitive as to the formation of another connexion.'

Charles Dickens, *David Copperfield*

11

'Good plum pudding'

MELBOURNE, 1840.
(From the original sketch by Mr. S. H. Haydon.)

I
F 1848 WAS A terrible year for John Brooks in Boston, he was
not alone. 1848 was also the year of failed revolutions throughout
Europe. Louis Philippe, king of France, was deposed and a
republic proclaimed in Paris. There were uprisings in Berlin, Buda-
pest, Cracow, Rome, Vienna and Prague. Karl Marx and Friedrich
Engels published their *Communist Manifesto*. Britain's contribution to
this 'Springtime of the People' was the last Chartist rally, in London
on 10 April. A huge gathering of Chartists was expected to gather

south of the Thames in Kennington, from where they would march across Westminster Bridge to present their petition to Parliament. Everything conspired against them: the attendance of some 20,000 people instead of the anticipated 200,000; the pelting rain; the massed forces of king and country; and the ludicrous embarrassment associated with much chicanery over the number of people who had actually signed this, their last petition.

But none of this mattered. The Chartists withdrew after this debacle, but in time every right they had demanded and fought for (except their strange wish for annual parliamentary elections) came to pass. The Chartists are largely forgotten today by the people they fought for, but they were the greatest mass movement of people in Britain in the nineteenth century. Many were transported or sailed as free immigrants to Australia, where 'they made a deep mark on Australian life'. In Britain, their spirit has risen up from time to time in the twentieth and twenty-first centuries to surprise and astonish the status quo: such subjects of the Crown are of course as British as the Bullingdon Club, remembered all too often, or the suffragettes. There is an aching gap for a monument to the Chartists in Trafalgar Square, where they led a crowd of some 10,000 supporters on Monday 6 March 1848. The protest became a riot which the police could not quell for three days. They gathered around Nelson's Column, the perfect place for a Chartist monument: they served their country, as he did.

A thousand men and women assembled in the Market Place in Leicester to support the last Chartist petition, but such activity was swallowed up in the great ocean of misery that constituted the years 1847 and 1848. A third of the city's population was on relief, and there was yet another epidemic of cholera in 1849.

> Bands of men paraded the town demanding, not asking, relief, bringing round carts to receive contributions of broken victuals; there was no playing of children. Groups of little creatures would gather together huddling on a doorstep, sitting closely but silently.

Rioting broke out in Leicester in May 1848 – the Bastille Riots, they were called – after the guardians of the workhouse implemented harsh

The cordial of laudanum assured an addictive life to come

changes to work relief. For three days, the inhabitants of Leicester's Wharf Street and its environs stoned the police, who retaliated by breaking down doors and belabouring anyone they encountered.

For four years Sary and her son Alfred had fended for themselves, a rare case of widow and child being spared the workhouse. One of the requirements of the 1834 Poor Law and its later exemption of widows from entering the workhouse, was the ability of a fatherless child to earn a living, and at the age of four, Alfred was too young for that. It is therefore likely that in his early years Alfred was left at home, or parked elsewhere during the long working day, and dosed with that deadly substance, Godfrey's Cordial, or some other opiate – 'Mother's Helper' and the like. Overdoses of such drugs killed many, but they were widely used to keep babies and children quiet while mothers were at work. For many of them the cordial of laudanum ensured a grim, addict's life to come. Laudanum also soothed many a mother's breast, not to mention father's, if such a man there was.

As the Hungry '40s drew to a close, new industries were establishing themselves in Leicester, as usual much dependent upon child labour. The manufacture of elastic webbing, and of boots and shoes – all adjuncts, in a sense, of the traditional trade of knitting hose – led the way. Footwear had been made in Leicestershire for many years: boots for the men serving in the Napoleonic Wars, and later for workers on the Midlands railways. The trade began to grow in the city in the 1830s as craftsmen and curriers set up small boot-making workshops, often in yards or sheds. Such workshops also served as places to doss down, and as 'sculleries, kitchens, dining rooms and even rabbit-houses'.

Boot-making remained a domestic industry until the 1860s, 'with vast numbers of men, women and children engaged at it'. Their workshops did not come under the control of the sequence of Factory Acts which slowly began to protect factory workers, most particularly children, who were forbidden to work before the age of nine. Sweatshop workers without such protection were crowded into

> dreadful places, underground kitchens [with] ceilings and walls
> black with gas soot; the faces of the workpeople, men and boys
> alike, colourless and grimy; the children literally in rags of the
> dirtiest description, the heat of the atmosphere almost unbearable.

Each man worked with a boy beside him to finish off and neaten the boots, and to learn the mysteries of the craft. No notice was taken of the Factory Acts, as was witnessed by the Children's Commission of 1842, which compared the employment of these children as being like the keeping of an infant school.

―――――――――――○‿○―――――――――――

After he became a free man in 1837, there are few traces of George Conquest until 1854. During those seventeen years British, penal New South Wales began, slowly, to disappear. These were the decades of the worst massacres of Aboriginals. Settlers, squatters and British investors were clamouring for labourers to work the land they had taken illegally, or with government permission. Convicts were still being shipped to Van Diemen's Land and Western Australia, but on the east coast everything was about to be transformed entirely. Gold had been found in New South Wales in the early years of settlement, including the areas where George served his sentence – the Bathurst region, and later near Goulburn and Bungonia itself. But the discoveries that turned Australia into a fool's paradise for the world's adventurers began in 1851, with discoveries in its terrain to the south, in what was then called the Port Phillip District with its lush, well-watered western region known as 'Australia Felix' for that reason.

British exploration into the interior, to the north and well to the south of the penal settlements of Sydney had always continued, in search of more grazing land. The fertile soil of the south-eastern edge of the continent, spreading out from the great bay of Port Phillip, produced perfect pasture for sheep. This coastal land, and the islands in Bass Strait, had been inhabited by Indigenous tribes for 60,000 years or more. Over the centuries European naval explorers had made fleeting sightings of, landings on and namings of its coastline as they negotiated the South Seas. Sealers, deep-sea whalers and the French were particularly present in the late eighteenth and early nineteenth centuries, as were Lincolnshire men of the sea: Matthew Flinders who circumnavigated the continent and named it Australia, George Bass who charted the strait named after him which separated Van Diemen's Land from the Port Phillip district of the Australian mainland, John Franklin, governor of Van Diemen's Land from 1837 to 1843, who in 1847 disappeared with his two ships and all their men in search of the North-West Passage.

Many other sailors and adventurers were products of Boston's links with seafaring. Commemorated today in the town's St Botolph's Church, their names jostle with the most famous man of Lincolnshire, the great botanist and president of the Royal Society, Sir Joseph Banks, who sailed with Captain Cook on the *Endeavour*'s expedition charting the coasts of New Zealand and eastern Australia. Lincolnshire names, like those of the French explorers, dot Australia's southern coastline: there is a Boston, a Point Boston, a Boston Island, a Boston Bay, a Stamford Hill, a Grantham, a Port Lincoln, and dozens more.

Settlers and missionaries from the penal colony on Van Diemen's Land had made their way across the strait well before the 1830s. They, together with sealers and whalers, and early English settlers such as the Henty brothers, who combined whaling with the pasture of sheep, presented the Indigenous inhabitants with some idea of their future nemesis well before a first serious attempt at a proper settlement was

launched in 1835, first by a farmer from Van Diemen's Land, John
Batman, and then by a Vandemonian ex-convict of most remarkable
resilience, John Pascoe Fawkner.

Batman sailed the short distance between Launceston on Van Diemen's Land to the head of Port Phillip Bay in 1835, taking land in the
country of the Kulin nation, a group of Indigenous tribes whose territory stretched well beyond Port Phillip. The region around the Yarra
Yarra River – an Aboriginal word for waterfall, although that was
ignored by white settlers when it came to the naming of it – where Melbourne was to arise, belonged to the Wurundjeri. Batman, an illegal
squatter, had come on behalf of a collection of prosperous Vandemonian financiers and adventurers who wanted more pasture for their
sheep. He set up camp on the banks of the Yarra, and 'induced the savages to put their marks' to a semblance of a treaty, in return for which
the Kulin received tomahawks, handkerchiefs and some flour.

Fawkner's arrival with fellow settlers from Van Diemen's Land followed shortly after. This extraordinary ex-convict was to have a life of
considerable achievement, making him one of those pioneers who could
be said to have laid down a template for the disputatious aspects of the
Australian personality. The governments in both London and Sydney
made little effort to stop the process of illegal land appropriation in the
early years. Official permission for sales and leases came from London
in 1837, and labour was provided by convicts and ex-convicts from Van
Diemen's Land, and by Aboriginals. Once these early pastoralists and
speculators were established, the country was taken from its owners and
a land rush began, dubious treaties quite forgotten.

Although the Colonial Office in London appointed 'Aboriginal
Protectors', and missionaries and more humane settlers gave battle
on their behalf, within fifteen years most of the Indigenous inhabitants were dead, not only from disease, but also because of the
ferocious speed with which these new white settlements and pastoral
runs were established – removing their sources of food and much
else. 'Eighty per cent of the indigenous population of Port Phillip
had been killed or were dead within thirty years; from all five clans
of the Kulin nation . . . only 200 individuals remained.'

Finance from Van Diemen's Land and the labour of the convicts
and ex-convicts – whom absentee owners sent over Bass Strait to work

their land, shepherd their flocks and guard their appropriated pastures –
opened up the territory that was to become the state of Victoria. Passing
names for the early encampment on Port Phillip Bay included 'The
Settlement', 'Batmania' and 'Bearbrass', the last a battered version of
the Aboriginal word for the place, all better than the final choice. In
1837, as George Conquest became a free man, and two years after Governor Bourke had declared the continent of Australia *terra nullius*,
Bourke visited the new settlement and renamed it after the then British
prime minister, Queen Victoria's favourite, Lord Melbourne. He also
ordered the region's land to be put up for sale. At that time there were
1,000 white settlers there, and 26,000 sheep. By 1842 the land was theirs:
there were 2,000 settlers and 1.4 million sheep. These animals flourished, while the native animals fared badly: one white trapper 'once
sold to a single buyer 7,000 wallaby skins, "very small, fine-furred, and
beautifully mottled", at a cost of thirty shillings per hundred'. At Port
Phillip Bay hundreds of ships were anchored at any time, and 'brickmakers earned 8s a day' building the town. In 1847, Queen Victoria
declared Melbourne a city, and four years later the south-eastern

In 1850, on the eve of the
discovery of gold, the Port
Philip District of New
South Wales becomes the
separate state of Victoria,
with Melbourne as its capital

portion of New South Wales took her name, becoming the colony of Victoria, with Melbourne as its capital, exporting wool to the value of £1 million annually.

Overlanders – the men who drove cattle and sheep inland and opened up unknown territory beyond the original settlements of New South Wales, hacked through thick scrub and bush, naming places already named – hence the Aboriginal names, some mangled, some not, which mark so many of the towns and rivers between Sydney and Melbourne. In 1836 a Vandemonian, John Gardiner, 'a superb bush-man and an excellent type of manhood', was the first to drive stock from Sydney overland to the Port Phillip district through the 'new country', where he took land on the south bank of the Yarra. In the following year he travelled north again to purchase 'four hundred cows and heifers' for his new pasture in Port Phillip from Dr David Reid, who sent his eldest son, also named David, to deliver the stock to Gardiner. Gardiner gave young David 'glowing accounts' of the land to the south, and on his return David told his father he planned to follow Gardiner's example and to set out 'for the unoccupied lands of Port Phillip District . . . to take up a squatting run'. The government set up a body of border police, made up of the flotsam of transported soldiers from the British Army, to protect these new set-tlers while the 'savages' white explorers encountered en route defended their lands without the benefit of guns and rifles – which means, or course, they lost.

Dr Reid, though warning 'What! Boy, the blacks will eat you', equipped his son with provisions for two years: everything from nails and axes to six horses, stockmen, and sixteen bullocks together with the men to handle them, and 'five hundred head of cattle, two bullock wagons and teams and six assigned servants'. Young David Reid was only eighteen when he set off in early 1838. There is evi-dence that George Conquest went with him as one of his stockmen. In February 1837 Dr Reid had signed George off as a free man, and his name seems to appear, misspelled, in biographical accounts of these events. George had been a waterman, and narratives of the early settlers of north-eastern Victoria are replete with floods, canoes and river crossings, and the negotiation of cattle and sheep over creeks, streams and rivers. Young David and his party had to ford the Murray, the continent's longest river, at the Hume crossing, first reached by the explorers Hamilton Hume and William Hovell in 1824. Crossing the Murray and its many tributaries with bullocks, horses, drays, goods and chattels was no mean feat.

Young David Reid first took possession of land along the Ovens River, over 150 miles north of Port Phillip, near what is now Wangaratta ('home of cormorants' or 'meeting of the rivers' in the local Aboriginal language). He married Mary Barber, a niece of Hamilton Hume, in 1844, and took more land to the north, near Yackandandah (a wonderfully short word for 'one boulder on top of another at the junction of two creeks'). Reid's acquisitions were on the tribal lands of the Yorta Yorta and Jiatmathang peoples, who exhibited 'an amount of excessive skill, and the exercise of military tactics, which is altogether without rivalry in the history of the early days'. If George Conquest was working Reid's newly planted wheat fields, he would have observed at first hand 'the cunning and the strategy of the Australian natives' as they fought to remove the invaders from their land.

The next time George Conquest's name appeared in the public record was in 1854, when his job was given as a carter, or 'on the diggings'. David Reid had to 'send all the way from Yackandandah a bullock team expressly' to Melbourne to bring up the heavy stones he needed to construct a watermill for his wheat. George could not only help build it but he had also become a 'bullocky', one of the men who with bullocks and drays became the essential lynchpin of early white settler Australia. Every other son and daughter of old Dr David Reid and his wife Agnes were to make their homes in Melbourne, and young David made many journeys there to trade his fat stock and his horses. He was a keen racehorse owner, and won his first race at Flemington in Melbourne in 1840 – horse racing, cricket and Australian Rules football being passions of the inhabitants of the city, then and now.

On his trips to Melbourne George would still have found many Aboriginals, some living on land which is now Melbourne Cricket Ground, near which he himself was later to live. A settlement was arising, clustered around the bay, invading the lush grasslands, gums, wattles and bush. Kookaburras (laughing), bellbirds (noisy), butcher-birds (pouncing), whipbirds (cracking) and a thousand other species observed convict labourers hacking away at trees and bush to make the grid of streets that makes up Melbourne today.

As the land was cleared, the centre of town became a hodge-podge of tents and huts, evolving into buildings, 'wretched in the extreme', made of wood, bricks and weatherboard. There was much dust and much, much mud, the freshwater Yarra River providing falls, swamps and floods. Across the river, reached at first by punt, then by Paddy Byrne's ferry, and from 1846 by a wooden bridge, George was to make his home, near the brickfields on the south bank. As one of the 6,000 ex-convicts who were Melbourne's earliest white inhabitants he could have seen, by 1850, seventy-one stone and brick quarries around the city.

When gold was discovered near Ballarat and Mount Alexander in 1851, many squatters and other landowners found themselves ruined overnight as their employees joined the rush to the diggings. Young David Reid managed to get his sheep sheared that year only by prom-ising his men that when the job was done he would take them to Mount Alexander, sixty miles north-east of Ballarat and on the way to Bendigo – these being the three great centres of gold fever. His party started digging first at Mount Alexander, then at Forest and Fryer's creeks to the south, an area so rich in gold that it became known as a 'bank till free to all'. They found as much or as little gold as the rest of the heaving multitude, some became exceptionally rich overnight, others enough to change their lives entirely. After Reid returned to his properties, gold was found on his and his family's land, which made the land impossible to raise stock, and his life took other directions.

The first railway line opened in Victoria in 1854 and many others followed throughout the following decades: only rail could conquer the vast distances between settlements and cities. Until then an experienced bullock driver or carter like George Conquest could make good money hauling bricks, timber and other materials to construct and supply the new gold-rush towns. They 'were paid from a hundred to one hundred and twenty pounds a ton for car-riage, and on the average taking some three or four tons of loading at each trip'. A digger's basic equipment consisted of 'cradle, picks, shovels, tin-dishes, tent and cooking utensils, together with a supply of flour, tea and sugar, beef and mutton', plus the extraordinary array of non-essentials inexperienced adventurers often cluttered themselves with as they toiled from Melbourne and its port to the diggings. Once the gold rush got going there were shops and stores, huts and townships galore in the mining districts, and everything had to be carted there on, at best, tracks 'of mud, dust and stone' with no bridges or fords over rivers and creeks.

> Where formerly was silence, only broken by the noise of the bellbird [now the] golden army [of] bullock-drays, bullocks, and bullock drivers, are shouting, roaring and swearing up the hill, or descending splashing through the once clear stream.

It was perfect work for George Conquest:

> All along the route from Melbourne to Mt Alexander the scene presented a most extraordinary appearance; it seemed in the day time like one long continuous street occupied by conveyances of every description and people travelling in every manner possible, with their various belongings, bullock-drays, horse-drays, pack-horses, and trucks and wheelbarrows carried along drawn by both men and women.

At Mount Alexander and its environs, a journalist wrote: 'The golden quartz lying in this soil I may liken to the fruit in a good plum pudding.' This news not only transformed the lives of the scruffy prospectors already digging in the area, but spread around the world. Gold could be found in the teeth of sheep, gold glittered in river and stream, gold was found by turning over a clod of earth or by prodding it with a pocketknife. Thousands flocked to the goldfields, a torrent of human beings on the march, deserting farms, villages, settlements and stations, coming from all over the world, including the Californian goldfields, which had triggered the global frenzy in the first place. The tents and stores of the diggers were soon bedecked with the flags of every nation.

Four days after the discovery of gold, Victoria became a separate

Zealous Gold Diggers, Bendigo, 1852, by
Samuel Thomas Gill, 'the artist of the goldfields'

state from New South Wales: at the time it had a white population of
nearly 80,000, twice as many men as women, and an Aboriginal
population reduced to 2,500. Port Phillip Bay became a crowded mass
of boats and ships, disgorging thousands who had not the faintest
idea of where exactly they were. A 'canvas town' was set up outside
Melbourne to house families left behind as the hopeful prospectors –
not all male by any means – trudged off to Ballarat, Bendigo, Mount
Alexander and all the likely turf between and around.

By 1861 half a million people lived in the state. Gold and the wealth
it brought was to dominate Victorian and Melbourne life until the
1890s, and the massive increase in population turned it swiftly into a
mishmash of peoples. This influx included Americans, Germans and
Scandinavians (all encouraged), Poles, Hungarian, French and other
refugees from the European revolts of 1848, and other Europeans and
people from places and countries unheard of by the motley crew of
ex-convicts and settlers already there. Japanese and Pacific Islanders

PACIFIC CHIVALRY.
Encouragement to Chinese Immigration.

Australians in the nineteenth-century encouraging Chinese immigration

arrived from the north. From India came merchants and coolies – the latter objected to, as were, most particularly, the many thousands of Chinese, welcomed in language and newspaper articles too racist to repeat. From 1855 the immigrants were taxed – the Chinese were charged £10 a head (over £1,000 in today's values) for a sea passage to Victoria, so they sailed to South Australia instead, and made their way eastwards to the Victorian goldfields by foot. This was the least of the ignominies heaped upon them in those years (redressed today by Chinese ownership of so many of the minerals and other precious substances beneath Australian soil).

Added to these were assisted emigrants. In the nineteenth century, 33 million emigrants, free and assisted passengers, left Britain for new worlds. Australia, an exceedingly distant place of refuge, received 1.6 million immigrants, the majority of them from the British Isles. This new system of ridding the country of its unemployed, underemployed and underpaid labouring, industrial and agricultural population replaced the convict system just as transportation to the east coast was coming to an end in 1840, and converted them into customers for British goods (by the 1840s 'every Australian consumed £7 worth of British products per year', a higher per capita return than any other overseas market). To this end, inducements were created to entice them to go. Assisted migration began in 1831– 'assisted' being as dubious a word as 'benefits' is today: both coming with many strings attached. This was financed for the most part by selling off the immense amount of colonial land the British government had expro-priated, with at least fifty per cent of the proceeds used to fund emigration to Australia.

From 1840 the Colonial Land and Emigration Commission man-aged this social engineering, doing so after 1856 in tandem with the emigration agencies of the colonies themselves, which in 1876 took over the choice of migrants entirely. Transporting its poorer subjects became a handsome source of profit for British shipping companies and merchants who were already invested in the colonies. It also expanded the demand for their goods there, and serviced their exist-ing business interests. British industries also poured their energies into emigration to Australia because the long sea trip there and back could be combined with the complex and profitable transport of cargo all over the world.

Apart from government schemes, the very considerable evan-gelical and benevolent forces of British society – including every church from the Wee Frees to the Salvation Army, from the Church Missionary Society to the Evangelical members of the Clapham Sect – contributed to this armada. Associations such as the Church of England Society for Empire Settlement, the British Ladies Female Emigrant Society, and numerous organisations for waifs and strays, distressed single ladies, needlewomen and salesgirls, trade unions, and most notably Charles Dickens' friend Caroline Chisholm's Family Colonisation Loan Society, put their hands to the wheel.

With vigorous assistance from sub-agents and from the Colonial

Offices in each Australian state, philanthropists of every stripe also took part in this removal. Parochial officers made arrangements for the emigration of their poor; employers and landlords also helped. Such a conglomeration of interested parties meant that the 'imperatives of Australian migration called into life an elaborate bureaucratic and commercial apparatus of most formidable proportions'. By the 1850s, the lure of the goldfields seriously depleted the Australian workforce, so there was an urgent need for working men, and for women not only to work as domestic and farm servants, but to provide sexual opportunities for the preponderantly male population of the colony.

Soon, however, bitter complaints were pouring in from the existing settlers, who were vehement about their preference for receiving more of their own kind, rather than the detritus of Britain's workhouses, poorhouses and streets, paupers selected by parish officers, miscellaneous orphans, or Ireland's 'popish serfs'. And so, pernickety attention came to be paid by all concerned as to the moral worth of proposed migrants, assisted or otherwise. But when it came to assessing the likes of George's brother Joseph, the strict criteria put in place by the authorities faltered, and disappeared.

Joseph was out of prison by Christmas 1850, and was again working as a brickmaker, his wife Mary as a stitcher. Their eldest son George was now sixteen, learning the shoe trade (which Sary's seven-year-old son Alfred was about to embrace). Their two middle sons, James and Thomas, aged fourteen and eleven, were already working as brickmakers. The widespread perception of the Australian colonies as a workers' paradise, with full employment, high wages and plentiful food, was a powerful temptation for such young men. And brickmakers were particularly in demand as Melbourne continued its rapid metamorphosis into the substantial city it became by the 1880s, by which time it had earned the temporary soubriquet of 'Marvellous Melbourne'.

Joseph was supremely qualified as a member of the labouring poor, but he and his family would have been a curate's egg as far as the British Colonial Emigration Society and its equivalents in Victoria were concerned. What they liked best were single men or women, and families headed by parents under fifty with sons and daughters old enough to work and to start families of their own more or less immediately. Though Eliza, Joseph and Mary's eldest, was of an age to undertake both these duties, their youngest son Alfred, aged four, would have been regarded as undesirable, not least because of the high death rate for such young children during the long voyage. A similar view would have been taken of Joseph's well-documented impoverished and criminal past.

Among the convoluted sequence of arrangements for emigration which succeeded each other over the years were passage warrants and a remittance system. The latter had nothing to do with those disgraced or drunken young Englishmen of standing despatched to the colonies by their angry parents. Rather, it enabled men like George Conquest to deposit

> money in the colony, on behalf of a nominated friend or relative
> who, if approved according to character, occupational, health,
> age, and gender criteria, was allocated an assisted passage . . .
> Remittances might also be sent via the 'military' or 'colonial'
> chest to London, to pay the deposit and/or outfit of a nominated
> relative or friend who applied under the ordinary regulations.

Although the obvious reasons for the despatch of such families as the Conquests to a distant colony 'revolved about the question of evacuating the poor and disorderly from British society', what the poor and disorderly did with this view of their capabilities is another story altogether.

There is a formidable spirit about these 'surplus poor'. They knew it was most unlikely that they would ever return, that they were leaving their family and their home for ever. Riff-raff or not, they needed considerable ingenuity, patience, courage and cheek to cope with the shoal of restrictions and instructions they received, the constant risk of danger and illness on the long, crowded and unventilated journey in the steerage bowels of a ship, crossing from their known world to the other side of the globe. Joseph Conquest is a typical example of so many emigrants who made it to Australia by the scruff of their necks. He was undeserving, not respectable, adventurous, literate to the point that he could read the Bible to his fellows in the workhouse, and had sufficient gumption to enable him to face down the formidable structures put in place to ensure that men such as himself did not get as far as the port of Liverpool.

Until the later months of 1852, when ships began to sail into Port Phillip from all over the world, George and his fellow ex-convicts, free labourers and settlers from the other Australian colonies, had the goldfields more or less to themselves. In some diggings such as Ballarat, deep sinking was required to get to the gold; men had to work together, as a single man had little hope of doing well, deep digging or not. It must have been at about the end of 1851 that, using the first of his bullocky or gold money, George sent for his brother Joseph. By then George would have known of the deaths of his father in 1846, of his mother in 1847 and of his brother Rice in 1851. Letters followed him as he moved from New South Wales: announcements that they were his to collect appeared in Sydney newspapers in January and April 1842, doubtless reporting that his brothers John and Joseph were in the Harborough workhouse and bringing him news of the assault of the Hungry '40s and all that they were to mean for his family.

Doctors, former employers and suchlike had to provide proof of good character for intended migrants. How Joseph managed to obtain the required documents can only be explained by the stolid figure of George supplying money and contacts who would speak for him, because of George's own proven value to the colony. The government subsidy paid the cost of the passage, including food, but George's nomination and remittances meant that immigration rules and regulations could be bypassed or ignored if the contribution towards the 'assisted' voyage was sufficient. George provided this for the near dozen members of his family who came to join him. By the end of 1851 the average earnings on the goldfields was about £40: sufficient to get Joseph, his wife and their six children from Yeoman Lane, Leicester to Port Phillip Bay, and if George did not find sufficient gold to provide this sum, he would have earned it as a bullocky. There is always a sense, with George, that his good luck was often finagled for him by the Reids and the other wealthy men of Melbourne for whom he worked.

Joseph and his family sailed from Liverpool on the Cunard line's steamship the *Europa* in June 1852. On the manifest Joseph transformed himself into a gardener, the kind of labourer much in demand at the top end of the colonial market. It seems to have been an uneventful journey, which was not always the case as shipwrecks, collisions, and other mishaps blighted many a passage, even in the second half of the nineteenth century.

They arrived at the port of Geelong, over fifty miles from the Ballarat goldfields, in time for summer. 'Serge frock, half-boots, cabbage-tree hat, and belt around the waist, attached to which was a quart tin pot for boiling tea' was the uniform of a digger, and so George would have appeared when he met Joseph and his family at the docks, bearded like most of his fellows, his Leicestershire patois quite changed by the convict argot learned after twenty-two years in the colony.

If Joseph took his entire family with him to the goldfields it would not have been unusual, but it was not to be for long. Amidst the

George Conquest, by the 1870s, would have looked like one of these men

labyrinthine shafts and diggings, tormented by flies and stung by the eternal mosquitoes, the diggers lived in tents and huts surrounded by yellow soil and dust, or slush and puddles. There was a constant inferno of noise: barking dogs, croaking frogs, gunshots, fights, drunken carousing, fiddles playing, the beating of wives and the killing of any animal that moved. 'One storekeeper nailed to his counter a human hand which he had chopped off when it appeared one night under the bottom of his tent.'

Colonial governments could participate in the sudden wealth of the goldfields only by taxation, and so imposed a licence fee on each digger of thirty shillings a month. Diggers who made a fortune, and those who scrabbled to find a tiny nugget, had to pay the same tax, and they did not have the vote. These licences and taxes, and the fines imposed for any departure from the copious rules and regulations, were paid to commissioners and superintendents, often corrupt, always hated. The peace was kept by the military and by police, mounted and on foot, always hated too. By late 1854 there was a constant state of near war between the diggers and the gentleman politicians of the Victorian colonial government, its military and its police.

The many names applied to the police, whom the diggers considered no more than government-armed robbers, were early examples of the Australian vernacular. There were mass petitions, riots, and simmering hostility towards the powers that be. The Victorian government reacted with fury – and terror of any repetition of 1848 European rebellion on colonial soil. This attitude, and the troops and officials who expressed it, were responsible for the 'agin the government' attitude of so many on the goldfields, which erupted in open rebellion with the Battle of the Eureka Stockade in December 1854. Three thousand diggers came to a meeting on 1 December, demanding a body of reforms. Military groups of diggers gathered, former Chartists were involved, republicanism was evoked, liberty and freedom acclaimed and demanded. One hundred and fifty of them, mostly Irish, built a stockade, hoisted a new flag, the Southern Cross, and swore 'by the Southern Cross to stand truly by each other and fight to defend our rights and liberties'.

The Eureka Stockade: Swearing Allegiance to the Southern Cross, December 1854

On 3 December British troops and colonial police charged the stockade and stormed the camp. Nineteen men were killed, five of whom were soldiers, the rest diggers – some of them, including a woman, had been hacked to death. Others died later and the numbers of the dead remain disputed. The battle was a short one, but it was carnage, and the miners were routed – but like the Chartists, the diggers achieved their aims. Public support for them was such that when the Eureka trials took place in 1855, all the defendants were acquitted of high treason. The diggers and the men and women involved in the rebellion of the Eureka Stockade provided their fellow citizens with a historic template, still celebrated (and attacked) today, still maintained as a part of the national psyche.

The British and Irish on the goldfields, which their establishment and government controlled, or tried to, were of George and Joseph's class, or at most one or two levels up the British class pyramid: migrants and ex-convicts who did not fancy any repetition of the entrenched inequalities of Britain. The Eureka Stockade brought about the end of the reviled government miners' licences, the loss of a much better Australian flag, electoral reform, and was also the beginning of the long process of unravelling imperial chains between Britain and Australia, still creaking on today. And the wealth from gold was to turn Melbourne into the splendid city it would be until the 1890s, when the golden years ended with the financial crash and depression of that decade. The Conquest boys did well. In 1854, the *Victoria Police Gazette* reported:

> Lost, or stolen, from the person of Mr George Conquest, near the Commercial Inn, Prahran, a large green pocket-book, containing a cheque in favour of G. Conquest, for £300, a cheque for £200, an order for £100, and £30 in ten-pound notes [about £69,000 today] Reward £30.00.

The money George made as a carter, and such gold as he found on the diggings, was not enough to stop him working as a bullocky, but enough to give his English family and the family he wanted for himself, much happier days. He was far removed from the rebels of Eureka – though perhaps his brother Joseph might have joined them had the brickfields of Melbourne not beckoned. George was always to be a cautious, modest man, he bought modest little houses, lived a modest life and helped the numerous members of his Conquest family, for Joseph and Mary's children – working as bakers, butcher, brickmakers – soon married and produced thirty grandchildren over the next decades. George helped them all but kept his money safely stowed, and growing.

In 1854, however, George had sufficient income to hire a firm of solicitors to deal with the loss or robbery of his pocketbook. The £300 cheque was made out to George by George Foord, working as a chemist and geologist on the diggings at the time, later to become the assayer for the Royal Mint in Melbourne. The cheque for £200 was from William Clarke, the owner of extensive lands outside Melbourne:

> known generally as 'Big' Clarke and 'Moneyed' Clarke, he was widely feared for his ruthless land hunger, but respected for his consummate ability in pursuit of fortune. He never meddled with

> agriculture but stuck to the 'raising of sheep' as a 'better paying game', and to his great profit he introduced the Leicester breed of sheep into Australia. The gold rush further increased his prosperity . . . and in time he acquired the reputation of being the wealthiest man in the country, this being regarded as a consequence of what his obituaries term 'parsimonious habits'.

Exactly the kind of adventurer who would have needed a bullocky like George Conquest.

George's £630 in cash and cheques were soon returned to him (we know this because five years later, in 1859, he appeared in court as a character witness to give an account of the honesty of the man who had restored it, Joseph Edeson, who was now accused of stealing £45). With this money, George set sail for England.

When George was in Australia, Sary and her son Alfred remained in Eaton Street, Leicester, for a year or two after Alfred's birth in December 1843. Their next lodgings were in Metcalf Street, with Sary's half-brothers Henry, John and William Allen and their families within shouting distance. The two streets ran side by side, and also by Wheat Street which edged the old cricket ground and was where Joseph and Sarah, parents of the Conquest boys, and Rice Conquest and his family had lived when Sary first moved to Leicester. All three streets were connected by Lead Street at one end, and at the other to Wharf Street, the heart of Leicester's nether regions and a centre of rumbustious shop and brothel, pub and pawnbroker life.

By 1851, when Alfred was eight, he and Sary were living in a one-up one-down tenement with Sary's step-nephew Joseph Smith, the stockinger son of her stepsister Ann, still living in Thurmaston. Around the corner, less than half a minute away, lived Sary's fifteen-year-old son John with his step-uncle William, both of whom were frame knitters. At the same time, most of the Conquest family who remained in Leicester were a five-minute walk away in a little slum side street, Yeoman Lane.

After the death of his parents in 1846 and 1847, Rice Conquest had gone back to work on the canals, and although this was well past the time when the railways began their onslaught on canal trade, he had done well. 'Any hand worth his salt soon became a master, of a slow-boat at least.' He had become a captain by the time he dropped dead in July 1851, while unloading at Loughborough. He was forty-three, the same age as Sary. John, Rice's eldest brother, had moved to Leicester after he and his family left the workhouse and was working as an ostler, his wife Elizabeth as a charwoman. They lodged at 143 Yeoman Lane, and a few doors away, at number 139, until George summoned them hence, lived Joseph, his wife Mary and their six children.

Sary no longer described herself as a seamstress or a knitter: she too was a stockingmaker. Famous Leicester names such as Richard Mitchell and Nathaniel Corah had opened factories with machines powered by steam, and Corah's new works in Granby Street were a whistle away from Wharf Street. By 1855 Corah's employed thousands of workers, and many other men of substance were also using the new machinery. Sary could not have afforded to invest in a frame for herself, and was now probably working in one of the new factories. If so, she was fortunate, for by the 1850s the law prescribed no more than a ten-hour working day for women. If not, she would have worked as so many Leicester knitters would continue to do – long hours in workshops or at home. This domestic frame-work knitting continued in Leicester for decades after Sary left.

While the hosiery industry was slowly changing, the slums remained the same. But warehouses, timber yards, boot, shoe and hosiery factories were beginning to overshadow the dismal passages and tenements of Wharf Street. Nearby were the gasworks, the Leicester canal and Cort & Bell's iron foundry, the first sign of the advent of engineering which was to be the salvation of Leicester. In 1851 the Great Exhibition in Crystal Palace celebrated the prodigious achievements of the Victorian age, and Thomas Cook shepherded over 150,000 of the curious by train from Leicester and places north, down to London to see it.

The summer of 1852 was exceptionally hot. Making his way through Leicester's rat-infested alleys and overflowing tenements, Joseph Dare, still the domestic missionary for Leicester's Unitarians, 'found one

poor old widow' in a hovel with no back door or window 'literally frying in her bed, which was reeking with her perspiration'. In the
following year Thomas Cook, the energetic Baptist, opened his spectacular Temperance Hall in Granby Street, not far from Wharf Street,
felicitously placed between two pubs, the Wagon and Horses and the
Nag's Head. Only its ban on alcohol and the price of a ticket would
prohibit visits to the music hall, housed in the same premises, and the
magic it offered.

Joseph Dare's accounts of the lives of the poor in Leicester illu-
minate many things, but above all why so many of them were
encouraged to leave. He fretted endlessly about the irreligion, the
drink, the crime, the fornication and the familiarities that were the
inevitable consequences of the sharing of common, and foul, privies –
and beds.

> I have found too little bed-clothing in poor families a great evil.
> There is no doubt that this leads directly to the demoralising
> practice of so many huddling together in sleep; they do so for the
> sake of warmth. I visited a family, consisting of the parents and
> three children, where there was but one up-stairs room, and but
> one wretched bed. The eldest was a daughter of about fifteen
> years of age. They all slept together . . . Numbers of large families
> are thus situated; and where this is the case, domestic decency and
> the nicer proprieties of personal conduct are out of the question.

Most particularly he bewailed the fact that so much energy was
being devoted by the authorities to removing single pauper women to
the other ends of the earth. By the 1850s, horror of prostitution (which
had become particularly rife in the Hungry '40s), and its dangers both
for the male of the species and the British race in general, were only
some of the reasons that made it desirable to spirit the eternal have-
nots of the British Isles off to happier climes. 1853 appeared to be a
comparatively good year for the respectable poor of Leicester: there
were 'Excursion trains, rural fetes, social meetings, with music and
recitations . . . and the pleasing fact, that no policeman was called in
amongst the twenty-five thousand who visited . . . promenade concerts on the Cricket Ground'. Many too poor or too unrespectable

for such diversions still scurried off for a bit of poaching, or to the 'more horrid orgies of the back room of the low tavern'. 'Drunkenness and prostitution remain, I fear, undiminished', Joseph Dare reported. In the same year, smallpox broke out in the slums: it was known to have been 'caused by the privy at the end of the row', and by two slaughterhouses nearby. Then, in 1854, as George Conquest set sail for England, cholera struck again.

12

'A perfectly new life'

Emigration as remedy, *Punch*, 1848

WHEN JOHN BROOKS' WIFE Mary Ann Winsall died in Boston in 1848, she left four children under the age of eight: her daughter Mary Ann was four years old. Two years later the four children had a stepmother, Mary Ann (yet another) Green, daughter of a cork cutter living in Boston's Pipe Office Lane, a step or two away from John's unwisely opened shop. Pregnant with her first child when she married John, and rarely in any other condition for the next decades, Mary Ann dropped the Mary, calling herself Ann Brooks, and provided John with a further seven children. A total of eleven children in all bore his name, though perhaps not all were the product of his loins. None of them could he afford to keep.

The severe winters of 1850 and 1851 meant two very bad years for the town and in 1853 Great Northern Railway had moved their headquarters from Boston to Doncaster in South Yorkshire, putting 700 Bostonians out of work, which increased the depression in the town. John Brooks rented a double-fronted shop, with a large room above it, in Dolphin Lane. Here he was in the very centre of Boston, surrounded by every variety of business: shops with dwellings attached, stables, sheds, yards, pubs, and artisans, and workmen and women of every calibre. For the next few years he managed to keep his head above water, as every year another baby was added to his household.

The 1850s began more decades of decline in Boston. John Brooks moved his home and brood frequently, but never more than a lane or two from his previous lodgings. He was only a watchmaker and silversmith now, the handsome Lincolnshire longcase clocks Bothamley's could have taught him to produce quite abandoned. He rented out portions of the shop in Dolphin Lane, and travelled frequently. 'Clocks cleaned in the country at the shortest notice' he advertised – this was made possible by cheap fares and the opening of the loop branch of the Great Northern Railway, giving Boston access to nearly every part of the country. These years saw the beginning of the peripatetic and cliff-edge existence that was to mark his future life.

It is tempting to imagine that John Brooks sought solace in alcohol, which might account for these Micawber-like years, but Lincolnshire, and Boston in particular, provide another explanation: the possibility that he took to opium, a favourite tipple in the Fens. The inhabitants of the low-lying, marshy, watery east coast of England suffered from the ague, from malaria, and nameless fevers, and opium was the medicine of choice. 'There was not a labourer's house . . . without its penny stick of opium, and not a child that did not have it in some form'. In 1850 the *Morning Chronicle* noted that its use had become ubiquitous. Poppies were grown in many a Fen garden, poppy tea 'was in frequent use, and was taken as a remedy for ague'. It was the Godfrey's Cordial of the Fens.

The county of Lincoln was a bastion of Methodism in the

nineteenth century, its Anglican counterpart wilting as the years went by, and Boston's numerous Wesleyan and Independent chapels contributed to the town's particularly enthusiastic temperance movement. As an alternative to alcohol, laudanum was easily available. You could buy it from market stalls, from grocers and from any druggist – as pills, grains or liquids, by the chunk, the ounce or the gallon. It was especially popular among the poor. John Brooks, master watchmaker, aspired to, but never achieved, a rung or two above that station of life: but he lived and worked amongst labourers and working people in the small streets and docks around Boston's market, amidst almost all of the chapels, meeting houses, and places of worship of dissenting Boston. Opium was cheaper than drink, so even for a poor man the amount consumed could lead to ruin. A malaria epidemic in 1858–9 increased its usage, and in Boston its port enabled easy participation in the Indo-Chinese opium trade should that be required. Many of its victims ended up in county asylums and workhouses.

In 1836, John Gardiner, the overlander who was to inspire young David Reid to move south, became the first settler of the pasture lands south of the Yarra. He took land on the banks of what is now called Gardiner's Creek, part of the Yarra River catchment, and as speculators and land grabbers followed him, the area surrounding his run and the creek took his name. Like many early Victorian settlers John Gardiner was a Nonconformist, an Independent. He was president of the Melbourne Temperance Society, which he set up only a year after his arrival there, an indication that the unbridled rum and ale consumption of the New South Wales colony had travelled south. That would not have been a problem for George Conquest, who did not share his brother Joseph's predilections, but by the time Joseph came to work in the brickfields, Gardiner had returned to England, and the usual drinking holes abounded in the area.

Part of the land John Gardiner had commandeered for himself came to be known as Prahran – a simplification of the native name 'Purraran', meaning 'land partially surrounded by water'. The enormous swathe of land Gardiner took displaced numerous Aboriginals, populous south of the river due to the excellent hunting available of 'large numbers of waterfowl, as well as kangaroos, wallabies and possums which grazed or foraged in the surrounding bush'. At first a section of bush was set aside as 'an Aboriginal reserve, within which it was hoped to contain the Aborigines, teach them English social habits, and convert them to Christianity'. The minister placed in charge of this Government Mission for Aboriginal People was instructed to regard 'the intermixture by marriage of the Aborigines among the lower order of our countrymen as the only likely means of raising the former from their present degraded and benighted state'.

This mission lasted less than two years. Some were formed into a Native Police Corps, others drank themselves into insensibility, took up begging or were felled by the usual imported European diseases. The appointment of a chief protector and later a 'Guardian of Aborigines', combined with neglect, did the rest. Other reserves followed, very much a mirror of the arrangements made for Native Americans in the USA, with similar results. In less than a decade British investment and British settlers had replaced Aboriginal homelands and hunting grounds with sheep runs, stations, fencing and cottages, huts and houses, wheat, woolsheds and gardens.

Centuries of flooding had produced deep clay deposits on both sides of the Yarra, making the swampy land, fringed with tea trees, ideal for brickmaking, and brickfields were established there in the earliest years of settlement. The brickmakers

> were also squatters and had to pay 10 pounds a year for being on Crown Land, 5 pounds for erecting a tent and 2 pounds 10s a year for using the clay.

These men were dismissed as the roughest of the rough in exactly the same words as those used to describe the canal boatmen of the Midlands – their brickfield settlement was notorious as 'the resort of a drunken, bloodthirsty, thieving crew'. Soon Joseph Conquest and his sons were back in their old trade, albeit in very different surroundings, amidst strange animals, gum trees and scrub, Indigenous Australians and a scattered community of small householders and market gardeners, ex-convict and emigrant workmen, the odd gentleman settler and the numerous taverns, hotels and inns that dotted the roads to the centre of Melbourne and the diggings. It was here in Prahran, near the brickfields, south of the Yarra, and four miles south-east of the centre of Melbourne, that George and the Conquests now settled. George added carting timber and bricks to his other activities, but when not on the road carting, George barely left its parameters until his death – with one exception.

In July 1854, a month after he had recovered his lost pocketbook and money, George set sail for England. Early steamships could make the voyage in eighty days or so by this time. Not for George the steerage quarters of assisted migrants: he sailed from Melbourne on the *Golden Era*, a packet boat owned by the White Star Line of Liverpool, doing excellent business during the gold rush. He certainly had sufficient funds to travel first class, with a steward to wait upon him. But had he done so, he would have been made most unwelcome: the presence of former convicts in first-class cabins was often commented upon, and not favourably. It is most unlikely that he did travel first class, but even steerage on the *Golden Era* would have been luxurious in comparison with the *Nithsdale*. George returned to an English winter and made his return remarkably brief, because in May 1855 he sailed back again from Liverpool on another of the White Star's speedy clippers, replete with 'unsurpassed ventilation, style and elegance', the SS *Merlin*. He had made two journeys of three months each, separated by only seven months in Leicestershire.

Sary was never able to do much more than sign her name, and though George improved in these matters after he became a comfortable man, there is no written record of how or exactly where they met or what the two of them felt. After twenty-five years in the Australian sun, George would have lost his English pallor. Hunger would have become unfamiliar to him. Handling a bullock team was tough work, so more muscle, more scars, more flesh on his body would have been only a few of the changes he presented to Sary and his family. After the mud and dust, hot sun, blue skies, pelting rain, bush tracks and tents he had become familiar with, back he came to the tenements of his youth, with:

> the numerous small, dark and dirty streets with their miserable huts and pestiferous atmosphere . . . its pale, thin, dull-looking people, who seem ready for eternity, yet are clinging to the streets.

When George met Sary again in the hurly-burly streets of the Leicester slums, he was forty-eight, and she was forty-six. It was nearly thirty years since they had seen each other. Their daughter Eliza would have been twenty-seven had she lived. Perhaps Joseph had told George that Sary had been a neighbour in Leicester for years past. Perhaps the Conquest family had never lost sight of her in the intervening years. Most likely is that the Conquest family came across Sary as a neighbour, or in the pubs and taverns around Wharf Street. The Conquest boys were unlikely to have forgotten the woman whose pregnancy had sent their brother on his convict way to Australia. But equally likely is that their children brought them together over the years. Sary's son Alfred was eleven in 1854, and well into the boot-making trade, as was Joseph Conquest's eldest son George. John Conquest's daughter Sarah was Alfred's elder by two years, Rice's son George by only two months, Joseph's fourth son Joseph by twenty months: they were all urchins of the same streets. When not at work they all hovered around the Sunday schools, charitable institutions, and less improving haunts that studded the Wharf Street tenements.

When George returned to Leicester in 1854, the advent of factories had begun to improve conditions for the knitters, but always in fits and starts. Wages had fallen, frame rents had risen again for those who worked in their homes, and a severe outbreak of smallpox was added to the usual afflictions. The winter of 1853 had been exceptionally bitter, and as it ended Britain entered the Crimean War, leading to rising prices. But it was the winter of 1857–8, when the Hungry '40s came back with a vengeance, that finally sent Sary on her way. Joseph Dare had been administering his mission in Leicester for thirteen years by then, more or less the same number of years Sary had lived and worked in the city. In his report for 1858 he described the winter just past as 'one of the most trying and difficult that I have ever experienced'.

But by now the Board of Guardians of the Leicester Union Workhouse had firmly put into practice the requirements of the New Poor
Law. Outside relief was no longer on offer. Adults and children were
begging on the streets with baskets around their necks, ranging far
and wide in search of food. Thomas Cook's soup kitchen could not
feed the number of unemployed. In October 1858 his music hall, also
the headquarters of the Leicester Temperance Society, presented
Charles Dickens reading his *Christmas Carol* to a 'highly respectable'
but sparse audience – for though Dickens always insisted that there
be shilling seats for the poor, it was still too high a price to fill the hall
to overflowing, as was usual.

By the spring, 1,378 people had applied for relief in Leicester, but
only a bare 202 could face the workhouse. The rest made other choices.
Sary left during the depression of 1858, and so never reaped the benefits of later times, which were to make Leicester one of the wealthiest
cities in England. Perhaps no such benefits would have come her way,
as, for persons like Sary, life expectancy hovered around forty years
until the 1870s. But the industrial poor of Leicester were never again to
know the desperate poverty of the years during which Sary lived there,
as its new industries helped turn the charitable and educational
impulses of this radical town, always there, towards slum and factory
improvements.

Nevertheless many of the villainies of the hosiery business were
not to be remedied for decades. The renting of frames was not forbidden by law until 1874, and only with the Education Acts of 1870 and
1876 were children removed from the great labour pool the industry
required. By that time Leicester had its first sewerage works and a
piped water supply. Yet as it turned itself into a flourishing late Victorian city, its slums lingered on: still pullulating in the 1870s, and
boasting the addition of pail closets, but with no running water well
into the 1950s.

Of the 33 million Britons who emigrated from their islands in the
nineteenth century, by far the largest number chose to go to the
USA and Canada. Emigrating to Australia cost money: while you

could sail to a new life in North America for about £5, an emigrant's fare to Australia in the 1820s was £30, and later settled to a steerage ticket cost which averaged £17, almost the annual wage of many a labourer. And the list of additional expenses the voyage required was formidable. This was where George's gold and carting earnings made all the difference to Sary and the Conquest family: many of Britain's poor made for a new life in Australia with the financial assistance of former convicts such as he. Two of his nephews were the first beneficiaries of his return visit. In January 1856 Thomas and James Conquest, sons of his Bedford brother Thomas, set off as assisted migrants on a lugger, the SS *Earl Grey*, from Deal in Kent. With their arrival in Geelong in June 1856, eleven Conquests were now in Victoria.

Sary's assisted passage was not so easily arranged, although she lived at a time when the Australian colonies were trying to entice immigrants from Britain by every means possible. The big shipping lines had agents in many a city and major town, and there were also selection agents working for the Colonial Land and Emigration Commissioners and agents-general of the colonies themselves. Cheap books and periodicals were widely available, with copious instructions as to how best to traverse the bed of nails involved in reaching this 'great Colonial Empire'. All instructions and advice were replete with wise homilies and sage advice as to how to navigate every step and cope with every official an emigrant was likely to encounter. Whatever information George sent her, Sary would scarcely have been able to read it, but she had access to many who could, for clergy, charitable ladies, emigrant societies and organisations provided exactly this assistance. For Sary, the custom of broadsheets and pamphlets being read aloud in taverns and social clubs could have brought the information to her. Alfred could always read and write better than she.

The Leicester newspapers were particularly enthusiastic about Australia, and the colonies' governments constantly advertised their need for workers in their pages. Thomas Cook's Temperance Hall presented 'musical and pictorial entertainments' about Victoria with titles such as 'Gold and Where to Get It'. Local dignitaries assisted many a migrant: clergy, MPs, Poor Law administrators – all supplied advice and information. There were squadrons of emigration charities, many of them Anglican, as Sary professed herself to be when asked. Most important was Dickens' *Household Words*, the magazine he launched in 1850, costing only tuppence. Widely circulated and read, its pages repeatedly exhorted its readers to leave for a better life in the new world. There were public readings, books, pamphlets, a barrage of advertisements, posters and leaflets, and regular articles and letters in local newspapers from happy – and fattened – emigrants.

> My dear mother . . . I must tell you that . . . I was never better in my life . . . meat is cheap here . . . Thousands in England scarcely know what it is to have a bellyful of beef . . . anyone that will work gets well paid . . . I wish I could send you a fat bullock.

> Those who choose to take employment can readily find it at high wages. Few servant girls get less than 20 pounds a year; those more experienced are sought after at considerable advance.

> let the people of England be assured that the Australian colonies are better than any painter has delineated them.

This was the age of print: broadsheets, journals, magazines, newspapers, books and many manuals instructed the newly literate how they should live their lives and save their souls. In so many newspapers, emigrants' accounts and letters home, it is not only higher wages, better weather and the possibility of permanent work that are frequently mentioned, but, constantly, food: the joy of having enough to eat – of having more than enough to eat. The pain of missing home, leaving family and friends for ever seems to have been assuaged by daily life spent without hunger.

Between 1853 and 1856 the Crimean War much affected emigrant shipping, and increased the cost of a steerage passage – if one could be obtained. Mail services to Australia, fitful and unsatisfactory even before the war, became much worse. But the probable reason Sary could not leave before 1858 was that the level of destitution had so increased in Leicester that 'applications for government passages to Australia have lately been so numerous, the Commissioners have declined to receive any further applications'. Besides which, Sary was not the type of woman the colonies wanted:

The London *Daily News*, writing on the necessity of sending
to Australia a superior class of female emigrants, says: The
Government Commissioners lose no opportunity of declaring
their growing sense of the importance of sending out women . . .
what classes of women are they thinking of? Single women of
course, as the married go with their husbands. But of what rank
and order? . . . They are thinking, if not actually of paupers from
the workhouses or poor needle women, of servant–maids . . . This
is all very well. Let them go, by all means, in numbers as large as
those of the working men, departing and already there, who will
be wanting wives. But what, we cannot but ask, are the prospects
of the Colony, if the mothers of the next generation are to be all
uneducated women?

Framework knitters, employed or otherwise, bore the taint of the
factory, and were not encouraged to emigrate. Sary was not a domestic servant, she was not a young marriageable woman – indeed, at
fifty she was older than they liked, with not that much profitable work
to be expected of her, with a womb that would produce no more children. However, 'Widows with no children under sixteen' were
occasionally permitted assisted passages. Alfred would be fourteen
when they sailed, so she lied about his age. On the other hand, however great the official insistence on a certain sort of immigrant, this
was by no means what they always got. George Conquest always finagled a species of assisted passage for those he nominated, however ill
they suited colonial specifications. For a government-assisted passage, application forms had to be filled in, selection procedures had
to be navigated, a deposit paid which could be as much as £15, and
there was also a compulsory 'kit', which could cost as much as £5,
which probably provided Sary and Alfred with more delightful paraphernalia than either had seen in their lives.

The 1851 regulations stated that:

The commissioners supply Provisions, Medical Attendance, and
Cooking Utensils at their Depot and on board the Ship. Also, new
Mattresses, Bolsters, Blanket, and Counterpanes, Canvas Bags to
contain Linen, &c, Knives and Forks, Spoons, Metal Plates, and

Drinking Mugs, which articles will be given after arrival in the Colony to the emigrants who have behaved well on the voyage.

The Emigrants must bring their own Clothing, which will be inspected at the Port by an Officer of the Commissioners; and they will not be allowed to embark unless they have a sufficient stock for the voyage, not less, for each Person, than –

For Males	For Females
Six shirts	Six shifts
Six pairs stockings	Two Flannel Petticoats
Two ditto Shoes	Two ditto Shoes
Two complete suits of exterior Clothing	Two Gowns

With Sheets, Towels, and Soap. But the larger the stock of Clothing the better for health and comfort during the voyage, which usually lasts about four months, and as the Emigrants have always to pass through very hot and very cold weather, they should be prepared for both; 2 or 3 Serge Shirts for Men, and Flannel for Women and Children, are strongly recommended.

They would have to get themselves to a port, in their case Liverpool, which by 1858 was perfectly accessible by rail – if one could afford the fare. On the ship's manifest Sary declared that she could read and write, but the awkward signatures which are the only evidence she has left behind intimate that 'scarcely' should have been added before these two claims. By the 1850s there were agents who would help putative emigrants for a fee, and George had the money to pay for the help she needed. Sary left a large family behind. In Leicester there were her half-brothers Henry, John and William Allen, and their families – framework knitters, cotton winders and seamstresses, with all the children over nine years of age already at work. Her mother was just alive, a pauper, in Thurmaston, where her other half-siblings and their numerous children still lived. Her son John was a grown man of twenty-two. She was never to see any of them again.

She sailed from Liverpool, by far the busiest port of departure for Britain's millions of emigrants, though it shared the gold-rush deluge with Plymouth, London and Southampton. Reaching the port from Leicester with Alfred in tow was simple enough, as George provided the money for the fare, but embarking on these emigrant ships was no simple business. The wait for boarding could be as long as ten days, and the lodging houses near the docks were fleapits no better than the tenement slums Sary and Alfred had just left, although by 1852 a special depot had been built at Birkenhead for emigrants to Australia.

Fraudsters hovered around, a common racket being the stealing of emigrants' luggage, returning it in time for boarding only on the payment of a considerable sum. George, however, enabled Sary and Alfred to sail on one of the better ships of the time, the SS *Rising Sun*, one of the Royal Mail packets of the Black Ball Line. Its fleet was advertised as having 'superior accommodations for all classes of passengers', 'unequalled by any other ship afloat', claims endorsed by Queen Victoria, and on this ship, on 18 March 1858, Sary and Alfred set sail.

To eyes accustomed to the slums of Leicester, what Sary and Alfred made of their first sight of the sea, their first experience of ports and docks and ships, can only be imagined. Considerably more courage was required to sail, packed in steerage, to the other side of the world across turbulent and endless seas, than for the shorter crossing of the Atlantic to North America. Yet for an emigrant, travelling to Australia was much safer than that voyage. Emigration to North America was carried out by private enterprise and their profit requirements meant dangerously unregulated ships, which led to thousands of deaths on board. It was Caroline Chisholm and her Family Colonisation Loan Society's representations about the primitive and dangerous conditions on earlier emigrant ships to Australia which had persuaded the British government, so experienced over the centuries in the transportation of convicts, slaves and soldiers, to pass the Passenger Act of 1852. By the time Sary and Alfred set sail, this ensured that the batches of poor souls they sent would arrive in suitable condition, able to perform a good day's work and populate the empire. This remarkable achievement was a taste of what the British could do for their own, if hearts and pockets were sensibly moved.

The voyage to Australia usually took three months or thereabouts, though it could take as long as four. By 1858 the shorter 'great circle

route', taking a more southern, near-Antarctic passage, had been discovered, reducing the journey to less than seventy days. But the
British government stuck to the old ways for the despatch of its
assisted emigrants. Unless provisions ran out or repairs were urgently
needed, the voyage was non-stop, meaning they set foot on no land
between Liverpool and Melbourne. They vomited in the Bay of Bis-
cay, passed Madeira, the Cape Verde islands and Cape Town, then
bounced on through the endless miles of the south Indian Ocean.
Often drenched and chilled to the bone, they saw flying fish and great
albatrosses, whales, dolphins, sharks and porpoises (much consumed),
immense skies and heaving seas, icebergs – hopefully avoided – and
strange shores glimpsed occasionally in the distance. What would
Leicester slum eyes have made of all this?

For perhaps a hundred days they were cramped in the malodorous
stench of the crowded steerage, storms and squalls above, seasickness
within. Ventilation remained primitive, and was not improved by the
animals caged or herded below decks, mostly for the benefit of the
captain's table. Cows, pigs, chickens, ducks, sheep, geese and goats
were all possible passengers, making the stomach retch and the heart
sick. All much worse in the doldrums of the blistering tropics, better –
though not for the animals – in the freezing southern latitudes. The
claustrophobia of their steerage bunks when confined below during
storms was accompanied by the banging and groaning of the pitching
ship, with vinegar and chloride of lime constantly in use to alleviate
the vile smell of vomit, and much else. Mountainous seas reminded
them of the many tales of shipwrecks, and of emigrants drowned or
lost at sea. Such stories were gloated over constantly in newspapers,
and recorded in journals and letters home:

> The wind Blew and the Sails tore and Chains and Ropes Rattled
> and the Seaman and Captain Run and hollwed about and the
> Women Cried and Prayed and men Run about onley with there
> shirts on and the warter Came into two hatchways By Streams
> and Sometimes the lamp was out and it Seems Verrey miserable
> and the Ship Roald heaved and Groand From one side to the
> Oather and now and then a Rat Squik and Run Oaver Some
> Bodey and then they would Sing out and then the Table and all

the Temprey Fixtures would Rattle and the tins Fall From the
Shelves and Tables Sometimes on Your head as you lie in your
Bed and the Jars and Books i had to hold in my Bed and Jar of
Red Cabbage Fell over and Wetted the Bed.

These terrors had been slightly ameliorated by the strict regulations in force after 1852, so Sary and Alfred's journey could not have
compared with George's experiences on the *Nithsdale*, or the dangers
encountered by emigrants bound for North America. On board they
would certainly have had more to eat and better medical care than
they had ever experienced in Leicester. Apart from the daily chores
they were required to do – sewing, scrubbing, cleaning, fumigating,
disinfecting, airing, cooking, serving and so forth – they were free to
learn, and even to be entertained when that was on offer.

Some assisted migrants left records, but not Sary or Alfred. They
had three months or so on board the *Rising Sun* to enjoy full stomachs,
weekly baths and be surprised by water closets: many an emigrant landed
in Australia a much plumper person. As with the British flagellation of
convicts, much was recorded and noted about each immigrant who for
this reason required a capacity to fib inventively, producing 'a tragi-
comedy of deception which featured endless stratagems from false
hair (to disguise age), to outright corruption.' Sary was comparatively
modest in her approach. On board and on her official documents she
described herself as an Anglican, a widow of forty-seven (she was actually
fifty), and listed Alfred as a boy of twelve (he was over fourteen), enabling him to travel at half the cost of an adult. Embarking in Liverpool
she described herself as a nursemaid, and changed that to a housekeeper
when addressing the immigration authorities on arrival. On the boat
they were Sarah and Alfred Grundy, but from the moment they landed
at Port Phillip Bay on 11 June 1858 Alfred became forever Alfred Allen.

Not for Sary the hiring procedure assisted migrants had to undergo
on arrival, on board, at the dock or at the immigrant depot. 'Gone to
friends, Melbourne' is all that was noted about her. She became
George's 'housekeeper' within hours of her arrival. They were never
parted again.

Apart from government control, which was considerable, the despatch
of single women to Australia became the charitable bailiwick of the kind
of middle- and upper-class woman Dickens portrayed so cruelly in the
character of Mrs Jellyby in *Bleak House*, though he himself also had a big
hand in it. Australia was very much a favourite with Dickens and he
wrote and published countless articles encouraging his fellow Britons to
emigrate. He sent two of his sons there, his fourth son Alfred d'Orsay
Tennyson Dickens in 1865, and his youngest and favourite son, Edward
Bulwer Lytton Dickens – always called 'Plorn' – in 1868. He never saw
them again. He gave the name of Port Middlebay to Melbourne in *David
Copperfield*. He sent Abel Magwitch, the Micawbers, Mr Peggotty, Little
Em'ly, Martha Endell and Mrs Gummidge to prosper there. Mr Micawber enjoyed even greater success than George Conquest, becoming a
most loquacious magistrate, and also the manager of the Port Middlebay
Bank, the kind of establishment at which George would have cashed his
carting cheques. Dickens also sent Uriah Heep, Mr Littimer and Wack-
ford Squeers to be punished there and John Edmunds in *The Pickwick
Papers* to become a shepherd. There are more.

  In 1847, with the wealthy banking heiress Angela Burdett-Coutts,
Dickens had founded Urania Cottage in Shepherd's Bush, London, as
a refuge for prostitutes and fallen women – for which Sary could certainly have qualified when young. For more than a decade he worked
tirelessly to reform and educate such women, and prepare them for a
new life in the colonies. In 1849 he wrote a leaflet, *An Appeal to Fallen
Women*, for distribution to the police who were charged with removing prostitutes from London's streets, to entice them to come first to
Urania Cottage, and then to take a ship for the colonies. He addressed
each woman personally, as someone

> who was born to be happy, and has lived miserably: who had no
> prospect before her but sorrow, or behind her but a wasted youth;
> who, if she is a mother, has felt shame, instead of pride, in her
> own unhappy child . . . As you are to pass from the gate of this
> prison to a perfectly new life, where all the means of happiness
> from which you are now shut out, are opened brightly to you, so
> remember, on the other hand, that you must have strength to
> leave behind you, all old habits.

As Sary was nearing the land to which Dickens so energetically wished to transport fallen women, Dickens' own domestic devils erupted to cruel effect: in May 1858 he banished his wife Catherine, the mother of his ten children, from his home, leaving her with 'no prospect before her but sorrow' for the rest of her life.

When Sary and Alfred arrived in Melbourne at the beginning of winter, June 1858, the gold rush and the rapidly increasing population had already begun the transformation of the small settlement into what was to become by the 1880s a golden city of the British Empire. Two days after they sailed from Liverpool the Allen and Conquest families could have read a report in the *Leicester Chronicle*:

> I give you a brief account of this now far-famed city, and of its rapid rise from comparative insignificance to its present state of great commercial and political importance. When I first came over here . . . the city of Melbourne had but a meagre appearance . . .
>
> The streets are now all formed, channelled, and macadamised; the footpaths in the principal thoroughfares are flagged; the city itself lighted with gas; in all directions lofty, elegant and substantial buildings are to be seen – Banks, Insurance Offices, Hotels – shops; that would throw no discredit on Regent Street, in London – the Houses of Parliament, the Town Hall, Hall of Commerce, Exchange, Custom House – Cathedrals, Churches and Chapels, completed and in progress – a University, a public Library, a Catholic College, a Mechanics' Institute – a Hospital, a Benevolent Asylum, an Exhibition building, three large Theatres, extensive Barracks and Docks.
>
> The Railways are already in operation, and doing an immense traffic; hundreds of miles of electric telegraph, by which the three colonies will speedily be put in communication are fixed up; and though last, not least, water is laid on throughout the city and suburbs . . .
>
> The streets of the city swarm with cabs, cars, omnibuses, and carriages of various descriptions, among which are some really

elegant equipages; and during the day, and often to a late hour at night, the footpaths are thronged with crowds of pedestrians, forcibly reminding one of the busy thoroughfares in the English metropolis . . . In immediate proximity with that is another extensive and thickly populated town named Prahran. This town also has a separate municipality, and in one part of it, where a few years ago nothing could be seen but trees and thick scrub, there now stands a Mechanics' Institute, supported by several hundred members.

———————————— ⌘ ————————————

When George returned to Melbourne in the winter of 1855, he had gone straight back to the diggings, to his carting business and to Prahran, where fortunes were being made from government land sales: 'A pound of gold, as payment for the purchase of Prahran land was not uncommon tender.' Both Joseph and George invested whatever gold they had found on the diggings, and their earnings as brickmaker and carter, in little plots of land in Prahran, some with cottages already built, some not, a small and safe portfolio which began his new position as a 'gentleman resident' of Prahran. By 1858, Joseph had three houses with land, and George double that number. And to a little weatherboard cottage in Robinson Street, Prahran, built or bought with some of that gold and those earnings, George Conquest took Sary and Alfred.

13

Skivvies

Emigrants off to Australia, 1840

I N 1858 JOHN BROOKS' sixth child was born. His four children by his first wife Mary Ann Winsall were no longer living at home. Their eldest boy, so hopefully named Charles Hickman after the Stamford clockmaker and patron of John Brooks' childhood, disappeared without trace at an early age. He later turned up in Australia, having reached there by means as mysterious as his future life was to be. John Brooks now housed his family in rented premises in Frampton

Place, a little outside the centre of Boston, although he still held on to his shop in Dolphin Lane. He was a man cursed by the times he lived in. He had trained as a clock- and watchmaker just as mechanisation was making that craft redundant. He went to live in Boston when it was in its prime, growing and prospering. He ran his shop in central Boston throughout its decades of decline after the arrival of the railways seriously weakened its coaching, port and maritime trade. He died two years before the town's fortunes revived in 1884 when a new, modern dock was finally built, and it became a thriving port again.

In the 1850s, however, Brooks was well placed socially, because as an Anglican whose first four children were raised as Independents he could draw customers from both persuasions in the religiously divided town. There were a considerable number of schools and Sunday schools for his children on offer from the town's Nonconformists. In later life Brooks' daughter Mary Ann swapped her religious affiliation from Congregational to Wesleyan as occasion demanded, making it likely that her education after the Independent Sunday school was the Wesleyan day school, which took all denominations, asked only a few pence a week, and offered free books and other necessities. A further advantage was that it was only three minutes away from her father's shop in Dolphin Lane, and the number of babies at home in Frampton Place made it probable that she and her siblings spent much of their time in the room above the shop. John Brooks supplemented his unreliable income by working as a travelling silversmith and jewellery repairer, and letting out parts of his shop to a hairdresser and a boot and shoemaker, contrary to the rules of the Charity Trustees from whom he rented it.

It is hard to imagine that there was much joy in the home arrangements for John Brooks' four older children after their mother's death. Those who were not members of the dissenting community, with its temperance movement and its Band of Hope, could divert themselves in a hundred ways in Boston, most particularly because both port and sea were to hand. For their father, opium and alcohol were always on offer, and in May visitors poured into town for the celebrated annual sheep fair. As well as travelling musicians and dancers, sideshows and stalls, the town's brothels and prostitutes – the police reported forty-four of the former and ninety of the latter in 1858 – cocked every snook at the disapproving Nonconformist community. Theatre was forbidden to them too, but children could always escape to pursue a little villainy along the quays and riverbanks, and to pester the carrier carts that crowded into the town on market day. And Boston's dissenting chapels and churches were ferocious providers of outings, Bible readings, hymn singing and other occasions of religious celebration and improvement.

Before the end of the decade John Brooks' three daughters by his first marriage disappeared into the maw of domestic service. This was by far the most common employment for women in Britain in the nineteenth century – there were about a million such maids and female servants in the 1850s, in a population of just over 18 million. Mary Ann Brooks was fourteen in 1858, and her younger sister Sarah Jane only twelve, but young girls could start domestic service as early as eleven, although thirteen or fourteen was the most common age. Girls such as Mary Ann and her sisters hardly had a childhood. They were the mules of the houses and estates of Lincolnshire's great landowners, whose holdings occupied a quarter of the county in the nineteenth century, and of its squires, landed gentry, lesser and greater, and the wealthy merchants, bankers, shipowners and professional notables. Mary Ann and her sisters entered a house in which

> the female staff was headed by a housekeeper, and included a
> cook, lady's maid, nurse, two housemaids, kitchen maid, scullery
> maid, dairy maid, stillroom maid, and laundry maid.

There were of course fewer servants in smaller homes, but the chores were the same, and many a skivvy worked as a maid of all work in a modest household.

There are no records of the lives of the Brooks girls as servants, but they probably obtained their positions at one of the May Day hiring fairs, which were still going strong in the marketplaces of Lincolnshire until the end of the century. However, their Nonconformist background may have disqualified them from some aristocratic or gentry households: 'As for dissenters,' wrote a lord to his son in 1850, 'I agree in the main with you. I detest them all, Catholics included.' And so, for seven years Mary Ann served as a notch in 'that scaffold supporting life in the British Isles'. As their stepmother produced annual babies, whatever pittance Mary Ann and her sisters could send home was needed, but by 1863, matters had become so much worse for John Brooks, his shop and his family that one of the numerous benevolent emigrant associations searching out distressed members of the female sex swooped down to rescue Mary Ann and her younger sister Sarah Jane. By the 1860s the demand for domestic servants in Australia had become overwhelming.

Mary Ann's Nonconformist schooling meant that she was more literate than many of her class, and she would have been able to read the abundance of emigration information and incessant advertising of the time. Each possession of the empire, and the United States, competed for these precious human acquisitions. Married couples, preferably indigent, preferably with one child, and single men were the most in demand. In the case of single women, however, most efforts were concentrated on keeping them out of the workhouse and off the streets: 'out-of-work servants were among the droves of women who turned to prostitution when they were down on their luck as an alternative to destitution or the workhouse'.

The 1851 census had revealed that there were nearly half a million more women than men in England, and that over a million of them were unmarried. These women were often described as 'surplus', and in the following decade, debate raged over what was to be done with them.

> How to provide for our multiplying population? . . . Something
> better should be done for numbers of our species than to
> imprison them in pauper-houses – those receptacles of sloth,
> inaction, misery, and degradation . . . In short we must organise
> an emigration of 230,000 souls yearly.

There was much emotional agonising about the dangers inherent in the large numbers of sexually deprived spinsters:

> Much of the evil results from the voluntary or enforced celibacy
> of the sterner sex, arising, in many instances, from poverty, or
> from emigration. For the first of these causes no remedy is
> offered, but for the second, it is strongly recommended that our

surplus female population be induced to emigrate to those places where the number of females is below that of the males. No doubt but that many of our suffering sisters might find ample and remunerative employment, either as domestic servants, or in the higher and nobler position of 'wife'.

Scores of organisations turned their attention to both respectable single women and their humbler sisters. The voices of my female ancestors barely surface above the commanding tones of the women of wealth and position who mothered their despatch through a profusion of female emigration societies. Many such societies were also run by men, and by clerics who were similarly motivated, but it was these women of the comfortable classes whose concern for the nation created much of the protected atmosphere under which Mary Ann and Sarah Jane sailed and were received.

This was a female imperial enterprise. The female poor, the unmarried mother and the street loiterer were scooped up and shipped off to indentured service in the colonies. Domestic servants of low breeding were needed to mate with the men of low breeding already in the colony, and also to enable settlers of good breeding the time and leisure to procreate and to raise worthy subjects of the state. 'Humble, pious and respectable working-class women' was what they wanted, and their purpose included not only a wish to civilise their empire and stock it with good British blood, but also to help the poor, and get them off the streets.

All this was balanced by the obvious and rare pleasure it gave women to be able to dominate at least one area of their Victorian world. The British Ladies Female Emigrant Society, the British Women's Emigration Association, the Female Middle-Class Emigration Society, the Society for the Overseas Settlement of British Women, the Girls' Friendly Society, the Ladies United Evangelical Association: in these and others can be seen the birth of the suffrage movement, often using the connections, status and money of the men in their lives, aristocratic or otherwise, to get a foot in the door. In 1861 Maria Rye of the Society for Promoting the Employment of Women founded, with Jane Lewin, the Female Middle-Class Emigration Society, through whose agency surplus British women were sent all over the world. She wrote that:

colonial governments ordered batches of women from Britain in a manner 'as peremptory and as defined as that of any Melbourne merchant writing to the corresponding house in London, about Manchester cottons or Bermondsey boots'.

In the case of Mary Ann and Sarah Jane Brooks, it was a benevolent man who whisked them away. They sailed under the auspices of one of Melbourne's remarkable early colonists, John George Knight, a renaissance man who was an architect, engineer, organiser of exhibitions, one of the great administrators of the Australian Northern Territory and an enthusiastic dabbler in gold mining, stocks and shares and the Royal Horticultural Society. He arrived in Melbourne from London in 1852, and the architectural partnership he formed there designed the early Legislative Assembly and Council Chambers of Melbourne, now Victoria's Parliament House. In 1861 he organised the Victorian Exhibition, which he took to the 1862 London Exhibition, and did the same for the Paris Exhibition of 1867.

As the other bodies in great demand were agricultural workers, many emigrants had already left Lincolnshire by the 1860s. 1862 was to be a peak year for the encouragement of female emigration. In the previous year the government of Victoria stated that there were 328,651 men

FROM GREAT BRITAIN TO SOLVE OUR DOMESTIC PROBLEM

The Party of Girls who arrived in Sydney this morning by the White Star liner Medic, and will come through to Canberra.

Still shipping off surplus women in 1927 – this time the result of the First World War in the state, and only 211,671 women. £78,000 was allocated to acquiring a substantial number of single women immediately. John Knight became honorary secretary to the Victoria Immigrants' Assistance Society, for which he wrote an ebullient description of the colony:

> The climate of Victoria is most genial, closely resembling that of
> Italy . . . the clearness and purity of the atmosphere exercising
> a strong influence on the habits and temperament of the inhabitants,
> who certainly appear more cheerful, buoyant and happy than
> those who dwell in colder latitudes . . . law, order and morality are
> as well, if not better observed . . . than in England.

The climate was not the only enticement. Victoria's wealth – its wool, its gold, its demand for workers, its higher wages – and its intimations to women of marriages to come, were drumbeats to every advertisement for emigration after the Hungry '40s and they reached a crescendo in their pursuit of single women servants.

Grantham Journal, 7 January 1869
Free Emigration to Australia

WANTED, FOR AUSTRALIA

Female Domestic Servants; also Married Agricultural Labourers
with not more than 2 children under 7 years of age or 3 under 10.
Young Females of good character will do well to attend to this
notice, as emigrants of this class especially are required, and their
prospects in Colonial Life are much better than in England.
. . . In the colony of Victoria alone the numerical preponderance
of men over women amounted to the astounding number of
134,000 in a population of 470,000. In other words there were only
about 168,000 women to 302,000 men, and this proportion was
becoming even more unfavourable.

Knight's search for likely emigrants concentrated on distressed areas in Lancashire and the other counties of the north-west affected by the Cotton Famine of the early 1860s, when overproduction and the collapse of the market in raw cotton impoverished the textile industry. It seems probable that it was through the activities of the Nonconformist communities of Boston, either Independent or Wesleyan, that Mary Ann and Sarah Jane Brooks were able to join this charitable caravanserai. Independents were more literate than most, and their chapels were run by exactly the kind of ministers who supported emigration, sincerely believing that the poor would be more or less sanctified, and certainly rehabilitated, if they went off to populate the British Empire. The prolific Regency novelist Catherine Gore summed up the situation: 'Everybody knows that Great Britain is the very fatherland of old maids. In Catholic countries, the superfluous daughters of a family are disposed of in convents.' More than the offer of rehabilitation, they would be married and their departure would not only relieve the country of its surplus of spinsters living abnormal and unhealthy lives, it would also spread the message of Christianity to the New World.

These exhortations were available to hear and read, religious tracts being only one of the methods of encouragement copiously available throughout these years. To receive an assisted passage, references from clerics, former employers or doctors were required. The Victoria Immigrants' Assistance Society did not 'grant free passages to other than single women qualified for domestic service'. And they had to be properly distressed women at that, as other migrants selected by the society and for emigration assistance in general had to pay some of the considerable costs of a passage to Australia. And they had to be respectable, moral, and experienced in domestic work, though in practice skivvies such as Mary Ann and Sarah Jane could pass muster, however rudimentary their skills, as their religious and moral qualifications promised progeny of the right sort. Domestic servants were perfect emigrants: they were used to having no home of their own, and to living in other people's houses. So, unlike Sary and the Conquest boys, in Mary Ann and Sarah Jane Brooks, housemaids, Australia would be receiving the type of immigrants it really wanted.

The Victorian government preferred Plymouth as the embarkation

point for its emigrants, as more rigorous control could be exercised
there than in the wilder waters of Liverpool. Their fares to the port
were provided, as were their lodgings before embarkation, and emigrants were accepted at the depot over two weeks before they departed.
Before sailing, their health and morals were thoroughly examined under
the supervision of a matron and a surgeon superintendent. Like all such
emigrants they travelled steerage, with single women separated from
the men. On 16 December 1863, Mary Ann, then aged nineteen, and
Sarah Jane, seventeen, boarded the SS *Coldstream*,

> which sailed from Southampton Wednesday for Melbourne,
> taking out 33 married couples, with 11 children and 7 infants,
> two single men, and 186 single women . . . The single
> women . . . have been chosen by Mr J. G. Knight, the special
> agent for selecting persons in distressed circumstances who are
> qualified for domestic service. These cases have been assisted in
> their outfit, embarkation and other expenses by the Victoria
> Emigrants' Assistance Society of London. The emigrants
> appeared to be a very superior class, and have been highly
> approved by the emigration officers. The Victoria Immigrants'
> Assistance Society have, as usual, provided on board the
> *Coldstream* a library of about 300 volumes of a useful and
> entertaining character, as well as copybooks and other works of
> elementary instruction.

'I have selected them', reported Knight,

> from the ranks of those receiving relief, but as much as possible
> from a class not closely identified with the work of the cotton mills,
> and well suited for domestic service on their arrival in the colony.

Seasickness dominated the first weeks for almost every emigrant,
before they became used to the rolling of the ship, the noise of its
flapping sails, and its strange and rarely enticing smells. Mary Ann
had at least seen the sea before, unlike Sary or Alfred. While at sea,
the emigrants were provided with

> those means of employment and instruction by which they may
> improve the leisure of a long voyage, and be trained in such habits
> of industry and self-discipline, as will make the Emigrant a better
> Colonist, whether as servant, wife, or mother.

Sewing, knitting, crochet, and, for low-level domestic servants, training in menial house duties were provided.

For many of the over 90,000 single women shipped to Australia
between 1860 and 1890 the journey was a grim experience: careful
spatial segregation, which limited women largely to their berths;
tight sleeping places; minimal toilet and bath facilities; daily drills
supervised by the matron; and dirt and vermin. Lice and fleas were
the most prolific pests, although rats and mice also plagued the
steerage passengers. Though segregated and guarded, on many
occasions men pounced, as men do. Women co-operated, or not, as
do they. Babies were born, and many, many children died on these
emigrant ships from measles, whooping cough, scarlet fever, or the
worst killer, diarrhoea. The more children on board, the unhealth-
ier the ship. In 1863, Thomas Small, a Scottish emigrant, recorded
in his journal:

> A child died at 8 o.c. & the father passed us with the little corpse
> in his arms going to put it out at one of the portholes on the quiet.

Adults who had survived Britain's factories, slums and workhouses
could better withstand these infections, and surgeon superintendents were paid for every emigrant delivered alive. There were
shipwrecks, fires and drownings. There are accounts of orgies, sadistic matrons and drunkenness. At least Mary Ann and Sarah Jane had
the great advantage of not being Irish, as forty of their fellow female
passengers and my other emigrant great-grandparents were:

> Single women occasionally complained against matrons who
> referred to them as 'nasty Irish beasts', or 'dirty Irish'. While there
> is insufficient evidence to confirm this empirically, it does seem
> that the majority of matrons were English, and a significant
> proportion of single women were Irish.

The two sisters would have shared a bunk or a canvas cot. They were regulated from dawn to dusk, experienced heat the like of which they had never encountered before as they sailed through the tropics, and saw the same magical fish and fowls that Sary and Alfred had seen. They had to clean and scrub and wash and cook, just as they had on land. But for these domestic servants, life on board offered more diversions than working as skivvies in other people's houses. There were games, singing, fiddlers and the occasional dance, and many religious services and lectures. Those who were not able to could learn to read and write, and to sew – a talent which both Mary Ann and Sarah Jane were to put to good use on arrival. There were celebrations and tomfoolery as they crossed the equator. The food was adequate and carefully measured and certainly more than they had been used to.

The *Coldstream* had a fine passage: six babies were born and no one died. She anchored in Hobson's Bay, Port Phillip, late on the evening of Wednesday 16 March 1864. On arrival the immigration agent boarded the boat, mustered the immigrants and meticulously noted the details of each one of them,

> including age, native place and county, parents' names,
> occupation, literacy, religion, marital status, state of health,
> complaints on treatment on the voyage, names of relations in
> the colony. A separate sheet recorded . . . baptism and marriage
> certification, and the names of the examining physician, referees,
> previous employers, selecting agent, and shipping contractor.

This done, they were put up in an immigrant depot or boarding house before being despatched to whatever jobs were on offer, sometimes after inspection by prospective employers in hiring rooms or the depot, something any Lincolnshire maid would have been well used to. The close scrutiny of the imperial ladies who shipped so many of the lower classes of their sex to the colonies was accepted, if not always welcomed.

The sisters were allocated jobs by the immigrant reception authorities. Mary Ann was sent to a Mrs Bell in Pevensey Crescent, Geelong. William Bell, a pioneer pastoralist and a former mayor of

Geelong, had built a large double-fronted house in the classical style, typical of much Melbourne architecture of the time. Mary Ann was employed as a housemaid, with an annual salary of £20. Her younger sister Sarah Jane was less fortunate, being sent to work at Mrs Popplewell's Church of England school in Emerald Hill, now South Melbourne. Mrs Popplewell already had four children and was about to give birth to her fifth. Sarah Jane's salary was £18 a year. Both would thus have been paid at least double the pittances they received in Lincolnshire. Even so, this would be the last time they offered their services so cheaply.

When Mary Ann was next heard of, three years later, she had moved on and was working in Prahran. Once she left Mrs Bell's employ she would have been, for the first time in her life, a free woman whose services were in demand. She could work for whomever she liked, no matron or benevolent society could tell her what to do, and she could spend whatever money she earned on herself. No more caps and gowns unless wearing them was worth it to her. She could throw as many teaspoons of tea as she liked into her teapot. The two sisters found lodgings in Errol Street – a dust track then – and set themselves up as dressmakers. Around the corner in Robinson Street were George and Sary Conquest – though not married, Sary had taken his name on arrival.

The reason for the 'distressed circumstances' that had led to the selection of the Brooks sisters as emigrants was revealed in a newspaper advertisement six months after their departure:

Boston Union – One Guinea Reward
ABSCONDED, about ten days since, John Brooks, watchmaker, aged 49 or 50 [he was forty-four] years, 5ft 8in. high, fair complexion, blue eyes, ginger whiskers, light hair, and rather bouncing gait. Left his wife and four children chargeable to the parish of Boston. One Guinea Reward and all reasonable expenses will be paid by the Board of Guardians for his apprehension. Henry Bates, Clerk. Boston, 12th July 1864

A month later the charity commission trustees put John's shop in Dolphin Lane up for rent. What his bankruptcy and bouncing gait were due to is not recorded, though a local doctor reported: 'Many never take their beer without dropping a piece of opium into it.' John Brooks was surrounded by people who could have helped him, however poor some of them were. Some were not: by 1861, aged only forty-five, his brother Charles had retired as a watchmaker and worthy subject of Stamford. He had moved to Peterborough, thirty-three miles from Boston, and easily within reach by railway. John also had relations in Stamford, and his wife's family in Boston to call upon. That he was abandoned to the workhouse suggests that he had permanently blotted his copybook.

In 1837 the prolific Victorian architect George Gilbert Scott, who had been a pupil of Samuel Kempthorne, the designer of Market Harborough's workhouse, had designed a new Boston Union workhouse in Skirkbeck Road. Scott was connected to Boston – he would also be responsible for the extensive restoration of St Botolph's in the 1840s and 50s – through his wife Catherine, the daughter of John Oldrid, whose draper's shop was two minutes away from Dolphin Lane. The new workhouse was constructed to house 350 paupers. An archway led to a central four-storey block for the master and matron, a three-storey wing to the east for the male inmates, to the west a two-storey wing for the women. There were also a chapel, an infirmary, a laundry and workshops. John Brooks would have known the place of old, as Bothamley's had been appointed to wind and repair the workhouse clock during the years he worked for them.

John Brooks' travails when he was incarcerated in this workhouse in 1864 would not have been as gruesome as the experiences of John and Joseph Conquest in Market Harborough in 1848, as it was said to be one of the better workhouses in England at the time, a modest distinction. Some improvements had taken place over the years. Charitable, philanthropic and friendly societies as well as individual benefactors had stepped in to succour the poor, but much depended on the nature of the master, matron and staff. However, workhouse regimentation remained quasi-monastic – silence when ordered, uniforms as ordered, prayers when ordered. Bells were rung to organise the day and the vile meals were eaten communally. There were malodorous cesspits and endless instructions. A diet of bread and water was the punishment for breaking the many rules that made up the daily routine of workhouse hours: it was an agonising life for a man already brought low. As only one pauper in a hundred entered a workhouse after 1849, low John Brooks had certainly fallen. The rapidity of his decline is revealed by the fact that only a few years before, when he was involved in a railway accident as a train left Peterborough for Boston, the local newspaper reported the 'miraculous escape' of the 'esteemed townsman' John Brooks.

An 1866 report gives some idea of what John Brooks would have undergone:

> The wards are for the most part dark, low, close, gloomy, and unhealthy; they are dangerously crowded with inmates, especially in the infirm and sick wards. Many of the infirm people, men as well as women, are sleeping together two in a bed. The sick have not all of them a separate bed to lie upon. In the 'venereal ward' the patients affected with syphilis are sleeping together two in a bed . . . Four patients, two men and two boys, were lately sleeping together in the same bed in the 'itch ward' . . . In the midst of this ward, and in full view of the others, boys and men, an adult patient was standing upright without a fragment of clothes upon him, whilst a pauper attendant painted him over with a brush dipped in an application for his disease. The 'itch ward' is at all times the most disagreeable to enter of any.

On the other hand, the Boston Guardians provided roast beef, plum pudding and ale for the Christmas of 1861. But whatever was offered in July 1864, it was not acceptable to John Brooks. The only record of his extremely short stay is a note that he had absconded with clothes belonging to the workhouse. That year was an active one for the Boston Union, most of its energies and money being devoted to removing lunatic paupers from the workhouse to county Pauper Lunatic Asylums, with meticulous attention being paid to the Lunatic Asylum Expense Account. There is an occasional record of payments made to the police for the apprehension of absconders, but no word at all about John Brooks.

This is unsurprising, as the inmates of Britain's workhouses left little but silence behind them. As the years went by more records exist, as the 1834 Poor Law and its workhouses did not come to an official end until 1930. They lingered on, in one guise or another, until the foundation of the National Health Service after the Second World War. But graffiti has a long life – and many a scrawl was left by the inmates of these 'Bastilles'. 'This bloody old hole is lousy' is as good a summary as any of the litany of hatred left behind by paupers on workhouse walls .

So, after a brief incarceration in the workhouse John Brooks scarpered, and disappeared for the next two years. He was not heard from again until 1866, when he popped up, in ebullient form, in Melbourne. Like his son Charles Hickman, he reached Australia mysteriously, and without any record of his presence on a ship, which was astute of him, because Victoria was still demanding only 'emigrants in good health, of sound mind, and of good character'. It is likely that, as a wanted man, he used a pseudonym for his voyage, and more than likely that he worked his passage, though how he did so is hard to guess. Escaping from Boston was not difficult; its port may have been sidelined by the railways, but its coasting trade continued, and he could easily have sailed away. Before he left he managed to impregnate his wife Ann again – at least, he was named as the father on the birth certificate of Augusta, their fifth child, born in March 1865. By then John Brooks was oceans away.

14

The Little Chapel

The first Independent chapel in Prahran, 1851

B Y 1858, WHEN SARY arrived in Melbourne, George Conquest
had become, in a small way, a man of property. He bought
land and cottages, always near Chapel Street in Prahran, so
called because of the little wooden hut that was the first gathering
place of the Independent congregation, and the first public building
there. Joseph Conquest did the same: Chapel Street was the centre of
their world. Before it was settled by the Conquests, Brookses, Allens
and their like, the area had been an important meeting place for Aboriginal tribes from all over the Port Phillip district, and corroborees were

frequently held there until the area became the site of the Aboriginal Mission in 1837.

In 1838 John Gardiner had welcomed the first Independent minister to arrive in Melbourne – by this time the name Congregational was beginning to replace the earlier term Independent for these Christians. The first Independent chapel in Melbourne gathered in Gardiner's house and was later built on his land. The little wooden hut was replaced by a small brick chapel between 1850 and 1852. There is no record that George or Joseph Conquest took any part in the building of it in 1850 or its enlargement in 1853 – with the gold rush, the congregation had grown to such an extent that many had to worship outside, under the gum trees – but it is most likely that they did, given Gardiner's connection to George's former master David Reid. And it is most likely that it was not only because of brickmaking but also because of the gathering of Independents in Prahran, that the Conquests and Mary Ann and Sarah Jane Brooks settled there.

The first minister of Prahran's little chapel was William Moss, one of those Nonconformists who can be a candle in a dark world. Born in Farnham, Surrey, he sailed to Melbourne on the SS *Yarborough* in 1850.

> It was the pastor, the Rev. William Moss, whose magnetic personality, charged with an abounding love of humanity, that lifted the Chapel into prominence, and made it the outstanding landmark in early Prahran . . . Children loved him, women trusted him, men honoured him.

This good man made his chapel the centre of a vigorous social life in Prahran. He turned his hand and gave his heart to every benevolent and instructive endeavour and was its pastor from 1852 to 1878. Included in an exhaustive list of his achievements was the minor one of baptising, marrying and burying many members of the Conquest and Allen families in the following years. Today there are Conquests scattered throughout Melbourne and the state of Victoria: the old family Christian names continued for many a generation. The little wooden chapel stood on stilts, and was reached by planks laid across the sodden ground. The swampy bush track – not yet a street – was

William Moss, minister and
philanthropist, the first
pastor of the Independent
Chapel, Prahran, 1851

dotted with a few shops and one or two hotels. This was Chapel Street,
soon to become the social centre of Prahran, even more so when Moss
added a Mechanics Institute in 1854.

In 1850, when the little chapel was built, Prahran was still bush,
with kangaroos, swamp, wattle, scrub and tall red gums. Aboriginals
still camped where they could. There was a huddle of tents and huts
near the Yarra, and boggy tracks led to houses and rough cottages,
many of which would be inhabited by the children of Joseph and
Mary Conquest or rented out by George or Joseph. Chapel Street was
linked to the other side of the Yarra first by a ferry, then in 1857, by
Church Street bridge, making life much easier for George as he carted
timber and bricks across the river. Deep clay deposits on both sides
of Chapel Street made the area a centre for brickmakers and their
yards and kilns. 'At the time of the gold discoveries bricks were selling at £20 per thousand ... The smoke by day, the glare by night of
the brick kilns, at all points of the compass, was a notable impression
of early Prahran.' Joseph and his sons George, Joseph and most particularly Thomas, who followed his father in many ways, set to
brickmaking in earnest and by 1869 the area where they worked had a
little Independent chapel of its own, which gave the street its name,
Union Street.

Bricks, carting and gold meant that poverty and slums were over for the Conquest family. In due course Thomas owned his own brickyard in Union Street, employing five brickmakers and producing up to 20,000 bricks a week. Although at one point he was brought to bankruptcy, and to the courts (for beating his wife Eliza, who drank), by the time he died he had risen again, leaving his widow haphazardly in charge of his brickyard, and £500 besides.

John George Knight, Mary Ann Brooks' benefactor, and his architectural partner Peter Kerr, were the principal architects of Victoria's State Parliament House, in 1865. It is tempting to think that some of the materials used in its construction were made by a Conquest hand, for many a Conquest brick adorns a Melbourne building built before 1900. But the brickyards and their kilns killed a number of the Conquest men, though their early lives in English workhouses and slums probably also contributed. Joseph was the first to die, in 1865. He was fifty-two. In his will, witnessed by George, he left his children three houses, a number of plots of land, and an estate worth

The funeral parlour which was constantly patronised by the Conquest and Allen families

£700, worth about £87,000 today. His fifth child, also called Joseph, with whom his mother had been pregnant in Market Harborough's workhouse in 1841, died in 1882 at the age of forty. His third son, Thomas, who had lived with his grandparents in the Leicester slums while his parents were in the workhouse, followed two years later, in 1884: he was forty-five. Joseph, their father, had been working on an invention at the time of his death in 1865, and a few weeks later his son Thomas published an announcement in the *Victoria Gazette* Patent number 825:

> Joseph Conquest and Thomas Conquest, both of Prahran, brickmakers, for an Invention 'for improvements having for its object the prevention of smoking chimneys'

The little wooden cottage in Robinson Street to which George took Sary and Alfred in 1858 was typical of the many workers' cottages in early Melbourne: one room wide, with a yard at the back where the dunny was, giving on to the night-cart lane.

Robinson Street, Prahran, where Sary and George settled

Unassuming as it was, it had very little in common with an English slum tenement. Bush, gums, flowers and birdsong surrounded these early dwellings, and above, almost always, was the high and so often bright blue sky. At right angles to Robinson Street is Errol Street, and by 1866 Mary Ann and Sarah Jane Brooks were living there, Mary Ann working as a dressmaker, Sarah Jane as a seamstress. Their lodgings were so near the cottage of George and Sary and Alfred that describing the distance as a stone's throw would be an exaggeration.

When George and Sary moved to Robinson Street there were still open spaces, market gardens, uncultivated paddocks and watery or dusty tracks, dotted with hotels and drinking spots. Australian Rules football, which was to dominate life in Victoria from that year to this, had just been invented in Melbourne. There was a billabong nearby, creeks trickling through the bush, and a large swamp where Chapel Street met the river.

But already Prahran was like a country town and Chapel Street offered butchers, bakers, grocers, undertakers, and much else. Besides William Moss's Mechanics Institute, the Prahran Hotel was the most popular meeting place, with its Saturday-night concert. Singsongs and music hall were the stuff of life to white Australians: women, however, were not allowed into public bars until the 1970s. Amongst many other instructive events and much jollier social occasions, the Mechanics Institute presented lectures on such topics as 'Is America or Australia the most advantageous to immigrants?' and 'Has the miser or the spendthrift been the most injurious to society?' William Moss's heart and personality transformed the usual good works of such endeavours into an irresistible meeting place for the young of Prahran at that time.

Within a few years of Sary's arrival there was gas street lighting, a bowling green, piped water, horse racing, railways and a free library. By 1859 the Little Chapel had now been rebuilt again, in a street even nearer to George, Sary, Sarah Jane and Mary Ann. There was a horse-drawn 'jingle cab' into the city – Prahran is four miles from the centre of Melbourne and you could take a boat down the Yarra to the centre of the city. The arrival of steam trains in 1859 brought about yet another onslaught by land purchasers and speculators, and cable trams followed. Within three years of Sary's arrival, Prahran had an elaborate Italianate town hall, and Chapel Street was well on the way to becoming the metropolitan thoroughfare it would be in the 1880s. The year before Sary's arrival, all men in Victoria had been given the vote, and George and Joseph and their sons had become citizens of the new state. Road levelling and surfacing had begun, and soon George and Sary could visit Joseph and Mary and the children without having to take a change of boots.

This was still the age of exploration of inland Australia, opening up new lands for cultivation and grazing. And as more and more land was taken from them, reserves were created for Aboriginals. Enforced removals to these would lead seamlessly to the Stolen Generations: as early as 1869 Victoria introduced an Aboriginal Protection Act, the protection taking the form of separating children from their families, particularly those with one white parent. George and Sary would have seen Indigenous people in Prahran, and many Chinese, still objected to, not only by British settlers and ex-convicts but also by the now burgeoning trade unions, which had already achieved an eight-hour day for workers by 1856. Many of George's rival carters were Chinese.

By 1866, presumably financed by George, Alfred had left home to open his first boot and shoe shop five minutes from Robinson Street, and he lived above it. While George Conquest could not have known Mary Ann Brooks' mother, Mary Ann Winsall, in Market Harborough, except as a child – for he was transported when she was only twelve – his family, including his brother Joseph, had been living very near the Winsalls in the centre of town in 1837 when she married John Brooks. Now all of them were neighbours in Prahran. The proximity of Errol Street and Robinson Street could be how Mary Ann met Alfred, but much more likely is that it was the exceptional pastoral care of William Moss and the social occasions which whirled around his chapel and his Mechanics Institute that brought them together.

The year after Joseph's death, in 1866 William Moss married Alfred Allen and Mary Ann Brooks in Alfred's lodgings; he was twenty-two and Mary Ann a year younger. John Brooks arose from the seas and god knows where else to lead his daughter to the altar, or at least to whatever served in its stead in Alfred's lodgings. His ebullient and rollicking signature on the marriage licence is unmistakeable. Shortly after he performed the same duty for Sarah Jane, who married a baker from Lancashire. John Brooks was next heard from in 1869, by which point he had crossed the seas, returned to Boston, impregnated his wife yet again and somehow managed to reopen his shop in Dolphin Lane, most likely with the help of his brother Charles.

Two years after Sary arrived in Melbourne, her mother Dorothy died, a pauper, in Thurmaston, and six years later, in 1865, her half-brother Joseph Allen, the probable father of Alfred, died in Thurmaston at the age of forty-two. News of his death must have reached Robinson Street, for at his marriage Alfred named Joseph Allen as his father, and his mother as Sarah Allen, another reason for suspecting that Sary may have been escaping family knowledge of incest when she left England. She now came into her own, for the newly-weds began the rapid production of nine children over the next thirteen years, with Sary acting as her daughter-in-law's constant midwife.

Sary identified herself as 'Sarah Allen' on her son's marriage certificate, otherwise she was Sary Conquest, except for their next official occasion when George Conquest, Gentleman, married Sary Grundy, housekeeper, in 1868. They married in a registry office, and as they were already thought to be a married couple there were no attendants or witnesses present. Perhaps George was beginning to feel the onset of his last illness. Common-law wives had no rights: marriage gave Sary legal protection, and allowed her to inherit his estate.

Alfred's shop was now in Chapel Street.

Shops for renting were plain and square. Entrance was from
the side of the single glass display window and a wide clapboard
above the shop bore the name and occupation of the shopkeeper.
Most were single-storied, built of brick, with galvanised iron
roofs. Dwelling quarters were behind the shop, with a small
back yard opening onto a right-of-way. Here the shopkeeper
lived, worked, and reared his family, all of whom bore their
share of the work.

By the 1870s Alfred was making something between £150 and £300 a
year, an unheard of sum in his profession in England, but more than
possible in the gold years of Melbourne.

Sary's first grandchild, Alfred Ernest, was born in 1867. John William came in the following year, but died at six months and William
Moss buried him. Next came Charles Arthur and the dead baby's
replacement John George, always known as George, who was to be
the support of Mary Ann's later years. Sary's life had become something she could never have dreamed of during her early years in
Leicester's slums: William Moss's Ladies' Visiting Society, Ladies'
Aid, Mechanics Institute and Town Mission provided endless social
occasions. There were concerts, bazaars, fetes and fairs, and now Sary
had the clothes to wear to them, as well as a full stomach and a flourishing family.

But by 1872 George Conquest was seriously ailing, and he died in
the following year. His death was announced in the Melbourne press,
the *Prahran Telegraph* reporting:

> another old resident of this town, George Conquest died at his
> residence Robinson-Street, Prahran, Last Sunday at 4 p.m. The
> deceased gentleman had reached his three score years and ten.
> He had been ailing for some time previous to his Last illness,
> and after eight days of intense suffering, having made his peace
> with God, he quietly breathed his Last.

George left everything to Sary and her heirs. He had bought a
substantial plot for his family in St Kilda Cemetery, one of Melbourne's oldest burial grounds, and there he was buried near the
grave of his brother Joseph. Alfred was his sole executor, handling on
Sary's behalf several allotments of land, five cottages and £1,136:
worth approximately £125,000 today. Sary now not only owned her
house in Robinson Street, but received regular income from her
rented properties.

Alfred and Mary Ann's next son, Joseph Edgar, was born in Chapel
Street in 1873. Joseph Conquest's widow Mary and most of her married
children were still living nearby. Names were swapped between the
Conquest and Allen families: there were Conquest children called

Sarah and Alfred, Allen children called George and Joseph, and this continued for many generations. When Sary came into her inheritance Alfred bought a family home and second shop in High Street, St Kilda, not far from his Chapel Street shop, but in an altogether more favoured district.

Sary went to live with them, the Robinson Street cottage being handed on to two of Joseph Conquest's surviving sons, George and Alfred, the latter living there until the end of the 1920s. This move to more handsome surroundings seems to mark the beginning of the end of their happy days. In April 1875 seven-year-old Alfred, their firstborn, picked some mushrooms in Brown's Paddock. He ate two of them, and took the rest home to Sary, who cooked them for him. He became ill immediately. Treated with vinegar and water and castor oil, he died after an agonising day and night, his wretched death covered in full and grim detail by Melbourne and state newspapers. The little boy was buried with George Conquest. There was an inquest at which his father Alfred said, 'I told him they ought to be red underneath.'

A year later, in 1876, Alfred and Mary Ann's first daughter, Alice Edith, was born. A girl, greeted rapturously by her mother, Alice died at the age of only ten months: this was a tragedy from which Mary Ann never recovered. Though she was to live for many years, she 'became all queer after the death of Alice in 1876'. Alfred sold the Chapel Street shop and moved his business entirely to St Kilda. Throughout the 1870s and 80s he was in and out of the local courts, as both plaintiff and defendant – for leaving a horse and cart untethered, for not having a light on his cart, or because someone owed him money, stole the boots he made, or gave him false cheques. This was the heyday of Victoria's bushranging years – 1880 saw the pursuit, capture and hanging of the most notorious bushranger of them all, Ned Kelly, in Melbourne Gaol. Sary and George lived together through the very best of Melbourne's gold and glitter years, its vivacity and glamour, such as it was, quite outstripping any such qualities in Sydney. After George's death Sary oversaw the birth of her last three grandchildren – Ernest Alfred, Alfred Ernest's replacement and my grandfather, and two more sons, Henry William and the last child, Frank Walter, born in 1881.

The following year Sary died at home with Alfred and Mary
Ann. She had survived George by nine years, and, attended by a
Congregational minister, and many Allens and Conquests, went to
join him, little Alice and little Alfred Ernest of the poisoned mushrooms in the family plot in St Kilda Cemetery. Sary and George
were tough people. Four of George's siblings had died before him,
as had a good half of Sary's half-brothers and sisters. George was
sixty-seven when he died, Sary seventy-four. Both had been born
at a time when life expectancy was about forty years, and it 'hovered stubbornly between forty and forty-one years for the next
seventy years'.

With Sary gone, Alfred inherited all of George Conquest's remaining money and property, and he bought a third boot and shoe shop in
St Kilda. But drink was to be Alfred's downfall, which is perhaps
unsurprising in view of his childhood dosage with 'Mother's Little
Helper' in the Leicester slums; while Mary Ann's activities took her to
another world. In pursuit of her dead children and in particular her
daughter Alice, with whom she remained in constant touch, she took
up spiritualism, which became exceptionally popular in Victoria in the
1870s and 80s. Regular advertisements for her work as a medium – 'Mrs
Allen's Circle' appeared in the *Age* and the seances themselves may
well have hastened Alfred along the road to inebriated insanity:

SPIRITUALISM – Mrs Allen holds Séance, Mrs Hardings,
69 Greville Street, Prahran station, Sundays only, 7.30. Private
sittings arranged for.

Mary Ann's father John Brooks died in 1884. He had made his
mysterious way back to England by 1869, when he impregnated his
wife Ann yet again, but a year later either she had thrown him out, or
he had abandoned her and his brood, and he set up shop again in
Dolphin Lane. Not a word was heard from him over the next dozen
years, except for the occasional report of a robbery of whatever stock
he still kept in his shop. Finally, in December 1883, with England at
its coldest – you can almost see him being gathered up as a vagrant on
the streets – he was admitted to Boston Workhouse once more. This
time he was too ill to abscond, and there seven months later he died

of bronchitis – bad lungs again. He was buried in a pauper's grave in St Botolph's churchyard on 16 July 1884: no headstone, just the location of his final resting place noted in the cemetery records.

By 1888 Alfred seems to have lost interest in his shoe shops. The gradual mechanisation of the boot trade affected his business, but his great affliction was his addiction to the drink. Matters worsened to such a degree that in 1888 Mary Ann, presumably in need of family support – because her sister Sarah Jane and their family had already returned to England – placed an advertisement for the attention of her brother, Charles Hickman Brooks, in the 'Missing Friends' section of the Melbourne *Age*.

> CHARLES BROOKS – Come or send address to your sister in St Kilda Mary Ann Allen. Important.

It seems that he did not answer her call – or if he did he was no help at all, for then came the spectacular financial crash of the 1890s as the investment boom that had created 'Marvellous Melbourne' collapsed, plunging the city into deep depression. In 1902 Alfred threw Mary Ann out of the house. She brought the case to court the following year:

> Mary Ann Allen, of 78 Union-street, Windsor, summoned her husband, Alfred Allen, boot dealer, of 91 Fitzroy-street, St Kilda, with failing to contribute towards her support. The parties are well up in years, and have long been residents of St. Kilda. Complainant stated that she had been married to defendant 37 years. They had had nine children, and there were six sons living. Defendant was addicted to drink. His conduct ultimately became unbearable and drove witness and her sons out of the house. She left on July 16 of last year. She offered to go back, but he called her filthy names, said he did not want her, and said he would give her no peace as long as she lived. She was staying with her sons. Defendant sold the furniture and piano on Friday last.
>
> Three sons gave evidence to show that defendant had refused to support his wife. When giving evidence each was in turn informed by the father that he was 'a liar'.

Defendant was ordered to pay 10/ per week, and to find a
surety of £25 and himself in a like amount, with 31/6 costs.

In 1903 Alfred sold his house, shops and stock and moved from
central Melbourne to the beach suburb of Beaumaris, well out of
shouting distance of his family. Eight years before, a photograph had
been taken, depicting what they had achieved, as distinct from the
chaos into which they had now descended.

Most of Alfred and Mary Ann's sons either fled or rejected
their father: all of them looked after their mother. Three became
bootmakers, one, my grandfather Ernest, a jeweller like his grandfather John Brooks; two went to fight in the Boer War and stayed in
South Africa.

In April 1907, at the age of sixty-three, Alfred was committed to
the Yarra Bend Asylum for the Insane. He is recorded as being 'inclined
to intemperance', 'suffering from senile dementia, lung disease, with

The Allen family. Front row: Henry, Frank; middle row: Charles, Mary Ann,
Alfred, Ernest (my grandfather); back row: John (George) c. 1895.

Alfred Allen, in the Yarra
Bend Asylum for the
Insane, Melbourne, 1907

delusions about having murdered a man'. 'Says he often thought of
suicide and would commit suicide if he got the chance.' He lasted sixteen months in the asylum. It was noted that one of his sons came to
see him shortly before he died there in August 1908, but his burial in
the new Melbourne Necropolis was not unlike that of his father-in-
law John Brooks. He was listed as 'Parents: unknown, married to
whom unknown. Issue: Unknown.'

Sary Conquest was my great-great-grandmother, and Alfred Allen
and Mary Ann Brooks my great-grandparents. They were matched
with Johanna O'Leary and James Keane, my Irish great-grandparents,
respectively from the little towns of Castletown-Kinneigh, in
Cork, and Borrisokane, in Tipperary. Both of them lived through the
great famine of 1845–9.

Johanna's parents Peter O'Leary and Norry (Honoria) Murphy
were born in Kinneigh and Kilmichael, eight miles apart in West
Cork. Peter O'Leary was a tenant farmer, like his father Jeremiah
before him. Being Catholics they leased land and a farm from their
landlord, the Earl of Bandon, where they grew potatoes, oats and

flax. Leasing their own land from those who had taken it away from them was a continuing affliction for Irish families like the O'Learys. In addition, they had to pay tithes to the Protestant Church of Ireland, ever a cause of resentment, particularly acute in West Cork in the 1830s. And they lived under the shadow of eviction and displacement as landowners sought to extract higher rents, choose Protestant rather than Catholic tenants, and free more land for pasture rather than tillage. Ascendancy landlords like Bandon delegated the management of their estates to agents and middlemen, whose repeated visits of inspection and threats of eviction were an affront to men like Peter O'Leary. My mother told me that he 'was a proud man, and resented not being able to own his own land'. His daughter Johanna told my mother that in those years 'If she had had a rifle and seen the absentee landlord, she'd have shot him.' The Bandon family seat, Castle Bernard, was burned down by the IRA in 1921.

Johanna was born in 1832 in the midst of the Tithe Wars that raged from 1830 to 1838. Johanna's childhood was spent living through, and observing, the suffering and death in Ireland during the Great Famine of 1845–9, the calamity which killed a million people, and the emigration of well over that number. She was Peter and Norry's first child, and between 1832 and 1853 she was followed by eight more: Mary, Jerry, Daniel, Timothy, Margaret, Honoria, Annie and Ellen, two of whom died in the famine. In 1851 Peter O'Leary and his family moved from Kinneigh to Caheragh, both villages in the district of Skibbereen in West Cork, which was one of the areas worst affected by the mass starvation. Johanna was thirteen when the famine began, so she grew up at a time when there was devastation and suffering on an unbearable scale – the 'uncoffined remains' of about 9,000 famine victims were buried in Skibbereen's Abbeystrewery graveyard, one of many other horrors she would have seen. According to my mother, she became a formidable woman, 'No one could get on with her, she was the kind of woman who would take a whip to a cat.'

After the Great Hunger, tenant farmers like Peter O'Leary were dissuaded from subdividing their plots, which meant that the land they rented could be passed on to only one son. The oldest daughter might get a small dowry, but what was to be done with the rest of them? Between 1846 and 1849, a large number of the Earl of Bandon's tenants emigrated, and as Lord Lieutenant and largest landowner of County Cork, he might well have arranged for some of them to do so. But the final push for Peter O'Leary's children came when another agricultural depression fell upon Ireland, from 1859 to 1864, a period of extreme distress in Cork. Alternate droughts and tremendous inundations led to a series of ruined harvests, blight, foot and mouth disease, sheep rot and a ruined butter market, an intimation of the return of the Great Hunger. This sent many more thousands of Irish men and women on their way.

Most Irish emigrants went to America and Canada. However, the United States was embroiled in civil war from 1861 to 1865, so Peter and Norry chose to send their children to Australia. To travel the great distance there, with the near-certain knowledge of never returning or seeing their families again, required human souls made of stern stuff, either the more courageous or the more desperate emigrants, who probably knew someone who had already taken the plunge. Between 1840 and 1914, 300,000 Irish men and women left for Australia, only five per cent of the total Irish emigration during those years, but they were to make up twenty-five per cent of Australia's population until the twentieth century, and to have a major influence on the development of the country's personality and language.

In August 1861, in Caheragh, Johanna married James Keane, from Borrisokane in Tipperary. The son of Patrick Cain and Biddy Hogan, James's surname was spelt every which way: Cane, Kane, Keane, Kean, Kain and Kaine. In Australia it would settle down to Kane for his first four children, Keane for the six who followed. His father Patrick may have been a labourer or a cottier, and as such is likely to have seen the inside of the Borrisokane workhouse, built in 1848 to cope with the famine. Johanna and James sailed to Australia on the SS *Hope* immediately after their wedding. They left three years after Sary and Alfred, and two years before Mary Ann and Sarah Jane Brooks. Johanna was the first of her siblings to go, and she was followed by Mary, Timothy and Annie O'Leary. All of them went as domestic servants, although in less favoured circumstances than Mary Ann Brooks and with a less enthusiastic reception from colonial Australia on arrival: at that time their view of the Irish mirrored England's imperial approach to the people of Ireland, their first colony. Happily for Australia this bigotry had simply withered away by the late twentieth century, no civil war required. It took time: distance in this case was not a tyranny, but a blessing.

Johanna and James sailed from Queenstown (now Cobh) as 3 million Irish emigrants and convicts did both before and after them, in conditions much akin to those to be found in Leicester's slums. They sailed steerage, as unassisted migrants. Besides Peter O'Leary's contribution, the reason they could drum up the fare was because nine years previously, at the age of twenty-one, James had made the big mistake of joining the Royal Irish Constabulary, although he was a Catholic. The following year he was sent to Cork, policeman number 14120, and he served for nine years – without promotion – which was more than long enough to destroy an Irish reputation. On the SS *Hope*'s passenger list James sensibly described himself as a labourer, and made no reference to his years as a policeman, then or later.

They arrived in Melbourne in January 1862, at a time when the Conquest men were labouring away at the brick-face in Prahran and Sary was three years into her new life in Robinson Street with George and the nineteen-year-old Alfred. They settled in Hawthorn and then Kew, to the east of Melbourne on the other side of the Yarra from Prahran, near to the Jesuit schools and the Faithful Companions of Jesus, a French order of nuns, who between them were to educate all their children. Both were employed as servants on arrival, but not for long. Scarcely had they landed than Johanna's womb began to bear fruit – she would provide James, who started life in Victoria as a gardener, then became a florist, with ten children in the next fourteen years: Michael, Peter Francis Xavier, Bridget, James, Honoria, Gertrude, Patrick, Norbert, Francis and Teresa. Michael would die in an earthquake in Valparaiso in 1906. Gertrude and Patrick died as babies. Norbert – named, it was said after a bottle of German whisky – disappeared to an early death in New Zealand, and Francis committed suicide by throwing himself off a boat in Port Phillip Bay in 1918, aged forty-six. Their father, James Keane, died in 1899: he was sixty-eight. Johanna lived on for twenty-four years a widow, naming her house in Melbourne 'Castletown Kinneigh' after the place of her birth.

Of Johanna's siblings who followed her to Australia, Timothy and Mary's story is one of late marriages, early deaths and dead children,

Annie O'Leary in her finery, stout and on the left, at her daughter
Ethel's wedding to Frank Whiteley, London, 1904.
William Whiteley, later to be murdered, is the mutton-chopped fellow.

but there was a much happier fate for their baby sister Annie. She married her widowed employer in 1874, when she was twenty-six and he seventy-four, immediately had two children and inherited all his money when he died two years after their wedding. Now a wealthy woman, in 1884 she married her husband's nephew, who had a shop in London, and decamped to live in Bayswater and Cheshire for the rest of her life. There her daughter Ethel married Frank Whiteley, the son of William Whiteley, the formidable fellow who in 1899 started the great department store in Bayswater that still bears his name and who was shot dead at his desk in 1907 by a young man who thought he was Whiteley's illegitimate son. Annie's worldly behaviour created a rift in the Australian O' Leary family that was never healed – not surprising, in view of Johanna's character and her adherence to the faith of her fathers.

Teresa – Tess – the baby of the Keane family, was my grandmother, a teacher. In 1905 she married Ernest Alfred Allen, the seventh child of Mary Ann Brooks and Alfred Allen and the replacement baby for Alfred Ernest who had died from eating the poisoned mushrooms. Tess was twenty-nine, though she claimed to be twenty-four, and Ernest twenty-eight, a jeweller like his grandfather. After marriage in the presbytery of St Joseph's Catholic Church near her home in Hawthorn (by special licence as he was a Protestant) the guests repaired to the Keane family home nearby where the drawing room 'was a glory of autumn leaves and golden and brown Japanese Chrysanthemums'. On this occasion the terrifying Johanna, dressed in 'a robe of silk poplin, with appliqué lace', confronted the Independent spiritualist Mary Ann Allen, adorned in 'black silk taffeta, with cream appliqué lace and velvet; black and mauve bonnet'. This was a victory for the Keanes, for barely an Allen was present, and an Irish Catholic world took over the lives of all the children to come.

My grandmother Tess inherited her mother's trousseau, linen sheets woven by the flax grown by her father in Ireland, and made her wedding bed with them. She told me they were so cold my grandfather leapt out of bed: she later made dresses out of them. After their marriage Tess and Ernest Allen moved to Elwood, a new suburb of Melbourne, built on reclaimed swampland where Aboriginals were still encountered – according to my grandmother they would come to the back door asking for charity. Elwood is very near the sea, and its long beaches were to be a great thing for Tess and Ernest's descendants. Their firstborn, in 1906, was my mother Lorraine. Each of their three children were raised within the bosom of the Catholic Church, despite rows between Tess and Ernie during the First World War and the Easter Rising of 1916 when divisions between Catholics and Protestants in Australia mirrored those of the land of their fathers – and mothers.

In 1922 a large family of prosperous emigrants from Lebanon, Anna and Peter Callil and their children, eight of the ten born to them, moved into a house across the road from Tess and Ernest. They were, or had been, Maronite Catholics, an Eastern rite of the Roman Catholic Church. Their children attended the local Catholic Church, St James's, as did Lorraine and her brothers.

The Maronite church was formed by St John Maroun in the fifth century AD. In the tenth century, persecution and the advent of Islam caused its adherents to hole up on the highest peak in Lebanon, in the village of Bsharri, directly under the Cedars of Lebanon, high above their sacred Qadisha Valley.

For centuries these ancient Christians lived in isolation, avoiding the attentions of the Ottoman Empire and its tapestry of so many unacceptable religions. Syria – in which today's Lebanon, Jordan, Palestine and Israel were subsumed – was under Ottoman rule from 1521 to 1918. The Maronites were not the only pre-Islamic Christians in Lebanon, though they were – and remain – the largest in number. The upper reaches and sides of the mountain, which drops precipitously down to the Qadisha Valley, were studded with monasteries and hermits' caves. These peasant people grew wheat and other grains on stony soil, vines, olive and mulberry trees, and herded goats up and down the mountain. They were ruled by feudal and monastic landlords and by a system of delegated Ottoman rule which in its complexity and discrimination – racial, religious and fiscal – fixed labourers and peasants at the bottom of the social and economic pyramid, cemented in by demands for both deference and taxes. During the crusades of the eleventh century the men of Bsharri fought with the invading Christians against their Arab brethren, for which they were not forgiven.

Bsharri was thus a bastion of Catholic Christianity, a fortress village, snowed in for six months of the year. Its people were ferocious defenders of their ancient faith: short, illiterate and mostly curly-haired, with mountain legs and fiery tempers. Maronites were a rare sect within the Roman Catholic Church because it allowed its priests (but not its monks) to marry – though only once. Protected by the French Empire, as their population grew they shared the mountain with the schismatic Muslim Druze, with Shia and Sunni Muslims and many other Christian sects – Syriac Orthodox, Melkites, Greek Orthodox, Greek Catholics and more.

Bsharri and the mountain's Christians were linked with Europe through many centuries of connection with France and the papacy – a Maronite College was opened in Rome in 1584 – and with Catholic religious orders which followed in the seventeenth century, including Capuchins, Carmelites and Jesuits. After 1831, when the first Jesuits started to teach in Lebanon, many convents, colleges and schools were established in the country, Protestant as well as Catholic. The influence of these institutions meant that the Lebanese, and particularly the inhabitants of its capital, Beirut, were Europeanised in many ways. As a result, Lebanese Christian immigrants to Australia were not seen as Arabs, but as Christians. They were therefore regarded as acceptable, if not ideal, immigrants. Muslims were not.

The nineteenth century was a period of extreme change for the Maronite people. The feudal system of the mountain was breaking up; Christians continued to be excluded from any official career under the Ottoman Empire. As Maronite peasants became more numerous and more powerful, they rebelled against both their Druze and Christian overlords. In 1840 near-civil war broke out between the Druze and the Maronites in the south.

This led to the division of the mountain into a northern Christian region and a southern Druze region. This solved little, as strife recommenced and led to civil war, which broke out in 1860, and which spread throughout Lebanon and Syria. There were massacres, pillaging, the razing of villages. Many thousands died, the number of Maronites being assessed as between 10,000 and 20,000. As the civil war reached Damascus, and the atrocities reported were so violent, the European powers intervened, the British keeping an eye on the Druze in support of the Ottoman Empire, the French protecting the Maronites. A French army landed in Beirut in 1860, and under the terms of a settlement arranged by the French and guaranteed by other European powers, Mount Lebanon became a semi-autonomous region within the Ottoman Empire, under French protection. This continued until the outbreak of the First World War.

My grandfather Butros Kahlil Fakhry, or Peter Callil as he would come to be known, was born in Bcharri in 1863, three years after the outbreak of the civil war. At this time the mountain's silk industry, which under French patronage had constituted a considerable part of its income, began to collapse in the face of competition from Japan and the invention of artificial silk. Disease attacked both their vineyards and, between 1875 and 1885, their silk worms. There was little work, and insufficient terraced land for the young men. The ancient Phoenician trading ports – Tyre, Sidon, Beirut, Tripoli – fell into decline with the opening of the Suez Canal in 1869. At and after this time Lebanese

Maronites set off for the four corners of the world: to North and South America – particularly to Brazil – to Africa, the Caribbean, Australia, New Zealand and many other less expected places. They were to make up the largest diaspora of any Arab country.

My grandfather was, it is said, the first Lebanese to emigrate to Australia, in 1881, though the historical record of these first Lebanese settlers is chaotic, as they did not speak English and their names were written down, if at all, with much Anglo-Saxon inaccuracy on ship, landing and government documents. He left a tiny country of some 400,000 people, and arrived in Melbourne, then a city of half a million inhabitants, speaking Arabic and French but no English and thinking he was elsewhere anyway. It is said that he had actually wanted to go either to the United States, the most desired destination of all emigrants, or to Brazil, where his elder brother was. These emigrants were exploited by corrupt brokers employed by various shipping lines, both French and British, which would ship the hapless emigrant to the farthest and costliest place. This was Australia or New Zealand, where many Catholic Lebanese settled in the late nineteenth century. Alternatively, unscrupulous captains would dump the migrants in Lisbon, or some other port, telling them: 'Here you are, this is America.'

Wherever my grandfather may have thought he was, the official who documented his arrival at Port Melbourne anglicised his first two names, Butros Kahlil, as 'Peter Callil' – though 'Kelly', which my oldest uncle was often called, might have been easier. He found a Frenchman who owned a hotel, worked for him as a roustabout, travelled and worked in Adelaide, Perth, Broken Hill, New Zealand and Tasmania, then returned to Melbourne and opened a very small warehouse there in 1884, with headed paper which read 'Importers of Fancy Goods'. He later enticed his older brother Latoof to come and join him, and the business was renamed Latoof & Callil.

The slum and red-light district of central Melbourne in which he started his business was known as 'Little Lon', close to Parliament House. Prostitution was the chief occupation of most of the inhabitants of this maze of little streets, which boasted some two dozen brothels, dominated by the matriarch of all brothel keepers, Madame Brussels. It was also occupied by emigrants of every hue and occupation: numerous Lebanese Maronites, Chinese cabinetmakers, English bellows makers, japanners, engineers, ironmongers, bootmakers. All the usual denizens of an Australian slum inhabited Little Lon, in many ways not unlike Sary's Leicester slums, but much easier to escape from.

Most Australian literature of the 1880s and 90s is set in the bush: tales of conquering the outback, settling the country, the loneliness and heartbreak of working the unforgiving land. In these stories a recurring character is the itinerant pedlar, whether Syrian, Indian, Chinese or Afghan. Sometimes there are illustrations of them: bearded, beak-nosed, brown- or yellow-faced, slit-eyed – whatever racial notions the sketchers of the time carried in their minds. These pedlars carried fabrics and laces, shoes and jewellery, perfume, drapery and a myriad bits and bobs – as well as news from homestead to homestead. Peter Callil, though illiterate, but neither beak-nosed nor slit-eyed, began to make his fortune through peddling.

In 1888 he returned to Lebanon to marry Henineh Yazbeck and

Left: my grandfather Ernest Allen, c. 1920s.
Right: my grandfather Peter Callil, c. 1900s.

brought her back to Australia. She was eighteen and is said to have been obtained from a Catholic orphanage on the mountain. In Australia she became Anna or Annie Callil. These Maronite mountain women from Bsharri were noted for their strength and forcefulness, and of the seven clans of the village, hers was far more warlike than that of my grand-father: she was to become a stern matriarch. She worked as the manageress of the factory which Peter began in his warehouse in 1889, adding to his fancy-goods business by manufacturing clothes in a very small way. Annie also made meals for its workers. Lebanese Maronites were always in two minds as to whether they were part of the Arab or the Western Christian world, but the finer points of the country's his-tory meant little to any Australian government official and in 1894 Peter Callil became an Australian citizen. He was described as a merchant with a hawker's licence who 'made a living by hawking fancy goods through the country districts with a horse and cart'.

Like all emigrants, as soon as they could afford to, Peter and Annie brought out sisters, brothers, cousins and in-laws. Most of them arrived on the SS *Yarra* in July 1889. With their help and under Peter's guidance the business prospered. It became a considerable clothing manufacturer, making nighties and much else for almost every citizen of Australia, owning six factories and twenty-five outwork establishments, buying cloth and doing business all over the world.

In 1912 Peter bought a block of land next to the warehouse in the centre of Melbourne and built a large four-storey brick building there, with his and his brother's names decorating its facade, succeeded in 1932 by an even more imposing edifice bearing the year in which he had founded the business, 1889: all now pulled down.

Some Lebanese immigrants in Australia experienced hostility during the First World War because of Lebanon's connections to Turkey and the tragedy of Gallipoli, where so many Australian and New Zealand young men died, but very little of this affected Peter or his family. They had burrowed themselves into Australia and into Melbourne, into its Catholic and business community, its sport and its way of life. The only exception was food and wine: theirs was always much, much better.

Peter made enough money to provide in varying ways for a very large family, for battalions of grandchildren and great-grandchildren,

Latoof & Callil in Exhibition Street, Melbourne, 1950s

for many more emigrants from the mountain, often unrelated to him. My mother said he was a very good man. Anna and Peter Callil had nine children: Joseph who was born and died in 1888 before they set sail. Next came Mary in 1889. Jim followed in 1891 – he fought in the First World War and died after and because of it and then came the first George, who was run over by a milk truck at the age of one. In 1895 came Rose. Madness or the Catholic Church was the lot of women of the first generation of these Lebanese emigrants, and the happiest of them chose the former. The following year brought forth another George, the replacement, then Philip in 1898 and a year later Frederick – my father – joined three years later by the last baby Alexander. All the boys except Alexander were sent back to Lebanon to be educated, generally in pairs, and there they stayed until their Catholic education was over, looked after by an aunt, a cousin, or a priest. My father would have been five or six when he went because my mother says he was so young he could not tie his shoelaces for himself.

In 1922 Anna and Peter and their family moved to Elwood, across the road from Ernest and Tess Allen. 'People used to visit other people in the street,' my mother told me. 'Were his parents pleased when you married?' I asked her. 'I don't think so,' was her reply, 'they liked them all to marry Lebanese.' But they would have met anyway at the local Catholic church, St James's, for Mass each Sunday. Both were dead by the time it burned down in 2015:

> Police are probing whether a fire that gutted one of Melbourne's oldest churches is related to a notorious paedophile priest. Police confirmed the fire, which largely destroyed the 123-year-old St James Church in Brighton on Monday morning, was being treated as suspicious. Detectives are now investigating if the fire is linked to the crimes of Ronald Pickering, who served as the church's parish priest from 1978 to 1993 before he fled to the United Kingdom, fearing prosecution. At least five people killed themselves after being sexually abused by Pickering between 1960 and 1980, according to research by Monash University's law faculty. Pickering died in 2012.

———————————— ⌀ ————————————

Johanna O'Leary, widowed in 1899, lived on until 1923, dying at the age of ninety-one. Alfred Allen's widow, my great-grandmother Mary Ann, lived on, and on, continuing to be much employed as a medium. She outlasted most of her sons, dying in a nursing home near my grandfather Ernest Allen's house in 1935, aged ninety-one. My mother told me:

> I went to see her when she was very old and felt very very sorry for her because she had to have her supper at half-past three in the afternoon. She had all those fine sons, but she never got over the death of her little girl [Alice Edith]. She came to stay with us and went round the streets picking up sticks for the fire saying, 'I'm picking up sticks for Ernie's fire.' Mother was NOT pleased.

Mary Ann was buried with George, Sary and her dead babies. The weather has all but worn away Sary's name. Alfred lies in a different cemetery, by himself.

Mary Ann Brooks, c. 1920s

Epilogue

W HAT DID THE BRITISH Empire do to the British, and in particular, to the English? What did their treatment of their own people in the British Isles, and others they subdued and invaded, do to them? Is it because the study of this history is so little taught and so rarely referred to, that the darker side of the British Empire forms so little part of the national story? Or why the stories of people like Sary and George are always so lost from the historical record? Is this great forgetting buried wilfully – and the reason why the chain of injustice and inequality clanks on in Britain today?

There is an aching void within the curricula of the British Isles where a warts-and-all history of the British Empire should be. Colonial history as a subject in British schools and universities is hard to come by, and when it is, it is often phrased in terms of its benefits – the rule of law, railways and so on – as though philanthropy and beneficence were the essence of British imperial purpose. Selective amnesia seems to afflict even serious historical assessments of the effects of empire on the British themselves, in their attitudes to their own people, and in how they live together today in their country to which the subdued nations gave so much. Would silence of this kind about the nation's past be accepted in modern Germany?

Surely there comes a point when knowledge of the Star Chamber and the Tudors and Stuarts should be balanced by contemplation of the famines, massacres and oppression of the Indian people in the colonial years, the torture and suffering caused by the colossal British involvement in the slave trade (800,000 slaves were legal property in Britain until 1833), the sad story of Ireland, the murky appropriation of so many countries in Africa? I could pen a much longer list of historical facts about British imperial history.

All imperial nations committed crimes but few ignore so much of their history and fail to teach the ambivalent legacy of empire. The

Australian experience, which pales beside the experience of so many other British imperial possessions, is only one of a multitude of colonial histories that should be as commonly known as the name of the heir to the throne or the Battle of Waterloo. It is said that one cannot judge history through the eyes of the present, but the desire for national and personal enrichment at the expense of others was the same then as it is now. Those on the receiving end of exploitation, racism, starvation and the whip felt the same then as they would now. The notion of inherited guilt is a waste of time, the notion of acknowledgement is not. Self-flagellation is not called for, self-knowledge is.

As for Australia itself, in recent years Australian historians have taken the narratives of the country's settlement by white Europeans by the scruff of the neck and shaken them to such a degree that its corpse of alternative truths is battled over in universities, the media, in Parliament and in public argument. Historians focusing on the misery and wretchedness of the convicts transported to the colony, on the Indigenous inhabitants who lost their land, the damage to their culture, to the land and to everything living and growing on it, do battle with others who concentrate on the reformative imperative within Britain's complex motives for founding the colony, on its success as a social experiment, pointing out the benefits of British civilisation and the remarkable achievements of a country which began as a penal colony. These rival versions of Australia's past can seem spurious and self-deceptive to those outside the realms of academe or politics, as all these reasons can be seen as ingredients in the un-Magic Pudding* of ideas which prompted the British government to send off the First Fleet.

Is there a connection between the brutality that characterised the early years of the penal colony in New South Wales and the failure of most subsequent attempts to make life better for Indigenous Australians? At the time of the arrival of the First Fleet, there were around half a million Indigenous Australians, speaking many hundreds of languages. Between 1788 and 1981, their population fell by seventy-seven per cent. The British and Irish who in time became Australians,

---

* *The Magic Pudding* is a classic Australian children's book by Norman Lindsay, published in 1918.

and the people of the hundreds of other nations who have since joined them, have struggled to do better and there have been considerable advances. But successive governments and parliamentarians, and so, the citizens who voted for them, have failed both Indigenous Australians and white Australians who fight for change.

It has fallen to later generations, both First Australians and the descendants of their invaders, to reconstruct Aboriginal civilisation, destroyed so soon after white settlement. We know now of their houses, their terracing, their use of food storage, of fire and water, the grains and crops they grew and harvested, their methods of irrigation and pasture, their prodigious fishing skills. We know too of how they fought the British invaders – settlers, convicts and troops – using strategic military tactics of their own.

These findings too are contested by certain Australian historians, on the basis that Britain, being civilised and Christian, managed the dispossession of the continent's original inhabitants more humanely than other nations would have done, and that insistence on justice for Indigenous Australians damages white Australian identity. John Howard, Australian prime minister from 1996 to 2007, called fussing about such matters 'the Aboriginal industry'. Others call it the 'History Wars'. But acknowledgement of the crimes of the British Empire does not mean that its finest hours, its considerable achievements, its civilisation and its gifts to the world – and there are many of them – cannot be recognised too. Nor that Aboriginal civilisation was perfect – just that it *was* a civilisation, and a remarkable one at that. Not enticing to European or Christian civilisations, perhaps, but as worthy of respect as any other.

The German people of the mid-twentieth century were Christian and civilised too. The use of the word 'holocaust' cannot be limited to describe only the most murderous example of all: the worst actions of humanity continue to need the word. Raphael Lemkin, the Polish-Jewish lawyer who coined the word genocide, defined it as 'the crime of destroying a national, racial or religious group' and this can be an act or a process. The appropriation of the land of Australia's Indigenous people, and the destruction of their way of life was a process of genocide, wrought by an empire with a limited view of what civilisation means, which considered it a duty to bring its own culture to the rest of the world, and to be handsomely paid for so doing.

The British near-destruction of the Aboriginal inhabitants of Australia, as with their destruction of the original populations of other lands they invaded, is often excused as 'not an encounter of civilisations, but a collision between a cultured people and a primitive and unredeemable race'. This was not genocide in the Nazi sense, it was not the official intention of the British government to wipe the Indigenous inhabitants of the Australian continent from the face of the earth (though the devastation of the Palawa people in Tasmania could be seen in this way). But in another sense, by the taking of their land, it *was* genocidal: genocide by a process of making the victim invisible. The British soldiers and settlers did the rest. 'Ethnic cleansing' is the modern term. Whichever, denial follows either definition like an apostle.*

The policies of subsequent Australian governments had similar attributes. The White Australia Policy, which aimed to keep out Asians, and the Chinese in particular (though its net also caught many a Czech or Russian), seems ludicrous now. Australians of my generation spent our childhood and youth in the sun, gazing at it without sunglasses or sun cream, in an attempt to become as brown – or black – as possible, while our parents silently accepted the white status quo. The Stolen Generations – the many thousands of twentieth-century Aboriginal children who were taken from their families to be brought up by white parents, or in orphanages – are the victims of the most tragic and shameful of Australian interventions (though the fates of British children shipped to Australia from 1947 to the 1970s – echoing the fates of my English great-grandmothers – and only coming to light in distressing detail now, show that the abuse of the powerless is no respecter of skin colour). Denial of historical villainies is no way to bind a people; historical amnesia is corrosive – as England now knows.

----------------ᴔ----------------

* The full range of the massacres of the First People can be seen on this interactive map on the website of the University of Newcastle, Australia: https://czlch.newcastle.edu.au/colonialmassacres/map.php

To paraphrase the noted Australian poet Adam Lindsay Gordon, who in 1870 killed himself on a Melbourne beach very near where I was born and raised:

> Life is mostly froth and bubble
> *Some* things stand like stone.

These are my stones:

First, there is an almost immutable tradition in British (especially English) civil life of harshness towards its lower, working, less wealthy, less educated classes – the great majority of its subjects – alleviated occasionally by radical advances such as the welfare state, but fought against decade after decade, by those at the top of the British class pyramid. This tradition reveals a great deal about its perpetrators. The despatch from Britain of its criminal and lower classes to Australia included many crimes against its own people. The British treatment of the original inhabitants of that continent was genocide. The Anglo-Celts who became Australians continued the tradition until recent years: it remains an ongoing struggle.

Secondly, it is impossible to read of the experiences of the First People of what is now called Australia, or of the British and Irish convicts transported there from 1788 to 1860, without horror; this is particularly true for the savage early years.

Thirdly, as to the country they were sent to, in time and in turn those open gates closed round this new world, which had promised such good things to the flotsam and jetsam of the British Isles and so many other countries. My Australian education taught me nothing about Indigenous Australians, their culture, and what had been done to them by the British, and by the Australians who followed them.

Charles Dickens could never have imagined that the hopes and fantasies he nourished for Australia's British convicts and emigrants, sent to the 'large open-air prison' of early white Australia, could so forget their origins. Nor that a country of white men founded on the lash and the triangle could lead to the historical amnesia and prejudice that permits and permitted detention centres like Nauru Island, Manus Island, Christmas Island and others. Nor the national shame that in the twenty-first century the long road to justice walked by Indigenous Australians still stretches ahead. What is one to say to the Aboriginals whose land was invaded by the persons the British considered to be the dregs of their earth, whose masters and 'betters' thus gained access to the natural riches of a continent that did not belong to them? As it did not belong to them, why can it not belong to refugees, asylum seekers and boat people?

Lastly, despite all this, for many of the impoverished, the criminal, the destitute, the disenfranchised, the poor and despairing inhabitants of the British Isles, the appropriation of Australia turned out to be their Happy Day. For those such as Alfred Allen and John Brooks, born and raised during England's Industrial Revolution and its Hungry '40s, nothing much could help them, but their descendants stand in contrast to their abused fellows – the superfluous poor, the convict and the Aboriginal. Their story is the happy Australian story; the unhappy story remains.

Appendices

Family Trees

The Brooks and Allen Families

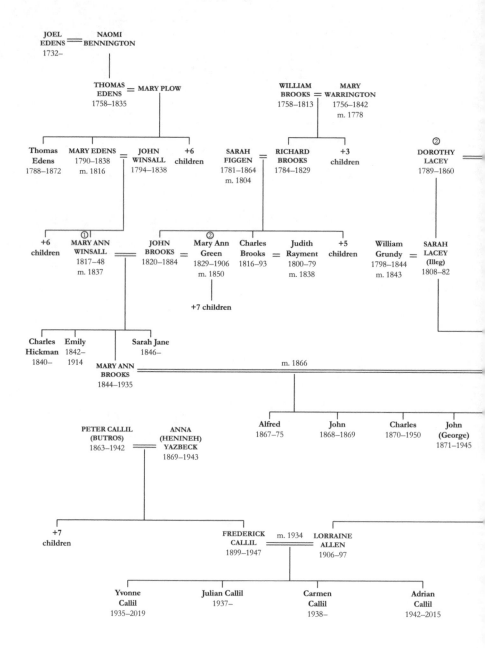

JOEL EDENS 1732– ═ NAOMI BENNINGTON

THOMAS EDENS 1758–1835 ═ MARY PLOW

WILLIAM BROOKS 1758–1813 ═ MARY WARRINGTON 1756–1842 m. 1778

Thomas Edens 1788–1872

MARY EDENS 1790–1838 m. 1816 ═ JOHN WINSALL 1794–1838

+6 children

SARAH FIGGEN 1781–1864 m. 1804 ═ RICHARD BROOKS 1784–1829

+3 children

② DOROTHY LACEY 1789–1860 ═

+6 children

① MARY ANN WINSALL 1817–48 m. 1837 ═ JOHN BROOKS 1820–1884 ═ Mary Ann Green 1829–1906 m. 1850 ②

Charles Brooks 1816–93 ═ Judith Rayment 1800–79 m. 1838

+5 children

William Grundy 1798–1844 m. 1843 ═ SARAH LACEY (Illeg) 1808–82

+7 children

Charles Hickman 1840–

Emily 1842– 1914

Sarah Jane 1846–

MARY ANN BROOKS 1844–1935

m. 1866

Alfred 1867–75

John 1868–1869

Charles 1870–1950

John (George) 1871–1945

PETER CALLIL (BUTROS) 1863–1942 ═ ANNA (HENINEH) YAZBECK 1869–1943

+7 children

FREDERICK CALLIL 1899–1947 m. 1934 LORRAINE ALLEN 1906–97

Yvonne Callil 1935–2019

Julian Callil 1937–

Carmen Callil 1938–

Adrian Callil 1942–2015

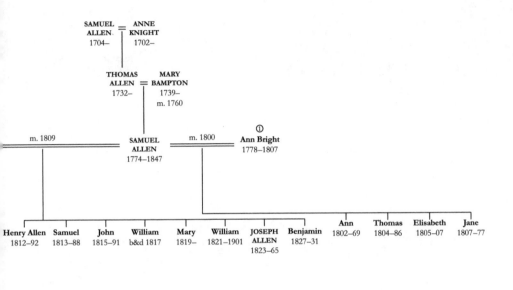

SAMUEL ALLEN 1704– ═ **ANNE KNIGHT** 1702–

THOMAS ALLEN 1732– ═ **MARY BAMPTON** 1739– m. 1760

m. 1809

SAMUEL ALLEN 1774–1847

m. 1800

① **Ann Bright** 1778–1807

| Henry Allen 1812–92 | Samuel 1813–88 | John 1815–91 | William b&d 1817 | Mary 1819– | William 1821–1901 | **JOSEPH ALLEN** 1823–65 | Benjamin 1827–31 | Ann 1802–69 | Thomas 1804–86 | Elisabeth 1805–07 | Jane 1807–77 |

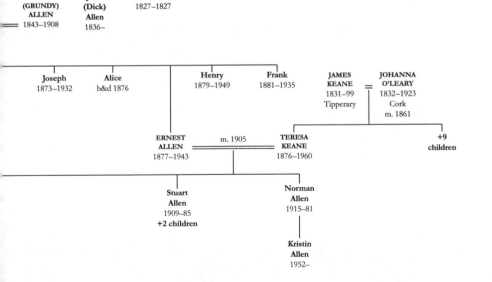

ALFRED (GRUNDY) ALLEN 1843–1908

John (Dick) Allen 1836–

Eliza Allen 1827–1827

| Joseph 1873–1932 | Alice b&d 1876 | | Henry 1879–1949 | Frank 1881–1935 | **JAMES KEANE** 1831–99 Tipperary | ═ | **JOHANNA O'LEARY** 1832–1923 Cork m. 1861 |

ERNEST ALLEN 1877–1943 ═ m. 1905 ═ **TERESA KEANE** 1876–1960

+9 children

Stuart Allen 1909–85 +2 children

Norman Allen 1915–81

Kristin Allen 1952–

The Brooks and Conquest Families

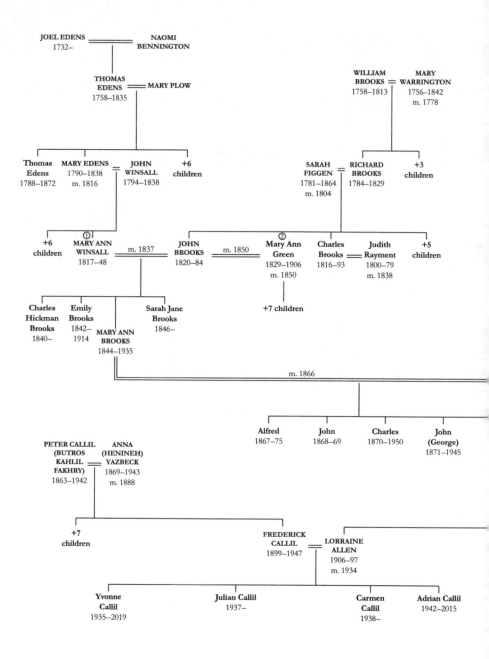

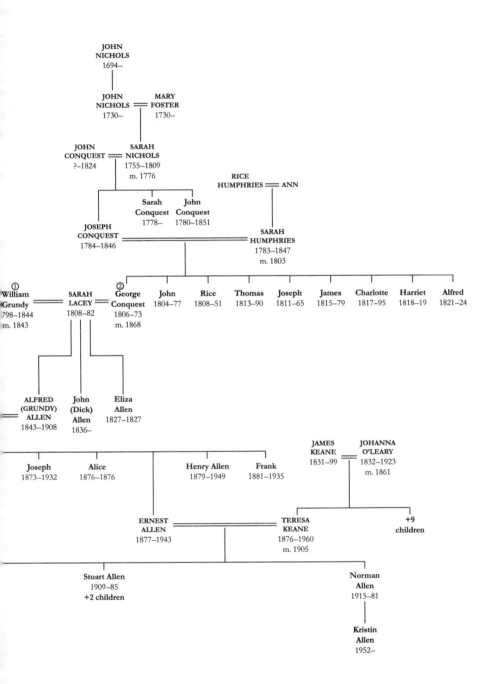

Acknowledgements

———————◀○▶———————

It is the natural state of the descendants of those who were despatched to Australia in the eighteenth and nineteenth centuries, or who finagled their way to *Terra Australis* under their own steam, to know nothing about their antecedents. These ancestors belonged to other countries, far away, and were mostly nothing to boast about. And anyway the full stomachs, reliable sun, blue skies, splendid animals, magnificent bush and sea of the new country made them forgetful of father- or motherlands – so burdened by ancient histories, entrenched habits of human classification and bad weather.

So my greatest debt is to my brother Julian, who first pointed out to me the strange collection of names on the tombstone of my great grandmother Mary Ann Allen. Who was Geoffrey Conquest? He did not exist, of course, but George did. Then, as time went on, our cousin Kristin Allen pounced upon the question, and, because she is younger, and so a mistress of the internet and the incredible resources it offers, it is she to whom this book owes the most. Her capacities were not limited to the mysteries of Australian library, archive and web records, but extended all over the world – no gravestone was left unturned in the Midlands, in Cork and Tipperary; no convict ship, newspaper or library record unexplored. This book could not have been written without the excellent stories my mother, Lorraine Allen, told me, the inaccurate family trees she left behind, or her reading aloud of Charles Dickens to her children during the Melbourne winters of my childhood. Nor could I have written it without the constant input from my friend Hilary McPhee, Australian publisher, writer and comrade-in-arms.

When I arrived in Britain in 1960, I knew nothing about this country, except for its literature. For this reason, the ideas in this book owe most to the men who gave me my first job in book publishing, John Boothe and William Miller, the editorial directors of Panther Books, part of the Granada Publishing Group, in the 1960s and early 70s, and to one of the authors they published, Angela Carter. Angie and I shared a fine rage. Rage is uncomfortable to live with, but it does give one an enquiring mind and an objecting spirit. She added genius and many other great qualities to this, and she was a born teacher. This book owes so much to her.

Angie. John and William. And Sonny Mehta, another member of the Granada stable at 3 Upper James Street, Golden Square, London W1, for whom I worked when he launched his paperback imprint Paladin in 1970. With his great friend, and mine, the writer and editor John Knowler, they were my real university: they taught me about the mysteries of England and English society. All of us, and many others, gathered every night at the John Snow pub around the corner, and talked endlessly about politics, class, justice, literature and life. They gave me the views and opinions I have today, and they would have been the first readers of this book. Not uncritical, but they would recognise what they taught me.

They are all dead – Sonny, too recently – and could not help me through the years when I researched and wrote this book. So many others did. I owe much to the meticulous research and delightful company of Henrietta Freeman-Attwood over many years. Before and after her, the research work of Lucille Andel, Peter Bennett, Tom Woolfenden, Rowana Mulholland and Virginia Wright was invaluable and I thank them all and most particularly Robert Lacey, who first honed my lengthy ms into tolerable shape with such patience and skill.

Research took me all over the East Midlands, and to many places in Australia. In Thurmaston I am particularly indebted to Jennifer Harris and to other members of the Thurmaston Heritage Group; to John Morrison, church warden, St John the Baptist Church, Hungarton; the Reverend Lorna Brabin-Smith, vicar of St Michael and All Angels, Rearsby; Peter Clowes, curator, Wigston Framework Knitters Museum; Richard Taylor, Welford Road Cemetery, Leicester; Robin Stevenson, Bishop Street Methodist Church, Leicester; Canon Barry Naylor, St Margaret's Church, Leicester; the Record Office for Leicestershire, Leicester and Rutland; Angela Scarsbrook of the Northamptonshire Family History Society; and the staff of Cheshire Archives and Local Studies. The mysteries of the English Canal system were often revealed through the kindness and assistance of various members of the Market Harborough Historical Society, most particularly Dr Len Holden, its secretary, but also Bob Hakewill, Pam Aucott and Mary Matts. I am also in debt to Mike Beech, curator of the Canal Museum at Foxton Locks, and to Richard Pickering of the Market Harborough Congregational Church.

Philippa Massey, former curator at the Stamford Museum, Tim Walker of Walker's Bookshop, Martin Smith, historian, and Stamford Library clarified much about the history of that city for me. Neil Wright's knowledge of the history of Boston was essential, and I am grateful to John Bird for information about Dolphin Lane, to Martin Potts for showing me around Boston Cemetery, to Kathy Lord of Scott House for showing me what was formerly the Boston Union Workhouse, and for the services of Boston Library, Boston Guildhall Museum, the Society for Lincolnshire History and Archaeology, Lincolnshire Family History Society and Fenland Family History Society.

I am indebted to Dan Byrnes and Jen Willetts for their remarkable websites and to Garth Hewitt for his CD of Chartists songs: *Liberty is Near*! For historical information about Bungonia I am grateful to Moira McGinity of the Bungonia and District Historical Society. My distant cousin Sheila Geary provided me with the photograph of my great-great-aunt Annie O'Leary, and the researches of my cousin Bernadette Keane into our Cork ancestors always set me, and my cousin Kristin, on the right path. My numerous Callil relations provided varied and colourful insights into the story of that family.

I could do, and could have done, nothing without my friends. In the twelve years it took me to write this book – years interrupted by attacks on my body by the usual diseases – listing the number of friends who helped me in one way or another would fell too many trees, and I hope I have not forgotten any of these human beings, the staffs of my life. Polly Devlin housed and fed me for many perfect writing weeks over the years, as did Gail Rebuck in France. Liz Calder and Louis Baum provided me with constant escapes to Suffolk, as did Julian Barnes to France. Without their company, and often too that of Rachel Cooke, Tony Quinn, Simon Hopkinson, Jancis Robinson, Nick Lander, Sophie and Stephen Browett, and Simone and James Herrick, I could not have survived.

No one should write a book without the regular company of Frances Stonor Saunders, an early reader, as were Diana Melly and Michèle Roberts; both were great encouragers and insisted that there was a world out there that might like to read it. Many others either read my work-in-progress, or continually entertained and supported me as the years rolled on: Hanan al Shaykh, Marie-Elsa Bragg, Anna Coote and Ian Gough, John Cox, Sue Crosland, Margaret Drabble and Michael Holroyd, Nell Dunn, Richard Evans, Peter Eyre, Jeff Fisher, Fiona Golfar and Robert Fox, Ian Jack and Lindy Sharpe, Sarah Jones, Kate Griffin and Christophe Egret, Georgina Hammick, Brian Jarman, Lotte Jarvis, Annalena McAfee and Ian McEwan, Virginia and Bill Nicholson, Polly Pattullo, Jessica Pulay and Victor Sebestyen, Marina Warner and Graeme Segal, Jane Wellesley, and Gus Skidelsky and the much loved members of our Cinema Club.

I owe the greatest debt to my agent Peter Straus of Rogers, Coleridge and White, and to all at that agency, in particular Gill Coleridge, who saw me through the book's early days, and my great friend Deborah Rogers, who was still alive when I began this book. A special thank you to my publisher Dan Franklin, my first reader at Cape, and to Rachel Cugnoni, and most of all to Bea Hemming, who could not be surpassed as an editor and comfort – such a calming and funny companion-in-words at all times. Thanks also to Daisy Watt, Emma Finnigan, Joe Pickering, the staff of Jonathan Cape and Vintage, in particular the brilliant Suzanne Dean who designed the cover. At home, Delfina de Freitas, Sophi Stewart, Hazel and Shannon Carey, and Effie, made my daily life possible.

What I learned over the years owes much to many historians and writers, chief among them Robert Hughes, whose classic and irreplaceable work, *The Fatal Shore*, reminded me of the terrible past of many of white Australia's citizens, about whose vicious treatment I used to weep when I studied their lives in the State Library of Victoria during my university years in Melbourne. The works of historians and writers are noted within the bibliography on page 317 but I would like to express a particular debt to some, most of them listed on that page, but some not: Alan Atkinson, James Boyce, David Cannadine, Inga Clendinnen, Linda Colley, John Docker, Roy Foster, Bill Gammage, Ian Gibson, Stan Grant, Robin Haines, Tony Judt, Coral

Lansbury, Alison Light, Stuart MacIntyre, Ned Newitt, Marilyn Palmer, Bruce Pascoe, Eric Richards, and Selina Todd.

Although I have learned so much from these and other historians, inevitably there will be errors in this story – for which I apologise, and, if found, will gratefully correct.

Carmen Callil, London, March 2020

Notes

<figure>◀○▶</figure>

CHAPTER I

4 **500,000–750,0000 people:** the figures vary, but this, I think, is the most recent assessment. Hughes, p. 9, says 300,000; others say the same.

4 **Heyer, 16 million population and social gradations:** Kloester, p. 3; the 16 million population figure includes Ireland.

5 **770 convicts:** estimates differ.

6 **The hoi polloi:** Chinnery, p. 6.

6 **in order to celebrate with his family:** Samuel had an aunt, Anne, and uncles Henry and John Bampton on his mother's side; and aunts Anne and Hanah on his father's side (plus a dead uncle, Samuel).

7 **'20000 poore people':** Chapman, p. 42, quoting Leicester Hall papers, fo. 245.

7 **'the indescribable sound of the stocking frame':** *Leicester Chronicle*, 25 June 1831; William Cobbett, *Rural Rides – Melton Mowbray to Leicester.*

8 **population of 9 million:** Hey, p. 120.

8 **increased by sixteen times:** Townsend.

9 **'I believe that some parts':** Park, p. 12.

9 **parish register records:** 'A List of all the inhabitants residing in the South End of Thurmaston in the County of Leicester, taken July 8th 1814', Record Office of Leicestershire.

10 **'Stay, Reader':** Nichols, p. 54.

11 **'crammed into basements':** Palmer, *Framework Knitting*, p. 23.

11 **Many families lived in just one room:** Royle, p. 55.

11 **No curtains:** for all this, and other information about Thurmaston, I am very grateful to Jennifer Harris of the Thurmaston Heritage Group.

11 **They carded the fibre:** Pinchbeck, p. 232.

11 **The child moved on to the frame at about nine years of age:** 'Mr Muggeridge's Report Upon the Condition of the Framework Knitters', *Leicester Chronicle*, 14 June 1845.

11 **By the age of twelve:** Hey, p. 157.

11 **'Mother will pin them':** Wardle, p. 55.

12 **It became more flexible:** Palmer, *Housing*, p. 71.

13 **'framework knitters':** Temple Patterson, *Radical Leicester*, pp. 277, 42.

13 **On Monday they walked back:** ibid., p. 48.

13 **They took on a variety of tasks:** British History Online, *A History of the County of Leicester*, Volume 4, pp. 303–14.

13 **'Stinting':** Royle, p. 54.

14 **Those on high:** British History Online, *A History of the County of Leicester*, Volume 4, pp. 303–14.

14 **William Smith:** *Leicester Chronicle*, 11 June 1842.

15 **'most expert poachers':** 'Mr Muggeridge's Report Upon the Condition of the Framework Knitters', *Leicester Chronicle*, 14 June 1845.

15 **As wages and the amount of available work fell:** Palmer, *Framework Knitting*. Much of the information in this chapter comes from this book and from the *Leicestershire Mercury*, 14 December 1844.

16 **Cut-ups were cheaper to manufacture:** much of the information in this section comes from Chapman, Chapter 3.

16 **'millionaires in both':** ibid., p. 87.

17 **The knitters fought constantly:** ibid., p. 111.

17 **Luddites:** Navickas, p. 284.

17 **men were hanged or transported:** Rudé, p. 124.

17 **Framework knitters' Declaration:** available on many websites.

19 **'circumstances of the most unparalleled distress':** available on many websites.

19 **'great rejoicings':** Navickas, p. 292.

19 **Slavery was finally abolished:** the Slavery Abolition Act of 1833 excluded the East India Company, Ceylon and St Helena. Slavery was abolished for them in 1843. The slave trade was abolished in 1807, but did not become illegal until the Slavery Abolition Act of 1833.

19 **To finagle the laws:** Temple Patterson, *Radical Leicester*, p. 108.

20 **Matters had worsened:** Chapman, pp. 94, 95, and Temple Patterson, *Radical Leicester*, pp. 104ff.

21 **'measures designed to meet this evil':** Henry Addington, 1st Viscount Sidmouth, Home Secretary, House of Lords, 30 November 1819.

CHAPTER 2

23 **Thurmaston . . . changed from an open rural hamlet:** Hey, p. 158.

24 **These might be thatched:** Hoskins, *Midland Peasant*, p. 274.

24 **Yards were often inches deep:** Wood, p. 19.

24 **Such cottages survived:** Jennifer Harris, Thurmaston Heritage Society, email and document sent to the author, December 2014.

24 **'three capital Messuages or Tenements':** *Leicester Journal*, 8 December 1815.

25 **By the time Sary left:** Hey, p. 159. In time, glove making was added to the repertoire; making hose led to the making of shoes and boots for suitably hosed feet, and this was the occupation of my great-grandfather Alfred.

26 **The marriage register of a Leicestershire village for the years 1837–50:** Levine.

26 **The thriving Wesleyan chapel:** Thurmaston Heritage Group, *Memories of Thurmaston Volume 1*, p. 28.

27 **'Relief is continually given':** *Leicester Chronicle*, 13 April 1833.

27 **Bett's Patent Brandy:** *Leicester Journal*, 28 September 1838.

27 **the Poor Rate:** Elliott, *Victorian Leicester*, p. 10.

28 **parish relief granted to households with four or more children:** Kidd, p. 15.

28 **'a pernicious effect':** *Leicestershire Mercury*, 12 August 1837.

28 **putting the unemployed and impoverished to useful work:** http://www.histo ryhome.co.uk/peel/poorlaw/plaa.htm; http://www.victorianweb.org.

28 **'reducing hills on roads':** *Leicester Chronicle*, 24 March 1827.

28 **county session at Leicester Castle:** ibid., 25 February and 28 April 1827.

29 **'The whole nine of us':** Muggeridge.

29 **'if these disturbances at Thurmaston':** *Leicester Chronicle*, 28 April 1827.

30 **One of many reasons offered:** Griffin, *A Short History of the Industrial Revolution*, pp. 36ff. 'The majority of the rising birth rate was caused by a drop in marriage age, the result of one section of the population marrying several years younger . . . the proportion of the population never marrying fell from 20 per cent to less than 10 per cent.' Improved fertility helped, perhaps improvements in wages enabled them to marry earlier, perhaps cottage industries helped . . . a hundred explanations are given.

30 **'Memorial' text and Privy Council's reply:** *Leicester Chronicle*, 7 April 1827.

31 **Nineteen were executed:** Wood, p. 78.

31 **Such activities were dangerous:** Rudé, p. 129.

32 **'I make no difference':** *Leicestershire Mercury*, 24 November 1838.

32 **'half work and full charges':** *Leicester Chronicle*, 26 May 1838.

32 **Sary's arrest in June 1833:** ibid., 29 June 1833.

32 **Leicester citizens transported:** Rudé, p. 129.

33 **'beyond the power of language to express':** Temple Patterson, *Radical Leicester*, p. 140, quoting the *Leicester Journal*, 20 January 1826.

33 **Adam Smith et al.:** Himmelfarb.

33 **Malthus believed:** Malthus. This is an inadequate summary of his propositions but a fair representation of what was current in parliamentary thought by the 1830s.

34 **'lie down like dogs':** Cobbett, 'The Poor man's friend'.

34 **forty per cent of the trade:** www.slaverysite.com, and many others.

34 **'the colonial church owned slaves and supported slavery':** Hirst, *Convict Society*, p. 23.

34 **46,0000 British slave owners:** review of BBC2 programme *Britain's Forgotten Slave Owners*, *Guardian*, 23 July 2015. Claimants included vicars, spinsters, many women – mostly widows – and the father of William Gladstone. Also Alan Frost, p. 82.

34 **'that curse and disgrace to humanity':** Leicestershire Town Council Meeting, reported in the *Leicester Chronicle*, 20 March 1841.

34 **'All relief whatever':** Kidd, p. 28, quoting S. G. and E. O. Checkland, *Poor Report of 1834*, p. 375.

36 **could not afford to damage their hands:** Royle, p. 55.

CHAPTER 3

37 **Leicester's population growth:** Haynes, p. 96, and Millward, p. 86.

38 **Nonconformist groups:** Moore, *Where Leicester Has Worshipped*.

38 **People's Charter, 1838:** the six demands, all of which had been advocated before, were: 1. a vote for all men over twenty-one; 2. a secret ballot; 3. electoral districts of equal size; 4. no property qualification to become an MP; 5. payment for MPs; and 6. annual elections for Parliament. Available on many websites, e.g. https://archive-shub.jisc.ac.uk/features/apr08.shtml.

38 **Leicester Anti-Persecution Union:** www.leicestersecularsociety.org.uk.

39 **Chartist petitions:** the first national petition of 1839 was signed by 1,280,958 people, making it the single biggest petition ever seen at that time. It was also notable for the number of women who signed – though the petition did not seek to give them the vote. The second national petition of 1842 was the largest of the Chartist petitions, with 3,315,752 names – an outstanding achievement considering that the adult population of England, Scotland and Wales was under 10 million. The third national petition of 1848 was the best known and most controversial, taken to Parliament on 10 April following the Chartist rally on Kennington Common. Famously Feargus O'Connor (at that time MP for Nottingham) told the House of Commons that the petition had 5.7 million signatures. Three days later, Mr Thornley for the Commons committee on public petitions responded that 'Upon the most careful examination . . . the number of signatures attached to the petition does not, in the opinion of the committee, exceed 1,975,496. (Hear.) It is further found, that a large number of the signatures were consecutively written in the same hand. It was also observed that a large number of the signatures were those of persons who could not be supposed to have concurred in its prayer; among those were the name of Her Majesty, signed Victoria Rex, the Duke of Wellington, Sir Robert Peel, &c., &c. There was also noticed a large number of names which were evidently fictitious, such as "Pugnose", "Longnose", "Flatnose", "Punch", "Snooks", "Fubbs", and also numerous obscene names, which the committee would not offend the house of its dignity by repeating but which evidently belonged to no human being'. (*Northern Star*, 15 April 1848). An outraged O'Connor replied that it would have been quite impossible for thirteen clerks to have counted even 1,900,0000 signatures in the time. He stood by his claim of 5.7 million names . . . Opponents of the Charter now joined the attack, the Earl of Arundel and Surrey maintaining that far from attracting 400,000 supporters, as O'Connor had claimed, the Kennington Common meeting had been attended by just 15,000. As further evidence of the petition's unreliability, it was claimed that 8,200 out of every 100,000 signatories were women.

39 **'borne on the shoulders':** https://www.tolpuddlemartyrs.org.uk/story/mounting-protest.

39 **Tolpuddle petition:** https://www.marx-memorial-library.org.uk.

40 **another year of depression set in:** Temple Patterson, *Radical Leicester*, 1825–6 and 1836 were depression years.

41 **'You have been living for centuries':** *Leicestershire Mercury*, 24 November 1838.

41 **'saw the rags and bones':** *The Victoria History of the Counties of England. A History of Leicestershire Volume* IV, xcvi.

41 **'the Shakespereans':** Roberts, p. 163.

42 **'Men of England':** Newitt (ed.), *Anthology*, p. 45; song by William S. Villers Sankey, published in the *Northern Star*, 29 February 1840.

42 **Walter Upton:** *Leicestershire Mercury,* 12 January 1839.

42 **'if he and his fellow-townsmen':** ibid., 9 February 1839.

43 **'I had to wait upon':** ibid., 29 June 1839.

43 **'a large arch-way', etc.:** *Leicester Journal,* 29 November 1839.

43 **'imprisonment presented no terror':** *Leicester Chronicle,* 11 June 1842.

44 **'suffering classes':** *Leicestershire Mercury,* 20 August 1842.

44 **'degradation, want, and misery':** *Leicester Chronicle,* 19 February 1842.

44 **'with labels round':** ibid., 20 March 1841.

44 **'Many persons':** ibid., 11 June 1842.

44 **the opening of a female lodge:** *Leicestershire Mercury,* 3 September 1842.

45 **marrying close relations:** Kuper, pp. 153, 178.

45 **'by inquiry in asylums':** Darwin, p. 175.

45 **'How can decency':** Haynes, quoting Joseph Dare, p. 43.

45 **'Young girls':** Kuper, quoting Beatrice Webb, *My Apprenticeship* (London, 1926), p. 275n.

46 **One of the first acts:** Millward, p. 110.

47 **'Being an old walled town':** Newitt (ed.), *Slums,* p. 33.

47 **The two-roomed tenements:** Elliott, *Victorian Leicester,* p. 110.

47 **'Out of 242 streets':** Newitt (ed.), *Slums,* quoting *Leicester Morning Chronicle,* 1841.

47 **Railways had supplanted canals:** Hadfield, p. 79. The Leicestershire and Swannington Railway opened in 1831.

47 **'perhaps the most unhealthy part of the town':** Newitt (ed.), *Slums,* p. 33.

48 **Under the new Poor Law:** Heydon; Haynes, p. 40; Cynthia Brown, p. 55.

48 **no women were appointed until 1875:** Anna Clark, p. 402.

48 **the city's streets were dotted:** Heydon.

48 **It was worse in the narrow streets:** Newitt (ed.), *Slums,* p. 33; Elliott, *Victorian Leicester,* p. 58.

49 **Though slum dwellers trudged:** Edwin Chadwick's 1842 *Report into the Sanitary Conditions of the Labouring Population of Great Britain* pinpointed drainage and the necessity of fresh piped water. Nothing was done. Royal Commissions were set up in 1844 and 1845, but not until the Nuisances Removal Act of 1846 did anything crawl forward. In due course Robert Peel's Public Health Act of 1848 established a Central Board of Health – the beginning, but only the beginning, of the way we live now.

49 **odour of tripe boiling:** Newitt (ed.), *Slums,* p. 9.

49 **'For foul and offensive':** Elliott, 'John Buck'.

49 **1844 was another year of great hunger:** Elliott, *Victorian Leicester,* p. 93.

50 **the life expectancy of the average stockinger:** Elliott, *Victorian Leicester*; Newitt (ed.), *Slums*; Temple Patterson, *Radical Leicester*; Palmer, *Framework Knitting*; Newitt (ed.), *Anthology,* p. iv; *Leicester Chronicle,* 3 August 1844. For the upper class, life expectancy was sixty-eight years and eight months.

50 **'the cotton berlins':** *Leicestershire Mercury,* 31 May 1845, quoting Muggeridge.

50 **'defenceless poverty':** Palmer, *Framework Knitting,* p. 15, quoting.

50 **'all that was needed':** Chapman, p. 112.

50 **'were less a lumpen proletariat':** ibid., p. 114.

51 **It is most unlikely that she could have afforded:** Steedman, *An Everyday Life*, p. 245.

51 **Others had built rows of houses:** Townsend, p. 304.

51 **more than a third of the old frames:** Millward, p. 93.

51 **by 1847 competent hosiers:** Chapman, p. 119.

51 **The 1847 Factory Act:** *Leicester Chronicle*, 12 June 1847.

51 **'Those pest-holes':** Simmons, 'A Victorian Social Worker', p. 73.

52 **Leicester Fancy Rabbit Club:** *Leicester Chronicle*, 12 March 1853.

52 **Penny dreadfuls:** Haynes, p. 68.

52 **'nothing else but a meeting place':** Elliott, *Victorian Leicester*, p. 90.

52 **gambling, betting, music:** Haynes, p. 63; Temple Patterson, *Radical Leicester*, p. 377.

52 **'Wright's wild beast-show':** *Leicestershire Mercury*, 15 October 1842.

52 **'scarcity of money':** ibid.

52 **sold everything from rabbits to concertinas:** Haynes, p. 74, and Cynthia Brown, p. 76.

53 **Wharf Street rang throughout the night:** King.

53 **'mothers addicted to drunkenness':** Haynes, p. 26.

53 **'blessed promises', etc.:** ibid., p. 36.

53 **'What filthy little wretches':** Tom Barclay, *Memoirs and Medleys: The Autobiography of A Bottle Washer* (1934), in Newitt (ed.), *Slums*, p. 76.

54 **Ladies' Working Society:** Haynes, p. 25.

54 **clothes could be had from the slop-shops:** Pinchbeck, p. 312.

54 **'We principally live on taters':** *Leicester Journal*, 17 January 1845.

55 **assaulting her in the street:** *Leicester Chronicle*, 7 November 1846.

55 **Thomas would come home drunk:** information in letter to author from Jennifer Harris, 19 January 2015.

55 **'the industrious poor':** Elliott, *Victorian Leicester*, p. 82.

56 **the city's imposing jail:** Kane.

56 **'depravity and licentiousness':** *Leicester Chronicle*, 16 January 1847.

57 **Baptists, Congregationalists, Bible societies, Methodists:** Moore.

57 **'be erased from the list of members':** Cynthia Brown, p. 70.

57 **a Methodist mission hall:** ibid., p. 95.

57 **little schooling was possible:** ibid., p. 96. By 1867 only fifty per cent of Leicester's children aged between six and fourteen were receiving an education.

57 **church, chapel and charities evangelised:** Muggeridge, and Ruddington Framework Knitters Resources, https://www.frameworkknittersmuseum.org.uk: pack.

57 **'many of the poor little things':** Haynes, p. 17

57 **'writing and summing' class:** ibid., p. 27.

58 **Advertisements offering a better life abroad:** ibid., pp 14–23.

CHAPTER 4

62 **as many as 2,000 beasts in the town:** Anderson.

62 **hounds met regularly:** *Leicester Journal*, 7 December 1810.

63 **tammies and shalloons:** Davies, *Bowden to Harborough*, p. 121.

63 'fancy hosiery . . . cotton and worsted': *Harborough Historian*, No. 29.

63 Clarke's Worsted and Carpet manufactory: *Leicester Chronicle*, 22 November 1828.

63 Mail wagons, curricles and stagecoaches: Day, 'Coaching Days'.

64 Turnpiked roads came to Harborough: Simmons, 'Public Transport', p. 109.

64 'The Honour of Waiting upon the Nobility': *Harborough Historian*, No. 17.

64 stocks, a whipping post: stocks were last used in England in 1872; the demise of the whipping post is hard to date because whipping continued for so long in Britain and its colonies – the final whipping of men in British prisons took place in 1948.

65 There were markets for much besides sheep: Davies, *Bowden to Harborough*, p. 42.

65 Animals of every kind: Davies, *Georgian Harborough*, pp. 28ff.

65 'King's Head-yard': *Leicester Journal*, 2 February 1849.

66 epidemics were almost constant: Gräf, p. 107.

66 'boasted two bathrooms': Kloester, p. 26.

66 a population of 1,801: Davies, *Georgian Harborough*, p 58.

66 'the Necessary House': ibid.

66 Independent preachers had been hard at work: Davies and Brown.

66 Independents in Harborough: Harrod, p. 26.

67 'in most of the dissenting houses': Davies and Brown, p. 69.

67 jailed for 'preaching the gospel': Market Harborough Congregational Chapel, p. A2.

68 many other small private schools: Davies, *Bowden to Harborough*, p. 128.

68 the labouring classes were otherwise occupied: Anderson.

68 Independent Sunday school: Davies, *Bowden to Harborough*.

69 'not distinguished by grasp of mind': Bogue and Bennett, p. 141.

69 Leicestershire . . . profited most: Gräf, p. 102.

70 2,600 miles of canals by 1815: Alan Frost, p. 21.

70 'a restless, rootless turbulent set of ruffians': Temple Patterson, 'The Making of the Leicestershire Canals'.

70 'wrote topical verses': ibid., p. 77.

70 So great was the fervour: ibid., p. 83.

71 'pleasantly complicated': Hadfield, p. 79.

71 'barge and two boats decorated with flags': Hadfield, p. 79.

71 'the centre of extensive navigable lines': Hadfield, p. 81, quoting the *Leicester Journal*. The Grand Union connected the new canal from Market Harborough through the Leicestershire and Northamptonshire Union Canal, to Leicester Navigation, which took them up through Leicester, where it joined Soar Navigation and well beyond. Such connections included one of the earliest canals, The Trent and Mersey, for which the great potter, Josiah Wedgwood, cut the first sod.

72 'with a hilarity': *Leicester Journal*, 1 August 1817.

72 the great- or great-great-granddaughter: the generations appertaining to the Nichols have to be guesswork. That she was his descendant is certainly true, but by how many generations I have been unable to discover.

72 their Nichols and dissenter neighbours: Davies, *Georgian Harborough*, p. 167.

72 We, the undersigned: *Northampton Mercury*, 15 July 1820.

73 'most substantial inhabitants', etc.: Davies, *Georgian Harborough*, p. 132.

74 his company forayed out only twice: Harrod.

74 the British volunteers melted away: Colley.

74 lump sum of £4 or £5: Davies, *Georgian Harborough*, p. 130.

75 'Joseph Conquest, for stealing a quantity of malt': *Leicester Journal*, 10 August 1811.

76 'the poor unhappy wretches': Davies, *Georgian* Harborough, pp. 104–5, quoting Harrod.

76 jails were known as dens of iniquity: Johnston, p. 89.

76 Bells, music, flags, and a band: *Northampton Mercury*, 18 June 1815, and *Harborough Historian*, No. 24.

77 'The work, which was sometimes undertaken by family groups or gangs': Samuel, pp. 30–1.

79 no more than seven feet wide: Freer.

79 flyboats: Hanson, p. 50.

79 The language of the canals: ibid., p. 12.

79 Lock and toll keepers were at constant war: ibid., p. 26.

80 'I spent my time': ibid., p. 63, n. 61.

80 'drunkenness, dishonesty, violence, immorality': Hanson, p. 47ff.

80 spent most of it on alcohol: Freer, p. 6.

80 'knocked violently at his door', etc.: *Leicester Chronicle*, 19 April 1828.

81 By 1832, Market Harborough had grown: *Harborough Historian*, No. 24.

81 one drinking den for every twenty families: Johnston, p. 17.

81 living in one such dwelling and working as a brickmaker: Boston Rating Book, 1834 (information from Len Holden, Market Harborough Historical Society).

82 Joseph was out just in time for Christmas: *Leicester Journal*, 7 November 1834.

82 'for they had *insulted*', etc.: ibid., 20 May 1836.

82 less the cost of a horse: Hanson, p. 59.

82 'Margaret Bryan, 24', etc.: *Leicestershire Mercury*, 1 July 1837.

CHAPTER 5

85 Buckled shoes, waistcoats, etc.: Davies, *Georgian Harborough*, p. 57.

86 food, drink and services: Davies and Brown, p. 81.

86 'DWELLING-HOUSE': *Northampton Chronicle*, 26 April 1845.

87 near 6,000 souls: Tebbutt, p. 10.

89 Some thirty stagecoaches: Philippa Massey, former curator of Stamford Museum: meeting in November 2011.

89 Bull-running, etc.: Tebbutt, p. 2, and many other books on Stamford.

89 decided by the Cecils' minions: Wright, *Lincolnshire Towns*, p. 13.

90 There, in view of the church spires: Smith, *Stamford Then and Now*, pp. 13, 81.

91 Cholera was rampant: author's research in Stamford, 2011.

91 'worthy of the rank': *Stamford Mercury*, 18 February 1820.

91 'a new version': ibid., 9 July 1830.

92 'I see before me': ibid., 30 July 1830.

93 'to all persons renting any property': ibid., 24 September 1830.

93 'My heart is with you': ibid., 15 September 1837.

93 'the most unfair and tyrannous means', etc.: ibid., 4 November 1836.

94 'whatever changes had taken place': ibid., 15 January 1836.

95 'Longcase painted dial clock': Wilbourn and Ellis, p. 24.

95 'the increasing demand for artificial teeth': *Mechanics Magazine*, 26 January 1839.

95 'a boy the age of twelve years': *Mechanics Magazine*, 26 January 1839.

95 More populous than Stamford: Boston population figures vary. A little over 12,000 after the Reform Act seems correct: twice the size of Stamford.

97 'venting their fury': Bagley, p. 204.

98 Reformers took over the corporation, etc.: Wright, *Boston. A Pictorial History*, pp. 108ff.

98 Queen Victoria's marriage to Prince Albert: *Stamford Mercury*, 17 April 1840 and 14 February 1840.

98 In Boston it presented its numerous forms: Wright, *Lincolnshire Towns*, p. 107.

98 Good Friday tea festivals well attended, etc.: *Stamford Mercury*, 28 March 1845, and Gurnham, p. 173.

98 fifty per cent of women: Olney, p. 83.

99 'BOTHAMLEY, Watch and Clockmaker': *Stamford Mercury*, 3 April 1838.

99 Liquorpond Street: Wright, *Boston. A Pictorial History*, illustration no. 119.

99 The street was newly paved, etc.: Bagley, p. 231.

100 the featherbed factory: ibid., p. 229.

101 'great distress in the town': *Stamford Mercury*, 28 April 1845.

101 The very cold weather, etc., and 'most seasonable relief': ibid., 26 April 1850 and 7 February 1845.

101 The very worst years of this decade: Olney, p. 86.

102 'New and Second hand Watches': ibid., 10 December 1847.

102 'insidious poison': ibid., 20 March 1840.

CHAPTER 6

103 'The *Catalogue of Offences*': *Leicestershire Mercury*, 5 January 1839.

105 'much ill-feeling has for a considerable time existed': *Leicester Chronicle*, 15 January 1842.

105 Mary's was bread and gruel, etc.: Horrell et al., p. 88.

105 'a pauper named Conquest', etc.: *Leicester Chronicle*, 15 January 1842.

106 'after leaving the dining room on that day', etc.: *Leicestershire Mercury* and *Leicester Chronicle*, 22 January 1842.

108 'one of the most heartless and wicked acts of sacrilege': *Leicester Journal*, 26 May 1843, *Leicestershire Mercury* 30 March 1850, and most other Leicestershire papers.

108 Harborough Bank failed, etc.: *Harborough Historian*, No. 29.

109 the riots of 1838: ibid., No. 24.

109 Thomas Cook moved to Leicester: Holden and Chambers, p. 87.

109 There were severe floods: *Leicestershire Mercury*, 18 July 1828.

111 'The following persons': *Leicester Journal*, 7 November 1834.
111 'The practices and litigation': Kidd, p. 174. See also Pinchbeck, pp. 81ff; Steed-man, *An Everyday Life*, p. 180.
111 overseer letter: Quoted by King, p. 254, Leicestershire Record Office, DE/1587/154/24, 25 February 1823.
112 the usual weekly maintenance of a shilling: Paley, p. 23.
112 'TRANSPORTED 7 YEARS': Cheshire Archives and Local Studies QJB 4/5, p. 619.
113 Over 16,000 subjects: www.thepotteries.org/focus/001.htm.
113 'The Quarter Sessions terminated yesterday', etc.: *Chester Courant*, 1 May 1829.
114 List of those tried with George Conquest: *Chester Chronicle and North Wales Advertiser*, 1 May 1829. Its editorial on these matters: 'The experience of all ages tends to shew, that the mere fear of detection and punishment is not, alone, suffi-cient to deter persons from the commission of crime. There must be better and higher motives; and we are persuaded that until a change can be wrought in the morals and habits of the peasantry of this country, all other means employed for the diminution of crime will prove nugatory, and will only swell the number of prisoners for trial at each session and assizes' (continues on to moan about the cost, not the plight of the peasantry).
117 Criminal trials in the nineteenth century: Alan Frost, p. 44.
118 'Crime was thought to be caused': Johnston, p. 11.
118 'To be removed, with all convenient Speed': Cheshire Archives and Local Stud-ies Ref QAB5/2/55-177 Part 2, 1822–1929.
119 'my long hair underwent the operation': Hughes, p. 139, n. 25. This pseudonym-ous actor was sentenced in 1839, and sent to Norfolk Island for fifteen years. It is unlikely that George's treatment, ten years earlier, would have been any different.

CHAPTER 7

121 'The end of all punishment': http://www.jenwilletts.com/scourgers.htm.
123 'transportation to any', etc.: Branch-Johnson, p. 3.
124 they studded the ports and dockyards of Kent, Hampshire and Devon: Chatham, Sheerness, Portsmouth, Gosport, Devonport, Plymouth. Hawkings, *Bound for Australia*, p. 61.
124 spent seven months on this hulk: National Archives, H08/22, 'Quarterly return of Hulks, December 1829, f152. "Ganymede" and "Dasher" Hulks, Woolwich. Geo. Conquest, age 22, conviction: stealing hemp, tried at Chester 27 April 1829, 7 years. Remarks: NSW 9 Dec. H011/7 Transportation Register "Nithsdale" 184 to NSW 26 December 1829'.
124 Sometimes the hulks were towed to the north shore: Campbell, p. 2.
124 'workshops, warehouses': https://www.maritimeheritage.org.
125 'fetters on each leg', etc.: Branch-Johnson, p. 4.
125 'the villains were dragged': Rigden, p. 8.
125 £32 per convict: ibid., p. 3.

125 **many of whom congregated around Blackheath and its golf club:** Byrnes. The Blackheath Golf Club makes no mention of its notorious connection to the slave trade on its website today.

126 **'at night, these men were fastened':** www.victorianlondon.org/publications5/prisons-08.htm.

126 **'a man whose one remembered comment':** Campbell, p. 57.

126 **'any fever or other disorder':** Branch-Johnson, p. 10.

126 **The diet for their prisoners:** Campbell, p. 23; Byrnes; Branch-Johnson, p. 16.

126 **'first the steward took his cut':** Hughes, p. 141.

126 **one prisoner in three died:** Rigden, p. 9.

126 **'A foul odour', etc.:** Branch-Johnson, p. 14.

127 **Aaron Graham:** Campbell, p. 82. Graham was Inspector of the Hulks from 1802 to 1815.

127 **'floating dungeons':** *Memoirs of James Hardy Vaux*, 1819, https://en.wikisource.org/wiki/Memoirs_of_James_Hardy_Vaux.

127 **Even the insane were flogged:** Rigden, p. 10.

128 **ravaged by scurvy, etc.:** ibid., p. 9.

128 **the earlier death rate of one in three had gradually ameliorated:** ibid.

128 **'robbery of the dead':** Branch-Johnson, p. 181.

128 **'Resurrection Men':** Rigden, p. 18.

128 **Bones, still encased in their irons:** ibid.

128 **nearly 5,000 men incarcerated:** Branch-Johnson, p. 89.

128 **'In the hospital ship':** Lee Jackson, *The Dictionary of Victorian London*, www.victorianlondon.org.

128 **John Henry Capper:** Campbell, p. 111.

128 **Robert Capper:** Branch-Johnson, p. 95.

129 **Bentham insisted that homosexual rape:** Campbell, p. 83.

129 **one of 350 men:** Branch-Johnson, p. 120.

129 **slops all too rarely replaced:** ibid., p. 116.

129 **'loading and unloading vessels':** ibid., p. 99.

130 **many the bribes paid:** Hughes, p. 140.

130 **'a disastrous year for labourers':** Dr Marjorie Bloy, 'A Web of English History: Rural Unrest in the 1830s', http://www.historyhome.co.uk.

131 *Household Words* **was often banned:** ibid.

132 **'repeat once a month' and 'two hundred and eighty':** Branch-Johnson, pp. 125ff.

132 **'evinced a becoming fortitude':** ibid., p. 135.

132 **A blind eye:** Campbell, p. 103.

132 **Parliamentary inquiries were launched:** ibid.

132 **'all sorts of iniquity', etc.:** Branch-Johnson, pp. 120, 117.

133 **'a lantern, supposed to be left burning':** ibid., p. 121.

133 **500 of the 3,000 convicts:** Campbell, p. 125.

133 **'Bodily State':** National Archives, H08/20.

133 **one in fourteen:** Campbell, pp. 218–19.

134 **'In 1841, the gross number of convicts':** Mayhew and Binny.

CHAPTER 8

136 **Indigenous Australians:** Clendinnen, p. 4. The British called them 'natives' or 'indians'; Clendinnen calls them Australians. White Australians were not so called until much later; in the early days they were Britishers.

137 **rise in population:** Hughes, p. 25.

138 **'perishing classes':** Mary Carpenter, 1851, quoted in Johnston, p. 12.

138 **increased in number more than sixfold:** Rudé, p. 14.

138 **Over 200 crimes were punishable by death:** Hirst, *Convict Society*, p. 9.

139 **'epic migrations':** Noel Pearson, quoted in the *New Statesman*, 14 January 2018.

139 **White Australia policy:** the WAP began in the 1850s when miners on the goldfields, who came from all corners of the earth, objected to the Chinese who came to do the same, and Queenslanders objected to Pacific Islanders who came to work the sugar plantations. It was a trade union and/or Brexit point of view: these migrants provided low-wage labour. Restrictions muddled on throughout the nineteenth century, but in 1901, when the separate states in Australia federated to form a nation, the Immigration Restriction Act of 1901 used circumlocutory language and conditions to prohibit all non-Europeans from settling in Australia. One of these conditions included a dictation test in which the migrant had to 'write out at dictation and sign in the presence of the officer a passage of fifty words in length in a European language directed by the officer'. The border immigration officer could choose any European language for this test, thus a Chinese applicant would be offered a text in Hungarian, and so forth. Immigration Restriction Act 1901, https://www.legislation.gov.au/Details/C1901A00017.

140 **'Black Caesar', etc.:** Frost and Maxwell-Stewart, pp. 33, 132.

140 **'The vineyard . . . ':** Dunbabin, p. 52.

140 **'A Sample of Protesters':** based on Rudé, pp. 9–10.

141 **those in charge of hulks, prisons and workhouses:** Frost, p. 83.

142 **'effectually disposing of convicts':** http://nzetc.victoria.ac.nz/tm/scholarly/tei-McNo1Hist-t1-b3-d5.html.

143 **'the serpent we are nursing at Botany Bay':** Francis Baring, principal of the East India Company, quoted in Byrnes.

143 **'deeply Christian outlook':** Alan Frost, pp. 56–7.

143 **'chilled to the bone':** Hughes, p. 145.

146 **'springtime of trust':** Clendinnen, p. 287.

146 **'amity and kindness':** Hughes, p. 273, quoting George III's instructions to Phillip.

147 **'I went with a party':** Tench, *A Narrative*, p. 41.

148 **gifts of smallpox, typhus:** Tom Griffiths, p. 36, and Atkinson, *Volume 1*, p. 92. The smallpox epidemic was in 1789.

148 **Treadmills later provided:** Atkinson, *Volume 1*, p. 97.

148 **Camden, Calvert & King:** Hughes, p. 145, and Byrnes.

149 **'were slung over the side':** eyewitness account by the chaplain of the First Fleet, the Rev. Richard Johnson: 'I beheld a sight truly shocking to the feelings of humanity, a great number of them laying, some half, others nearly quite naked, without either bed or bedding, unable to turn or help themselves. Spoke to them as I passed

along, but the smell was so offensive that I could scarcely bear it . . . The landing of these people was truly affecting and shocking; great numbers were not able to walk, nor to move hand or foot; such were slung over the ship side in the same manner as they would a cask, a box, or anything of that nature. Upon their being brought up to the open air some fainted, some died upon deck, and others in the boat before they reached the shore. When come on shore many were not able to walk, to stand, or stir themselves in the least, hence some were led by others. Some creeped upon their hands and knees, and some were carried upon the backs of others.' Quoted at: https://dictionaryofsydney.org/entry/second_fleet.

149 'so emaciated, so worn', etc.: Bateson, p. 138, quoting Governor Phillip.

149 the government in London now took note: McDonald and Shlomowitz, pp. 287ff.

149 'a convict found guilty': Clendinnen, p. 188.

149 'modified form of slavery': Hughes, p. 108.

150 seventy-eight such individuals: Atkinson, *Volume 1*, p. 77.

150 This land was free of rents and taxes: Hirst, *Convict Society*, pp. 80ff.

151 As these successful men rose in status: Atkinson, 'The Political Life of James Macarthur', pp. 134–9, 158, and 'The Parliament in the Jerusalem Warehouse', pp. 75–104.

151 'an unplanned straggle of shacks': Hughes, pp. 296ff.

152 'sink of iniquity': Atkinson, *Volume 1*, p. 291.

152 'a man of great physical presence': Atkinson, *Volume 2*, p. 32.

153 The flogging of women ceased in 1817: ibid., p. 196.

153 Macquarie lowered magistrates' sentencing power to a hundred lashes: Hirst, *Convict Society*, p. 111.

156 convicts lived under a British system of law: an alternative view is presented in Hirst, *Convict Society*, p. 109: 'The magistrates had a general interest in maintaining convict discipline, but they were superior men both in wealth and education and so were free from any personal ties or obligations to the middling and smaller masters.'

156 5,000 men who arrived in New South Wales: Johnston, p. 8.

156 the *Nithsdale* sailed from Sheerness on Friday 1 January: Rudé, p. 158, 'Most English ships sailed from Portsmouth and Spithead; but others – including Irish Fenians and three of the four "Canadian" ships – sailed from London, while Irish ships sailed nearly all from Cork – or more properly, from the Bay of Cobh – until 1837 and switched to Dublin between 1838 and 1852.' Willetts gives 1 January from Sheerness, then to Deal and leaving 3 January. Many different dates are given for the departure of this ship.

156 typhus and dysentery caused the most deaths: McDonald and Shlomowitz, p. 286.

157 Four women were on board, etc.: Willetts. Much of the information about the *Nithsdale* comes from Willetts' invaluable website.

157 warmer clothes for winter: Rudé, p. 159.

157 'and (when in irons)', etc.: Hughes, pp. 54, 133.

157 The *Nithsdale* sailed by the direct route: information about the voyages of all convict vessels is incomplete (see McDonald and Shlomowitz), but as there was so little trouble on the *Nithsdale*, I am assuming it took the route which enabled stops such as

Cape Town, and that in doing so, the convicts were somewhat occupied below, when not suffering from dysentery and so forth, with the goods obtained in these ports.

157 **'Two rows of sleeping-berths'**: Bateson, p. 69, quoting Peter Cunningham, naval surgeon.

158 **the ship's steward sued the captain**: Willetts.

158 **By 1830 50,000 people lived there**: Eric Irvin, 'Tag-Rag and Bob-Tail', *Push from the Bush*, No. 2, November 1978, pp. 50–1.

158 **'In 1828, the *Sydney Gazette* announced'**: Atkinson, *Volume 2*, p. 64.

158 **flying jewellery in the skies**: as described by Angela Carter.

158 **'I have seen young children practising'**: Harris, p. 24.

159 **two were gibbeted**: in England, gibbeting (also known as 'hanging in chains') peaked in the 1740s, and was officially mandated by the 1752 Murder Act, which required bodies of convicted murderers to be either publicly dissected or gibbeted. Between 1752 and 1832, 134 men were hung in chains. It was formally abolished in 1834.

159 **'Coal, which makes it very valuable'**: *Maitland Mercury and Hunter River General Advertiser*, 16 August 1851.

160 **'1834, October: Governor Stirling'**: https://australianmuseum.net.au.

160 **Newcastle had ceased to be a secondary penal colony, etc.**: Barker, p. 20.

161 **many convicts were shipped to the Hunter Valley**: Hirst, *Sense & Nonsense*, p. 31.

161 **'they were too fond of drink'**: ibid., p. 99.

161 **'The lash had to do the work'**: ibid., p. 69.

161 **'the plain fact is that the majority of eighteenth-century convicts'**: Alan Frost, p. 54. Also see Hirst, *Convict Society and Its Enemies: A History of New South Wales*, pp. 28ff.

162 **'conspiring to raise wages'**: Rudé, p. 181.

162 **Those assigned with George from the *Nithsdale***: Willetts.

CHAPTER 9

165 **regularly sent reports of military abuse**: Atkinson, *Volume 2*, p. 55.

165 **'The breaking point came'**: Hirst, *Convict Society*, pp. 29ff. Chapter 2, 'Masters & Servants', is an exquisite example of Australian revisionist history, revealing much about its writer and little about the experience of convicts – and others of the time.

166 **many descriptions of the horror of the first flogging**: Atkinson, *Volume 2*, p. 155.

167 **'Death or liberty!'**: ibid., p. 116.

167 **The Ribbon Gang**: www.barossa-region.org/Australia_2/Bathurst-s-bushrangers---Ribbon-Gang.html.

167 **'Whenever the British were behaving despotically'**: Niall Ferguson, quoted in Parish, p. 124.

169 **David and Agnes Reid**: Carroll.

169 **George working for Dr David Reid**: this is not certain, but highly probable.

169 **'tyranny of the worst kind exercised to the full'**: Ogier, p. 3.

170 **'one of the old magistrates'**: quoted in Harris, p. 247.

170 'most extraordinary' results: Carroll, and Ogier.

170 'sometimes had as many as forty assigned servants': Cullen and Cullen, Chapter 4.

170 'With the help of four convicts': Carroll.

170 The homestead was built from rock quarried on the property, etc.: Cullen and Cullen, Chapter 4.

171 'There were at times up to forty': Carroll.

171 'blacksmiths, carpenters, shoemakers': Ogier, p. 3.

171 'bed made from straw and ticking', etc.: Joseph Mason, in Kent and Townsend (eds), p. 44.

172 'one light suit': Leitch, p. 85.

172 'slaves make the most tyrannical masters': Ogier, p. 6.

172 The murderers were hanged and gibbeted at Goulburn: ibid., p. 7.

172 He saw captured bushrangers brought to Dr Reid, etc.: ibid.

173 'The masters hereabout': quoted in Harris, p. 298.

173 In George's time Inverary had a school, etc.: for the historical information about Bungonia I am grateful to Moira McGinity of the Bungonia and District Historical Society.

175 'Thousands of letters were written': Frost and Maxwell-Stewart, p. 3.

175 he could leave Inverary and return to England: return from transportation ceased to be a capital offence in 1834; see Johnston, p. 62.

176 'To families there are some very serious drawbacks': Nicholas and Nicholas, pp. 104–5.

178 Macquarie's and Campbell's letters: Hawkings, *Bound for Australia*, pp. 144–8.

CHAPTER 10

181 British imperial legacy: for the 'glorious empire' school of British history, read Niall Ferguson, Lawrence James and Andrew Roberts, for example.

183 In 1835, the colony's convict population of 27,000: Hirst, *Convict Society*, p. 58.

183 piano wire was used in Jamaica in 1865: Gibson, p. 169.

183 Although flogging was abolished in France in the nineteenth century, etc.: ibid., p. 166.

184 'Flagellomania, while almost totally absent in France': quoted in ibid., pp. x, 45.

184 In English prisons this continued until the 1960s: ibid., p. 167.

184 'In 1878 alone': ibid., p. 154.

184 'chaplains, judges': William Dalrymple, *Sydney Morning Herald*, 31 May 2003.

185 '100 lashes': quoted in Hughes, p. 480.

186 'declined to join him at Newcastle': Willetts.

186 'The convict flagellator at this time': www.pogues.com/forum/viewtopic. php?f=38&t=8312.

186 1,500-lashes-before-breakfast punishment: Atkinson, *Volume 2*, p. 115.

186 'a total of 268,013 lashes': V. G. Kiernan, review of Robert Hughes's *The Fatal Shore*, *London Review of Books*, Vol. 9, No. 6, 19 March 1987.

186 'RETURN of Corporal Punishments': Willetts.

CHAPTER II

194 **they made a deep mark on Australian life':** Atkinson, *Volume 2*, p. 309.

194 **A thousand men and women assembled:** Temple Patterson, *Radical Leicester*, p. 357.

194 **Bands of men paraded:** Lott, p. 46.

195 **For three days, the inhabitants of Leicester's Wharf Street:** Temple Patterson, *Radical Leicester*, p. 361.

196 **'sculleries, kitchens, dining rooms':** *Leicester Chronicle*, 27 March 1847.

196 **'with vast numbers of men, women and children engaged at it':** Samuel, p. 36.

196 **'dreadful places, underground kitchens':** British History Online, *The City of Leicester: Footwear Manufacture*, quoting from *2nd Report Children's Commission 1842*, footnotes 61, 62.

196 **like the keeping of an infant school:** ibid., footnote 71.

198 **'induced the savages to put their marks':** Sidney, p. 87.

198 **'Eighty per cent of the Indigenous population of Port Phillip had been killed':** Malcolm Turnbull, review of James Boyce's *1835: The Founding of Melbourne & the Conquest of Australia*, the *Monthly*, July 2011.

199 **At that time there were 1,000 white settlers there, and 26,000 sheep, etc.:** James Boyce in conversation with Peter Moses, Melbourne Writers Festival, August 2011, YouTube

199 **'once sold to a single buyer 7,000 wallaby skins':** Atkinson, *Volume 2*, p. 123.

199 **'brickmakers earned 8s a day':** Sidney, p. 89.

200 **exporting wool to the value of £1 million annually:** Serle, p. 2.

200 **'a superb bushman':** John Butler Cooper, *History of Malvern*, p. 2.

200 **'four hundred cows and heifers':** Ogier, p. 20.

200 **'for the unoccupied lands of Port Phillip District':** Carroll.

200 **'savages':** Ogier, p. 23.

200 **'five hundred head of cattle':** ibid., p. 21.

200 **his name seems to appear, misspelled:** ibid., p. 68.

201 **'an amount of excessive skill':** ibid., p. 24.

202 **'wretched in the extreme':** Carter, *Botany Bay*, p. 215, n. 35, quoting John Cotton (*c*.1801–49), *The Correspondence of John Cotton, Victorian Pioneer, 1842–1849 in three parts*, ed. George Mackaness (Dubbo, NSW: Review Publications, 1978), p. 22.

202 **As one of the 6,000 ex-convicts, etc.:** Serle, p. 3, and Annear, p. 47.

202 **'bank till free to all':** http://www.fomad.org.au/history-overview.html.

202 **'were paid from a hundred':** Ogier, p. 67.

202 **'cradle, picks, shovels, tin-dishes':** ibid., p. 48.

203 **'Where formerly was silence':** Sidney, p. 155.

203 **'All along the route from Melbourne to Mt Alexander':** Hanson, p. 53, n. 61.

203 **'The golden quartz lying in this soil':** Sidney, p. 165.

203 **it had a white population of nearly 80,000, etc.:** Serle, p. 2.

204 **By 1861 half a million people lived in the state:** https://en.wikipedia.org/wiki/History_of_Victoria.

206 **received 1.6 million immigrants:** Richards (ed.), *Visible Immigrants: Two*, pp. 2ff, and Haines, Kleinig et al., p. 235.

206 **'every Australian consumed £7 worth'**: Broeze, p. 239.

206 **Assisted migration began in 1831:** Richards (ed.), *Visible Immigrants: Two*, p. 5.

207 **Parochial officers made arrangements for the emigration:** Richards, 'How Did Poor People Emigrate', p. 266.

207 **'imperatives of Australian migration called into life':** Richards (ed.), *Visible Immigrants: Two*, p. 1.

207 **Ireland's 'popish serfs':** Huntsman, p. 811, quoting Patrick O'Farrell, *The Irish in Australia* (Sydney, NSW: University of New South Wales Press, 1987), p. 71.

208 **'money in the colony, on behalf of a nominated friend or relative':** Haines, *Emigration and the Labouring Poor*, p. 274.

208 **'revolved about the question of evacuating the poor':** Richards (ed.), *Visible Immigrants: Two*, p. 3.

209 **Letters followed him as he moved from New South Wales:** the January letter would have been written by September 1841 at the latest, and the April 1842 letter by 1 January at the latest. *Australasian Chronicle*, 22 January and 14 April 1842; *Government Gazette*, 14 January and 12 April 1842.

209 **average earnings on the goldfields was about £40:** Serle, p. 24.

210 **'Serge frock, half-boots, cabbage-tree hat':** Atkinson, *Volume 2*, p. 322, n. 51.

211 **'One storekeeper nailed to his counter':** Serle, p. 82, quoting n. 43.

211 **thirty shillings a month:** Atkinson, *Volume 2*, p. 330.

213 **'Lost, or stolen, from the person of Mr George Conquest':** *Victoria Police Gazette*, 24 May 1854.

213 **'known generally as "Big" Clarke':** *Australian Dictionary of Biography*.

214 **five years later, he appeared in court as a character witness:** the *Argus*, Melbourne, 19 November 1859 – 'George Conquest, a carter in Prahran, said that he had known the prisoner for some time, and gave an account of his honesty in returning a pocket-book containing a sum of money when the witness had left it behind.'

215 **'Any hand worth his salt':** Hanson, p. 60.

215 **no more than a ten-hour working day for women:** Pinchbeck, p. 90.

215 **This domestic frame-work knitting continued:** Haynes, p. 61 and footnotes.

215 **factories were beginning to overshadow the dismal passages:** Cynthia Brown, and Millward, p. 95.

215 **'found one poor old widow', etc.:** Haynes, p. 43.

216 **Temperance Hall:** Moore, p. 4.

216 **'I have found too little bed-clothing':** Haynes, p. 42.

216 **'Excursion trains' etc.:** ibid., pp. 63ff.

217 **'caused by the privy':** *Leicester Chronicle*, 12 March 53.

CHAPTER 12

219 **Great Northern Railway had moved their headquarters:** Gurnham, p. 200.

219 **'Clocks cleaned in the country at the shortest notice':** *Stamford Mercury*, 10 December 1847.

219 **'There was not a labourer's house'**: Berridge, p. 294, quoting L. M. Springall, *Labouring Life in Norfolk Villages* (London, 1936), p. 59.

219 **'was in frequent use, and was taken as a remedy for ague'**: Berridge, p. 296, quoting Charles Lucas, *The Fenman's World. Memories of a Fenland Physician* (London, 1930), p. 52.

220 **Many of its victims ended up in county asylums**: Berridge, pp. 307–8.

221 **'large numbers of waterfowl'**: 'Prahran Character and Conservation Study 1992', https://www.stonnington.vic.gov.au/. Also see Tibbits.

221 **'an Aboriginal reserve'**: Tibbits, *History of the Development of Prahran*, p. 4.

221 **'the intermixture by marriage'**: Stonnington's Indigenous history, p. 14, https://www.stonnington.vic.gov.au/.

221 **'were also squatters and had to pay'**: Tibbits, *History of the Development of Prahran*, p. 6.

221 **'the resort of a drunken, bloodthirsty, thieving crew'**: Finn, p. 544.

222 **'unsurpassed ventilation, style and elegance'**: *Liverpool Mercury*, 4 and 20 May 1855.

222 **journeys of three months each**: sailing packets of the White Star Line averaged between eighty-four and ninety-three days. See Ullwood and Putnis. *Merlin* arrived in Melbourne 20 August 1855 (*Liverpool Mercury*, 17 November 1855).

223 **'the numerous small, dark and dirty streets'**: a Polish refugee quoted in Temple Patterson, *Radical Leicester*, p. 367.

223 **Wages had fallen, etc.**: *Leicester Chronicle*, 12 March and 7 May 1853.

223 **rising prices**: Simmons, 'Victorian Social Worker', p. 69.

223 **'one of the most trying and difficult'**: quoted in Haynes, p. 31.

224 **Adults and children were begging on the streets**: ibid., pp 30–1.

224 **Thomas Cook's soup kitchen**: Simmons, 'Mid-Victorian Leicester', p. 28.

224 **life expectancy hovered around forty**: Griffin, *A Short History of the British Industrial Revolution*, p. 159.

224 **The renting of frames was not forbidden, etc.**: Royle, p. 58.

225 **the annual wage of many a labourer**: Haines, *Emigration and the Labouring Poor*, p. 14.

225 **with the financial assistance of former convicts**: Richards (ed.), *Visible Immigrants: Two*, p. 9.

225 **'great Colonial Empire'**: *Emigration, its necessity and Advantages* (1840), https://collections.museumvictoria.com.au/items/245458.

225 **'Gold and Where to Get It'**: *Leicester Chronicle*, 5 September 1857.

226 **'My dear mother . . . '**: ibid., 23 December 1857.

226 **'Those who choose to take employment'**: ibid.

226 **'let the people of England be assured'**: ibid.

226 **'applications for government passages to Australia'**: *Liverpool Chronicle*, 8 November 1856.

227 **'The London *Daily News*, writing on the necessity'**: *Goulburn Herald & County of Argyle Advertiser*, 23 October 1852.

227 **Framework knitters, employed or otherwise**: Gothard, *Blue China*, p. 63.

227 **'Widows with no children under sixteen'**: ibid., p. 22.

227 **For a government-assisted passage, application forms, etc.:** Richards, 'How Did Poor People Emigrate', p. 263.

227 **'The commissioners supply Provisions':** Haines, *Emigration and the Labouring Poor*, p. 26.

229 **a common racket being the stealing of emigrants' luggage:** Maritime Archives & Library, National Museums Liverpool, Information Sheet 64, 'Liverpool and Emigration in the nineteenth & twentieth centuries'.

229 **'superior accommodations for all classes of passengers':** *Leicester Journal*, 5 March 1858.

229 **'unequalled by any other ship afloat':** *Liverpool Mercury*, 26 February 1858.

230 **'The wind Blew and the Sails tore':** William John Adams, quoted in Charlwood, p. 355, n. 15.

231 **These terrors had been slightly ameliorated by the strict regulations:** Haines, *Life and Death in the Age of Sail*, p. 28.

231 **'a tragi-comedy of deception':** Richards (ed.), *Visible Immigrants: Two*, p. 16.

231 **enabling him to travel at half the cost of an adult:** Charlwood, p. 112.

232 **'who was born to be happy':** quoted in Hartley, pp. 243–5. *An Appeal to Fallen Women* is available at http://dickens.jp/etexts/dickens/others/sonota/fallen.

233 **'I give you a brief account':** *Leicester Chronicle*, 20 March 1858.

234 **'A pound of gold':** John Butler Cooper, *History of Prahran*, p. 99.

234 **'gentleman resident':** *Prahran Telegraph*, 9 September 1873.

CHAPTER 13

236 **forty-four of the former and ninety of the latter:** Gurnham, p. 220.

237 **occupied a quarter of the county:** Olney, p. 22.

237 **'The female staff was headed':** ibid., p. 32 (1851 census).

237 **'As for dissenters':** quoted in ibid., p. 39.

237 **'that scaffold supporting life':** Light, *Mrs Woolf*, p. 4.

238 **'out-of-work servants were among the droves of women':** Light, *Common People*, p. 144.

238 **'How to provide for our multiplying population?':** *Leicester Chronicle*, 26 August 1853.

238 **'Much of the evil':** *Lincolnshire Chronicle*, 9 May 1862.

239 **'Humble, pious and respectable working-class women':** Family & Colonialism Research Network, www.colonialfamilies.wordpress.com.

240 **'colonial governments ordered batches of women from Britain':** Gothard, 'Compromise with Conscience', p. 39, quoting Maria Rye.

240 **many emigrants had already left Lincolnshire by the 1860s:** Olney, p. 170.

240 **328,651 men in the state, and only 211,671 women:** *Louth and North Lincolnshire Advertiser*, 12 July 1862.

241 **'The climate of Victoria is most genial':** quoted in Carment, Wilson and James, p. 16.

242 **'Everybody knows that Great Britain is the very fatherland':** Gore.

242 'grant free passages to other than single women': *Hertfordshire Guardian, Agricultural Journal and General Advertiser,* 26 December 1863.

242 they had to be properly distressed women: *Grantham Journal,* 21 January 1865.

243 'which sailed from Southampton Wednesday for Melbourne': *Hampshire Advertiser,* 19 December 1863.

243 'I have selected them from the ranks': *Maitland Mercury and Hunter River General Advertiser,* 20 August 1863.

244 'those means of employment and instruction': quoted in Gothard, *Blue China,* p. 93.

244 'careful spatial segregation': ibid., pp. 109ff.

244 'A child died at 8 o.c.': Thomas Small journal, 1863, quoted in Charlwood, p. 189.

244 'Single women occasionally complained against matrons': Gothard, *Blue China,* p. 143.

245 'including age, native place and county': Haines, *Emigration and the Labouring Poor,* p. 301.

246 'ABSCONDED, about ten days since': *Stamford Mercury,* 15 July 1864.

247 'Many never take their beer': report by Dr Henry Julian Hunter, 1863, quoted in Berridge, p. 297.

248 'The wards are for the most part dark': Higginbotham, p. 134, Preston Workhouse 1866, quoting Mr R. B. Cane, a workhouse inspector.

248 roast beef, plum pudding and ale for the Christmas of 1861: Bagley, p. 281.

249 'This bloody old hole is lousy': Higginbotham, p. 40.

249 'emigrants in good health': *Louth and North Lincolnshire Advertiser,* 13 July 1861.

CHAPTER 14

251 'It was the pastor, the Rev. William Moss': John Butler Cooper, *History of Prahran,* pp. 42–3.

252 'At the time of the gold discoveries': John Butler Cooper, *History of Malvern,* p. 94.

254 'Joseph Conquest and Thomas Conquest, both of Prahran, brickmakers': *Victorian Government Gazette,* No. 71, 23 June 1865.

255 women, however, were not allowed into public bars: Malone, *Early Prahran,* p. 7.

255 the Mechanics Institute presented lectures: www.prov.vic.gov.au/provenance/no5/PrahranTechPrint.

257 'Shops for renting were plain and square': Malone, *Chapel Street,* p. 17.

258 There were concerts, bazaars, fetes and fairs: Malone, *Early Prahran,* p. 20.

258 'another old resident of this town, George Conquest': *Prahran Telegraph,* 9 September 1873. None of them had much idea as to how old they were. George was not seventy, but Sary thought he was, and the gravestones of many others bear little relation to their birth records. In addition St Kilda General Cemetery lists George as 'Geoffrey' Conquest, which made him rather hard to track down.

259 'I told him they ought to be red underneath': Deposition of Alfred Allen, Coroner's Inquest, St. Kilda, Public Record Office Victoria, file 1875/407.

259 'became all queer after the death of Alice': according to my mother.

259 **covered in full and grim detail by Melbourne and state newspapers:** *Argus*, 28 April 1875.

260 **'hovered stubbornly between forty and forty-one':** Griffin, *A Short History of the Industrial Revolution*, p. 48.

260 **'SPIRITUALISM – Mrs Allen holds Séance':** *The Age*, 23 April 1898.

261 **'CHARLES BROOKS – Come or send address':** ibid., 14 July 1888.

261 **'Mary Ann Allen, of 78 Union-street, Windsor':** ibid., 8 July 1903.

262 **'inclined to intemperance', etc.:** 1907–8 documents from Yarra Bend Asylum for the Insane (1848–1928), https://prov.vic.gov.au.

264 **'uncoffined remains':** https://roaringwaterjournal.com/tag/abbeystrewry-graveyard.

265 **Irish agricultural depression 1859–64:** Donnelly.

268 **'was a glory of autumn leaves', etc.:** *Melbourne Punch*, 5 May 1905.

270 **the mountain's silk industry:** Karpat, p. 178.

275 **'Police are probing whether a fire':** *The Age*, 30 May 2015.

EPILOGUE

278 **in recent years Australian historians have taken the narratives:** Robert Hughes and Manning Clark are the two Australian historians whom revisionists object to most strenuously. There are many more. (The revisionists and/or objectors include: Michael Sturma, John Hirst, Alan Frost, Geoffrey Blainey, Keith Windschuttle, Portia Robinson, Marian Aveling, John Carroll and Alastair Davidson.) George Conquest did not see the horrific brutality of the secondary penal settlements. But he saw and experienced horrific things, and what he saw, Hughes wrote about accurately, and is available to all to read in archives, memoirs, letters, books, libraries, online. These revisionist historians forcefully attack a historical narrative that reports transportation, convict life and its punishments and the terrible condition of men and women who suffered from inequality and poverty in Britain as a British act of injustice, cruelty and repression. They are prone to disregard the chronic fear of its large population of impoverished subjects that Britain's governing classes felt and acted upon. They put forth the view that the despatch of so many of its subjects created 'a land of opportunity and redemption' for the generally lower-class convicts sent there, men and women who were a low class of person in general. George Conquest could be considered one of these and stealing hemp a criminal activity worthy of hulk, convict ship, and a seven-year sentence on the other side of the world. The British world that victimised him in England continued on in the treatment of convicts and aboriginals in Australia. And of its British poor – notably its single women – shipped out all over the world in the second half of the nineteenth century. This approach is extended, by some of these historians, to denial of the widespread murder of Indigenous Australians, and some revisionists' views that nothing ill happened to the Aboriginals have in recent years reached David Irving proportions. See, for example, the work of Keith Windschuttle.

My view is that any narratives of transportation and convict life must take into account what they tell us about the people, the country, and the governments that sent them to the penal colony; that any account of the British Empire should include proper examination of its involvement in the slave trade, its massacres, its land appropriation, to name only some of the evils of British imperialism. These facts, as well as imperial grandeur and achievements, need to be part of the national curriculum, part of the national story. The tragic effects of empire on those it conquered and invaded should be contemplated, studied, and accepted, side by side with its glories, as part of British – perhaps mostly English – history. Misunderstanding – not being honestly taught – its own history damages English society.

278 **speaking many hundreds of languages:** Hughes, p. 9 says about 500; Hirst, *Sense & Nonsense*, says 500 or 600.

279 **We know too of how they fought the British invaders:** two key books are Pascoe, and Gammage.

279 **'black armband' view and 'History Wars':** Hirst, *Sense & Nonsense*, p. 81; Griffiths, p. 134; Atkinson, *Volume 1*, p. xxiii.

279 **Raphael Lemkin:** I am indebted here to the work of Raphael Lemkin and Professor John Docker. The key point for Lemkin and others is that the Holocaust was an *act* of genocide, but that of, say, the destruction of the Aboriginal way of life was a *process* of genocide. Lemkin stated: 'It can be an act and a process.' The act of genocide carried out on over six million Jewish human beings is what makes their terrible deaths so exceptionally – is there a stronger word? – unbearable.

280 **'not an encounter of civilisations':** Griffiths, p. 109.

280 **The Stolen Generations:** from 1905 to 1969/70 government agencies and Church missions removed 'half-caste' children of Indigenous Australian and Torres Strait Islander descent from their families. These children were put into care, adopted, instructed to forget their language and culture, and often abused. Well documented on the web, yet contested by Australia's revisionist historians, their stories are harrowing to read. Some 20,000–50,000 children are estimated to have been involved.

280 **'Life is mostly froth and bubble':** the original lines by Adam Lindsay Gordon (1833–70) read: 'Life is mostly froth and bubble, / Two things stand like stone. / Kindness in another's trouble, / Courage in your own.'

281 **'large open-air prison':** Lansbury, 'Terra Australis Dickensia', p. 14.

Bibliography

◄o►

Books

Annear, Robyn: *Bearbrass. Imagining Early Melbourne*. Melbourne: Black Inc., 2014

Aspinall, A. and Smith, E. Anthony (eds): *English Historical Documents, XI, 1783–1832*. New York: Oxford University Press, 1959

Atkinson, Alan: *The Europeans in Australia. A History. Volume 1*. Melbourne: Oxford University Press, 1997

Atkinson, Alan: *The Europeans in Australia. A History. Volume 2*. Sydney: New South Wales Publishing, University of New South Wales Press Ltd, 2016

Atkinson, Alan: *The Europeans in Australia. A History. Volume 3*. Sydney: New South Wales Publishing, University of New South Wales Press Ltd, 2014

Bagley, Geo. S.: *Boston. Its Story & People*. Boston: Richaprint, in association with the History of Boston Project, 1986

Barker, Theo: *A Pictorial History of Bathurst*. Bathurst: Robert Brown & Associates (Aust.) Pty Ltd, 1985

Barker, Theo: *A History of Bathurst*. Goolwa: Crawford House Press, 1992

Bateson, Charles: *The Convict Ships 1787–1868*. Glasgow: Brown, Son & Ferguson Ltd, 1985

Batrouney, Andrew and Batrouney, Trevor: *The Lebanese in Australia*. Blackburn, Melbourne: Australasian Educa Press Pty Ltd, 1985

Blanning, T. C. W. (ed.): *The Nineteenth Century. Europe 1789–1914*. Oxford: Oxford University Press, 2000

Bogue, David and Bennett, James: *History of Dissenters, from the Revolution in 1688, to the Year 1808, Vol. 4*. London: Printed for the Authors, 1812

Boyce, James: *1835: The Founding of Melbourne & the Conquest of Australia*. Melbourne: Black Inc., 2013

Branch-Johnson, W: *The English Prison Hulks*. London: Christopher Johnson, 1957

Briggs, Asa: *Victorian Cities*. London: Penguin, 1990

Briggs, Asa (ed.): *Chartist Studies*. London: Macmillan & Co. Ltd, 1959

Brown, Cynthia: *Wharf Street Revisited. A History of the Wharf Street Area of Leicester*. Leicester: Leicester City Council Living History Unit, 1995

Butt, Stephen: *Leicester at Work. People and Industries Through the Years*. Stroud: Amberley Publishing, 2018

Butt, Stephen: *Secret Leicester*. Stroud: Amberley Publishing, 2013

Campbell, Charles: *The Intolerable Hulks. British Shipboard Confinement 1776–1857*. Arizona: Fenestra Books, 2001

Cannadine, David: *Victorious Century. The United Kingdom, 1800–1906*. London: Allen Lane, 2017

Carment, David; Wilson Helen J. and James, Barbara: *Territorian. The Life and Work of John George Knight*. Darwin: Historical Society of the Northern Territory, 1993

Carter, Paul: *The Road to Botany Bay*. London: Faber & Faber, 1987

Carter, Paul: *Living in a New Country. History, Travelling and Language*. London: Faber & Faber, 1992

Cazamian, Louis: *The Social Novel in England 1830–1850*. London: Routledge & Kegan Paul, 1973

Charlwood, Don: *The Long Farewell. The perilous voyage of settlers under sail in the great migrations to Australia*. Melbourne: Penguin Books Australia, 1983

Chapman, Stanley: *Hosiery and Knitwear. Four Centuries of Small-Scale Industry in Britain c. 1589–2000*. Oxford: Oxford University Press, 2002

Chilton, Lisa: *Agents of Empire. British Female Emigration to Canada and Australia, 1860s–1930*. Toronto: University of Toronto Press, 2007

Chinnery, Allen: *The Church of St John the Baptist, Hungarton*. Wymondham: Sycamore Press, 1983

Clark, Manning: *History of Australia*, abridged by Michael John Cathcart. London: Chatto & Windus, 1993

Clendinnen, Inga: *Dancing with Strangers. The True History of the Meeting of the British First Fleet and the Aboriginal Australians, 1788*. Edinburgh: Canongate, 2005

Cobbett, William: *The Poor man's friend; or, A defence of the rights of those who do the work and fight the battles*. London: Printed by W. Cobbett, 1826; Cambridge: Cambridge University Press, 1882

Colley, Linda: *Britons. Forging the Nations 1707–1837*. London: Pimlico, 1994

Cooper, John Butler: *The History of Malvern. From its First Settlement to a City*. Melbourne: The Speciality Press, 1935. Available on the City of Stonnington website, http://www.stonnington.vic.gov.au/Discover/History/History-of-Stonnington/Local-history-publications

Cooper, John Butler: *The History of Prahran from its First Settlement to a City*. Melbourne: Modern Printing Co. Pty. Ltd. 1911, revised 1924, reprinted 1935. Available on the City of Stonnington website, http://www.stonnington.vic.gov.au/Discover/History/History-of-Stonnington/Local-history-publications

Cooper, Thomas: *The Life of Thomas Cooper,* 1872. Leicester: Leicester University Press, The Victorian Library, 1971

Cullen, Jill and Cullen, Vaughan: *Australian Van Trip*. USA: Xlibris, 2014, ebook

Curzon, Brian J. and Hurley, Paul: *Middlewich*. Images of England Series. Stroud: Tempus Publishing Ltd, 2005

Davies, J. C.: *Bowden to Harborough. The Story of the Town of Market Harborough and its Two Villages, Great Bowden and Little Bowden*. Market Harborough: Wellanside (Photographics) Ltd, 1964

Davies, J. C.: *Georgian Harborough*. Market Harborough: Wellandside (Photographics) Ltd, 1969

Davies, J. C. and Brown, Michael C.: *The Book of Market Harborough*. Buckingham: Barracuda Books Ltd, 1984

Davison, Graeme: *The Rise and Fall of Marvellous Melbourne*. Melbourne: Melbourne University Press, 2004

Davison, Graeme, Dunstan, David and McConville, Chris: *The Outcasts of Melbourne. Essays in Social History.* Sydney: Allen & Unwin, 1985

Derry, John (ed.): *Cobbett's England. A Selection from the Writings of William Cobbett.* London: Parkgate Books Ltd, 1997

Dickens, Charles: *Charles Dickens' Australia. Selected Essays from Household Words 1850–1858. Book One: Convict Stories. Book Two: Immigration. Book Four: Mining and Gold.* Researched and presented by Margaret Mendelawitz. Sydney: Sydney University Press, 2011

Dickens, Charles: *David Copperfield.* 1849–50

Dickens, Charles: *Hard Times – For These Times.* 1854

Drabble, Margaret: *For Queen and Country: Britain in the Victorian Age.* London: Andre Deutsch, 1978

Dunbabin, Thomas: *The Making of Australasia. A Brief History of the Origins and Development of the British Dominions in the South Pacific.* London: A & C. Black Ltd, 1922

Eidelson, Meyer: *The Melbourne Dreaming. A Guide to the Aboriginal Places of Melbourne.* Canberra: Aboriginal Studies Press, 1997

Elliott, Malcolm: *Victorian Leicester.* Stroud: Amberley Publishing, 2010

Finn, Edmund: *'Garryowen': The Chronicles of Early Melbourne, 1835 to 1852: Historical Anecdotal and Personal.* 2 vols. Melbourne: Fergusson & Mitchell, 1888

Frost, Alan: *Botany Bay. The Real Story.* Melbourne: Black Inc., 2012

Frost, Lucy and Maxwell-Stewart, Hamish: *Chain Letters. Narrating Convict Lives.* Melbourne: Melbourne University Press, 2001

Fullerton, Susannah: *Brief Encounters. Literary Travellers in Australia 1836–1939.* Sydney: Picador, 2009

Gammage, Bill: *The Biggest Estate on Earth. How Aborigines Made Australia.* Sydney: Allen & Unwin, 2012

Gibson, Ian: *The English Vice. Beating, Sex and Shame in Victorian England and After.* London: Duckworth, 1978

Gothard, Jan: *Blue China. Single Female Emigration to Colonial Australia.* Melbourne: Melbourne University Press, 2001

Grant, Stan: *Talking To My Country.* Melbourne: Scribe, 2016

Griffin, Emma: *A Short History of the British Industrial Revolution.* Basingstoke: Palgrave Macmillan, 2010

Griffin, Emma: *Liberty's Dawn. A People's History of the Industrial Revolution.* New Haven and London: Yale University Press, 2013

Griffiths, Tom: *The Art of Time Travel. Historians and their Craft.* Melbourne: Black Inc., 2016

Gurnham, Richard: *The Story of Boston.* Stroud: The History Press, 2014

Hadfield, Charles: *The Canals of the East Midlands.* Newton Abbot: David & Charles, 1966

Haines, Robin: *Emigration and the Labouring Poor. Australian Recruitment in Britain and Ireland 1831–60.* Basingstoke: Macmillan Press Ltd, 1997

Haines, Robin: *Life and Death in the Age of Sail. The Passage to Australia.* Greenwich: The National Maritime Museum, 2006

Hanson, Harry: *The Canal Boatman 1760–1914.* Manchester: Manchester University Press, 1975

Harris, A.: *Settlers and Convicts. Recollections of Sixteen years Labour in the Australian Backwoods by An Emigrant Mechanic.* London: C. Cox, 1847

Harrod, William: *The History of Market Harborough. In Leicestershire, and its Vicinity, 1808.* Whitefish, Montana: Kessinger Legacy Reprints.

Hartley, Jenny: *Charles Dickens and the House of the Fallen Women.* London: Methuen, 2008

Hawkings, David T.: *Pauper Ancestors. A Guide to the Records created by the Poor Laws in England and Wales.* Stroud: The History Press, 2011

Hawkings, David T.: *Bound for Australia. A Guide to the Records of Transported Convicts and early Settlers.* Stroud: The History Press, 2012

Haynes, Barry: *Working-Class Life in Victorian Leicester. The Joseph Dare Reports.* Leicester: Leicestershire Libraries and Information Service, 1991

Hey, David: *Family History & Local History in England.* Harlow: Longman Group UK Ltd, 1989

Higginbotham, Peter: *Voices from the Workhouse.* Stroud: The History Press, 2012

Higgs, Micheline: *Tracing Your Servant Ancestors. A Guide for Family Historians.* Barnsley: Pen & Sword Books, 2012

Hirst, John B.: *Convict Society and Its Enemies: A History of Early New South Wales.* Sydney: George Allen & Unwin, 1983

Hirst, John B.: *Sense & Nonsense in Australian History.* Melbourne: Black Inc. Agenda, 2009

Hodge, Jane Aiken: *The Private World of Georgette Heyer.* London: The Bodley Head, 1984

Holden, Len and Chambers, L.: *Market Harborough. Landscapes and Legends.* Donaghadee: Cottage Publications, 2008

Hoskins, W. G.: *The Midland Peasant. The Economic and Social History of a Leicestershire Village.* London: Macmillan & Co. Ltd, 1965

Hughes, Robert: *The Fatal Shore. A History of the Transportation of Convicts to Australia 1787–1868.* London: Collins Harvill, 1987

Hunt, Tristram: *Ten Cities that Made an Empire.* London: Penguin, 2014

Jenkins, Robin and Ryan, James: *Leicestershire Past & Present.* Stroud: The History Press, 2012

Johnston, Helen: *Crime in England 1815–1880. Experiencing the criminal justice system.* Abingdon: Routledge, 2105

Jupp, James (ed.): *The Australian People. An Encyclopedia of the Nation, Its People and Their Origins.* Sydney: Angus & Robertson, 2001

Kent, David and Townsend, Norma (eds): *Joseph Mason Assigned Convict 1831–1837.* Melbourne: Melbourne University Press, 1996

Kidd, Alan: *State, Society and the Poor in Nineteenth-Century England.* Basingstoke: Macmillan Press Ltd, 1999

Kloester, Jennifer: *Georgette Heyer's Regency World.* London: Heinemann, 2005

Knight, John George (comp.): *A Few Particulars relative to The Colony of Victoria (Australia).* London: The Victoria Emigrants' Assistance Society, 1863, original copy owned by the National Library of Australia

Lansbury, Coral: *Arcady in Australia. The Evocation of Australia in Nineteenth-Century English Literature.* Melbourne: Melbourne University Press, 1970

Lazarus, Mary: *A Tale of Two Brothers. Charles Dickens' Sons in Australia.* Sydney: Angus & Robertson, 1973

Leckey, John Anthony: *Low, Degraded Broots? Industry and Entrepreneurism in Melbourne's Little Lon 1860–1950.* Melbourne: Australian Scholarly Publishing, 2004

Leitch, Brenda: *Through Women's Eyes at Pioneering Days – Some Women of Wangaratta and District.* Wangaratta: Business and Professional Women's Club of Wangaratta, 1985

Light, Alison: *Mrs Woolf & the Servants. The Hidden Heart of Domestic Service.* London: Fig Tree/Penguin Books, 2007

Light, Alison: *Common People. The History of an English Family.* London: Fig Tree/Penguin Books, 2014

Longmate, Norman: *The Workhouse. A Social History.* London: Pimlico, 2003

Lott, F. B.: *The Centenary Book of the Leicester Literary and Philosophical Society.* Leicester: W. Thornley & Sons, 1935

Malthus, Thomas: *An Essay on the Principle of Population, 1798.* Available online

Martin, R. E.: *The Legends, Folklore and Dialect of Leicestershire with an Introduction on the General History of the County.* https://www.le.ac.uk/lahs/downloads/Martinlegends-PagesfromVolume17.pdf

Mastoris, Steph: *Around Market Harborough in Old Photographs.* Gloucester: Alan Sutton, 1989

Mayhew, Henry and Binny, John: *The Criminal Prisons of London 1841.* Available in numerous reprints and online

Millward, Roy: *A History of Leicestershire and Rutland.* Chichester: Phillimore & Co. Ltd, 1985

Moore, Andrew: *Where Leicestershire Has Worshipped.* Leicester: Laurel Publishing House, 2008

Murphy, Brian: *The Other Australia. Experiences in Migration.* Melbourne: Cambridge University Press, 1993

Newitt, Ned: *A People's History of Leicester. A Pictorial History of Working-Class Life and Politics.* Derby: The Breedon Books Publishing Company Limited, 2008

Newitt, Ned (ed.): *The Anthology of Leicester Chartist Song, Poetry & Verse.* Leicester: The Leicester Pioneer Press, 2006

Newitt, Ned (ed.): *The Slums of Leicester.* Derby: The Derby Books Publishing Company Limited, 2009

Nicholas, F. W. and Nicholas, J. M.: *Charles Darwin in Australia.* Melbourne: Cambridge University Press, 2008

Nichols, John: *The History and Antiquities of the County of Leicester Volume III, Part 1.* SR Publisher in collaboration with Leicestershire County Council, 1971

Ogier, J. C. H.: *Reminiscences of David Reid as Given to J. C. H. Ogier (In Nov. 1905) Who Has Set Them Down in The Third Person.* www.davesact.com/p/reid-crypt.html, and at the National Library of Australia, http://nla.gov.au/nla.obj-52773898/view?partId=nla.obj-89055323#page/no/mode/1up

Olney, R. J.: *Rural Society and County Government in Nineteenth-Century Lincolnshire.* Lincoln: The History of Lincolnshire Committee, 1979

Paley, Ruth: *My Ancestor was a Bastard.* London: Society of Genealogists Enterprises Ltd, 2004

Palmer, Marilyn: *Framework Knitting.* Shire Library 119. Princes Risborough: Shire Publications Ltd, 2002

Parish, Chris: *Being British. Our Once and Future Selves.* Alresford: Chronos Books, 2016

Pascoe, Bruce: *Dark Emu: Black Seeds: Agriculture or Accident?.* Broome: Magabala Books, 2016

Pinchbeck, Ivy: *Women Workers and the Industrial Revolution 1750–1850*. London: Virago 1981, reprint of 1930 edition

Rearsby Local History Society: *Rearsby. The Story of a Village*. Leicester: Oldham & Manton, 1984

Reedman, Les and Walker, Margaret: *Early Architects of the Hunter Region. A Hundred Years to 1940*. Brooklyn, NSW: Les Reedman & Margaret Walker, 2008

Religious Tract Society: *The Emigrant's Friend. A Selection of Tracts being a Companion for the Voyage and a Manual of Instruction in His New Home*. London: 1834–59

Reynolds, Henry: *This Whispering in our Hearts Revisited*. Sydney: New South Wales Publishing, University of New South Wales Press, 2018

Rigden, Reg: *The Floating Prisons of Woolwich and Deptford*. London: London Borough of Greenwich, printed by Gravesend and Dartford Reporter Ltd, 1976

Rudé, George: *Protest and Punishment. The Story of the Social and Political Protesters transported to Australia 1788–1868*. Oxford: The Clarendon Press, 1978

Sanders, Mike: *The Poetry of Chartism. Aesthetics, Politics, History*. Cambridge: Cambridge University Press, 2009

Serle, Geoffrey: *The Golden Age. A History of the Colony of Victoria 1851–1861*. Melbourne: Melbourne University Press, 1968

Sidney, Samuel: *The Three Colonies of Australia: New South Wales, Victoria, South Australia. Their Pastures, Copper Mines and Gold Field*s. A Project Gutenberg Australia ebook, 2014, from London: Ingram, Cooke & Co., 1853

Smith, Martin: *Stamford Then & Now*. Stamford: Paul Watkins, 1992

Smith, Martin: *The Story of Stamford*. Stamford: Martin Smith in association with Walker's Books Ltd, 2000

State Library of Victoria: *All The Rage. The Poster in Victoria 1850–2000*, narrative by Christine Downer. Melbourne: The Authors and the State Library of Victoria, 2001

Steedman, Carolyn: *Labours Lost. Domestic Service and the Making of Modern England*. Cambridge: Cambridge University Press, 2009

Steedman, Carolyn: *An Everyday Life of the English Working Class. Work, Self and Sociability in the Early Nineteenth Century*. Cambridge: Cambridge University Press, 2013

Steinbach, Susie: *Women in England 1780–1914: A Social History*. London: Weidenfeld & Nicolson, 2005

Stevens, Philip A.: *The Leicester Line. A History of the Old Union and Grand Union Canals*. Newton Abbot: David & Charles, 1972

Tebbutt, Laurence: *Stamford Clocks & Watches*. Stamford: no publisher given, 1975.

Temple Patterson, A.: *Radical Leicester*. Leicester: Leicester University Press, 1975

Tench, Watkin: *1788*, edited and introduced by Tim Flannery. Melbourne: Text Classics, 2009

Tench, Watkin: *A Narrative of the Expedition to Botany Bay: With an Account of New South Wales, its Productions, Inhabitants*, 1789. Avaliable online

Tench, Watkin: *A Complete Account of the Settlement at Port Jackson, in New South Wales, Including an Accurate Description of the Situation of the Colony; and of its Natural Productions; Taken on the Spot*, 1793. Available online

Tharoor, Shashi: *Inglorious Empire. What the British Did to India*. London: C. Hurst & Co. (Publishers) Ltd, 2017

Thompson, E. P.: *The Making of the English Working Class*. London: Penguin, 2013

Tibbits, George: *History of the Development of Prahran*. Melbourne: Nigel Lewis and Associates, 1983 & Prahran Conservation Study History of the Development of Prahran, 1992. https://www.stonnington.vic.gov.au/

Todd, Selina: *The People. The Rise and Fall of the Working Class*. London: John Murray, 2014

Traboulsi, Fawwaz: *A History of Modern Lebanon*. London: Pluto Books, 2007

Trollope, Anthony: *The Last Chronicle of Barset*, 1867

Vaux, James Hardy: *Memoirs of James Hardy Vaux, written by himself, in two volumes*. London: John Murray, 1819. Available online

Vicinus, Martha: *The Industrial Muse. A Study of Nineteenth Century British Working-Class Literature*. Barnes & Noble Books, USA: 1974

Vicinus, Martha: *Independent Women. Work and Community for Single Women 1850–1920*. London: Virago, 1985

Vincent, William Thomas: *Woolwich. Guide to the Royal Arsenal*. (Reprint of 'Warlike Woolwich'.) *Tenth Thousand*. London: British Library, Historical Print Editions, 1885

Wardle, David: *English Popular Education 1780–1975*. Cambridge: Cambridge University Press, 2009

Wells, E. A.: *The British Hosiery and Knitwear Industry. Its History and Organisation*. Newton Abbot: David & Charles, 1972

Wilbourn, A. S. H. and Ellis, R.: *Lincolnshire Clock, Watch and Barometer Makers*. Lincoln: Hansord, Ellis & Wilbourn, 2001

Williams, Daniel (ed.): *The Adaptation of Change. Essays Upon the History of 19th-Century Leicester and Leicestershire*. Leicester: Leicestershire Archaeological and Historical Society and Leicestershire Museums, Art Galleries and Records Service, 1980

Wohl, Anthony S. (ed.): *The Victorian Family Structure and Stresses*. London: Croom Helm, 1978

Wood, Anthony: *Nineteenth Century Britain 1815–1914*. Harlow: Longman Group Ltd., 1982

Wright, Neil: *Boston. A Pictorial History*. Chichester: Phillimore & Co. Ltd., 1994

Wright, Neil R.: *The Railways of Boston. Their Origins and Development*. Boston: Richard Kay publications, in association with the History of Boston Project, 1971

Wright, Neil R.: *The Book of Boston*. Buckingham: Barracuda Books, 1991

Wright, Neil R.: *Lincolnshire Towns and Industry 1700–1914*. Lincoln: The History of Lincolnshire Committee, 1982

Articles, Journals, Pamphlets, Theses, Broadcasts and Talks

Anderson, John: *Bygone Market Harborough*. Blaby: Anderson Publications, 1982

Ashton, T. S.: 'The Standard of Life of the Workers in England, 1790–1830', *Journal of Economic History*, Vol. 9, Supplement 'The Tasks of Economic History', 1949, pp. 19–38

Atkinson, Alan 'The Political Life of James Macarthur', PhD thesis, Australian National University, 1976, pp. 134–39, 158

Atkinson, Alan: 'The Parliament in the Jerusalem Warehouse', *Push from the Bush*, No. 12, May 1982, pp. 75–104

Attwood, Bain: 'The Founding of Aboriginal History and the forming of Aboriginal history', *Aboriginal History*, Vol. 36, 2012, pp. 119–71

Aucott, Pam: 'Aldwinkle's Yard in 1809', *Harborough Historian*, No. 29, 2012, pp. 46ff

Ballyn, Sue: 'The British Invasion of Australia. Convicts: Exile and Dislocation', *Lives in Migration: Rupture and Continuity*, www.ub.edu/dpfilsa/2ballyn.pdf

Bennett, J. D.: 'Dickens in Leicester', *Leicestershire Historian*, No. 37, 2001

Berridge, Virginia: 'Opium in the Fen in 19th-century England', *Journal of the History of Medicine and Allied Sciences*, Vol. 34. No. 3, July 1979, pp. 293–313

Blair, Sandra: 'The Felonry and the Free? Divisions in Colonial Society in the Penal Era', *Labour History*, No. 45, November 1983, pp. 1–16

Broeze, Frank J. A.: 'Private Enterprise and the Peopling of Australasia, 1831–50', *Economic Review of History*, New Series, Vol. 35, No. 2, May 1982, pp. 235–53

Buck, Anne M.: 'Clothes in Fact and Fiction 1825–1865', *Costume*, Vol. 17, 1983, pp. 89–104

Bungonia and District Historical Society: 'Bungonia Village Historical Sites', http://bungonia.com.au/contact.htm

Carroll, Diane: *Mrs Agnes Reid, Parts One and Two*, https://lists.rootsweb.com/hyper-kitty/list/aus-vic-high-country@rootsweb.com/thread/33708194/

Clark, Anna: 'Wild Workhouse Girls and the Liberal Imperial State in Mid-Nineteenth Century Ireland', *Journal of Social History*, Vol. 39, No. 2, 'Kith and Kin: Interpersonal Relationship and Cultural Practices', Winter 2005, pp. 389–409

Clifton-Taylor, Alec: *Alec Clifton-Taylor's Stamford*, BBC, 1984

Cockayne, Steve: 'The Market Harborough Workhouse', *Harborough Historian*, No. 27, 2010, pp. 20ff

Cookson, J. E.: 'The English Volunteer Movement of the French Wars, 1793–1815: Some Contexts', *Historical Journal*, Vol. 32, No. 4, December 1989, pp. 867–91

Curthoys, Ann: 'Disputing National Histories. Some Recent Australian Debates', *Transforming Cultures,* ejournal, Vol. 1, No.1, March 2006, http://epress.lib.uts.edu.au/journals/TIC

Daedalus (Journal of the American Academy of Arts and Sciences): 'Australia: Terra Incognita?', Vol. 114, No. 1, Winter 1985

Darwin, George H.: 'Marriages Between First Cousins in England and Their Effects', *Journal of the Statistical Society of London*, Vol. 38, No. 2, June 1875

Day, Ken: 'Coaching Days in Market Harborough', *Harborough Historian*, No. 17, 2000, pp. 13ff

Day, Ken: 'The Harborough Bank and The Carpet Factory', *Harborough Historian*, No. 29, 2012, pp. 27ff

Docker, John: 'Raphael Lemkin, creator of the concept of genocide: a world history perspective', *Humanities Research*, Vol. 6, No. 2, 2010, special issue edited by Ned Curthoys, 'Key Thinkers and Their Contemporary Legacy', pp.49–74

Docker, John: 'Raphael Lemkin's History of Genocide and Colonialism', talk given 26 February 2004, United States Holocaust Memorial Museum, Center for Advanced Holocaust Studies, Washington DC, https://www.ushmm.org/confront-genocide/speakers-and-events/all-speakers-and-events/raphael-lemkins-history-of-genocide-and-colonialism

Donnelly Jr, James S.: 'The Irish Agricultural Depression of 1859–1864', *Irish Economic and Social History*, Vol. 3, 1976, pp. 33–54

Doust, Janet L.: 'Exploring Gentry Women on the New South Wales Frontier in the 1820s and 1830s', *Women's History Review*, Vol. 18. No. 1, pp. 137–53

Elliott, Malcolm: 'John Buck: Pioneer of Preventative Medicine and the Care of the Mentally Ill', https://www.le.ac.uk/lahs/downloads/Elliott2voluMELXIV-7sm.pdf

Evelyn, Lord: '"Weighed in the Balance and Found Wanting": Female Friendly Societies, Self Help and Economic virtue in the East Midlands in the Eighteenth and Nineteenth Centuries', *Midland History* (University of Birmingham), Vol. 22, 1997

Felkin, William: *History of the Machine-Wrought Hosiery and Lace Manufacturers*. Cambridge: W. Metcalfe, 1867

Foster, Gill: 'The Power of the Word. How Writings about boat people affected perceptions', http://www.spellweaver-online.co.uk/index.php/2

Freer, Wendy: 'Canal Boat People 1840–1870', DPhil thesis, University of Nottingham, 1991, http://eprints.nottingham.ac.uk/10946/1/281065_vol1.pdf

Gillen, Mollie: 'The Botany Bay Decision, 1786: Convicts, Not Empire', *English Historical Review*, Vol. 97, No. 385, October 1982, pp. 740–66,

Gore, Catherine: *A Bewailment from Bath*, Project Gutenberg ebook of *Blackwood's Edinburgh Magazine*, Vol. 55, No. 340, February 1844

Gothard, Jan: 'A Compromise with Conscience: The Reception of Female Immigrant Domestic Servants in Eastern Australia 1860–1890', *Labour History*, No. 62., May 1992, pp. 38–51.

Goulburn and District Historical Society: *Bungonia: The Spot on the Creek*, Goulburn, 1985

Gräf, Holger T.: 'Leicestershire Small Towns and Pre-Industrial Urbanisation', *Transactions of the Leicestershire Archaeological and Historical Society*, Vol. 68, 1994

Gurney, Peter J.: 'The Politics of Consumption in England during the "Hungry Forties"', *Past & Present*, No. 203, May 2009, pp. 99–136

Haines, Robin, Kleinig, Margrette, Oxley, Deborah and Richards, Eric: 'Migration and Opportunity: An Antipodean Perspective', *International Review of Social History*, Vol. 43, No. 2, Cambridge University Press, August 1998, pp. 235–63

Haines, Robin: 'Misfits or Shrewd Operators? Government-assisted Emigrants from the United Kingdom to Australia, 1831–1860', *Population Studies*, Vol. 48, No. 2, July 1994, pp. 223–47,

Hamilton, Paula and Gothard, Janice: '"The Other Half": Sources on British Female Emigration at the Fawcett Library with Special Reference to Australia', *Women's Studies International Forum*, Vol. 10, No. 3, 1987, pp. 305–9

Harborough Historian (Market Harborough Historical Society), Nos. 24, 23, 32, 18, 25, 28 and others, https://www.marketharboroughhistoricalsociety.org. All numbers indexed on website and some articles available for download

Head, Peter: 'Putting Out in the Leicester Hosiery Industry in the Middle of the Nineteenth Century', https://www.le.ac.uk/lahs/downloads/HeadSmPagesfroms mvoluMEXXXVII-5.pdf

Henriques, U. R. Q.: 'Bastardy and the New Poor Law', *Past & Present*, No. 37, July 1967, pp. 103–29

Heydon, Susan: 'The provision of medical care for the poor in Leicester in the 1830s', https://www.le.ac.uk/lahs/downloads/MediaclPagesfromvoluMELV-7.pdf

Himmelfarb, Gertrude: 'The Idea of Poverty', *History Today*, Vol. 34, Issue 4, April 1984

Hirst, John: 'An Oddity From the Start', *Monthly Essay*, July 2008

Holden, Len: 'The Rise and Decline of the Coaching Trade in Market Harborough', *Harborough Historian*, No. 34, 2017, pp. 28ff

Horrell, Sara, Humphries, Jane and Voth, Hans-Joachim: 'Stature and relative deprivation: fatherless children in early industrial Britain', *Continuity and Change*, Vol. 13, Issue 1, 1998, pp. 73–115

Hoskins, W. G.: 'The Origin and Rise of Market Harborough', https://www.le.ac.uk, taken from Hoskins' *Provincial England* (London: Palgrave Macmillan, 1963)

Huntsman, Leone: '*Bounty* Emigrants to Australia', *Clogher Record* (Clogher Historical Society), Vol. 17, No. 3, 2002, pp. 801–12

Kane, Jacqueline L.: 'Prison Palace or "Hell upon earth": Leicester County Gaol under the Separate System, 1846–1865', *Transactions of the Leicestershire Archaeological and Historical Society*, Vol. 70, 1996, pp. 128–46

Karpat, Kemal H.: 'The Ottoman Emigration to America, 1860–1914', *International Journal of Middle East Studies*, Vol. 17, No. 2, May 1985, pp. 175–209

Kercher, Bruce: 'The Law and Convict Transportation in the British Empire, 1700–1850', *Law and History Review*, Vol. 21, No. 3, Autumn 2003

King, Steven: 'Friendship, Kinship and Belonging in the Letters of Urban Paupers 1800–1840', *Historical Research*, Vol. 33, No. 3, 2008, pp. 249–77

Knight, John, I.: *Mechanics Magazine*, Vol. 39, January 1839, available at https://books.google.co.uk

Kuper, Adam: 'Incest, Cousin Marriage, and the Origin of the Human Sciences in Nineteenth-Century England', *Past & Present*, No. 174, February 2002, pp. 158–83

Lane, Penelope: 'Work on the Margins: Poor Women and the Informal Economy of Eighteenth and early Nineteenth-century Leicestershire', *Midland History* (University of Birmingham), Vol. 22, 1997

Lansbury, Coral: 'Terra Australis Dickensia', *Modern Language Studies*, Vol. 1, No. 2, Summer 1971, pp. 12–21

Levi, Neil: 'No Sensible Comparison. The Place of the Holocaust in Australia's History Wars', *History and Memory*, Vol. 19, No. 1, Spring/Summer 2007, pp. 124–56

Levine, David: 'The Demographic Implications of Rural Industrialization: A Family Reconstitution Study of Shepshed, Leicestershire, 1600–1851', *Social History*, Vol. 1, No. 2, May 1976, pp. 177–96

Lockwood, R.: 'British Imperial Influences in the Foundations of the White Australia Policy', *Labour History*, No. 7, November 1964, pp. 23–33

Longmuir, Anne: 'Emigrant Spinsters and the Construction of Englishness in Charlotte Bronte's Villette', *Nineteenth Century Gender Studies*, Issue 43, Winter 2008

Loomis, Brian and Loomis, Joy: 'Collecting Antique Clocks: The Bothamleys of Boston, Lincolnshire, and an unusual wall clock', https://www.brianloomes.com/collecting/bothamley/index.html

McDonald, John and Shlomowitz, Ralph: 'Mortality on Convict Voyages to Australia, 1788–1868', *Social Sciences History* (Cambridge University Press), Vol. 13. No. 3, Autumn 1989, pp. 285–313

McDougall, Jill: 'Church, Community and Change. Religion in Prahran 1836–1984 Melbourne', *Prahran Historical Studies Series* (Prahran Historical and Arts Society), No. 6, 1985

Macintyre, Stuart: 'The History Wars', *Sydney Papers*, Vol. 15, Issue 3–4, Winter/Spring 2003

Macintyre, Stuart: 'Reviewing the History Wars', *Labour History*, No. 85, November 2003, pp. 213–15

McQueen, H.: 'Convicts and Rebels', *Labour History*, No. 15, November 1968, pp. 3–30

Malone, Betty: 'Early Prahran 1850–1863', *Prahran Historical Studies Series* (Prahran Historical and Arts Society), No. 1, 1982

Malone, Betty: 'Chapel Street, Prahran. Part One 1834–1918', *Prahran Historical Studies Series* (Prahran Historical and Arts Society), No. 4, 1983

Market Harborough Congregational Chapel: *The Years Between. The History of our Church 1662–1987*, n.d.

Matts, Mary: 'Foxton Locks: Past, Present and Future', *Harborough Historian* (Market Harborough Historical Society), No. 17, 2000, pp. 30ff

Matts, Mary: 'The Canal Comes to Market Harborough', *Harborough Historian* (Market Harborough Historical Society), No. 24, 2007, pp. 43–7

Mayberry, Peter: 'Bathurst's Bushrangers & Ribbon-Gang', https://soc.genealogy.australia-nz.narkive.com/xl1jyg6F/bathurst-s-bushrangers-ribbon-gang

Navickas, Katrina: 'The Search for General Ludd: the Mythology of Luddism', *Social History*, Vol. 30, No. 3, August 2005

Nicholas, Stephen and Oxley, Deborah: 'The Living Standards of Women during the Industrial Revolution, 1795–1820', *Economic History Review*, Vol. 46, No. 4, 1993, pp. 723–49

Palmer, Marilyn: 'Housing the Leicester Framework Knitters', *Transactions of the Leicestershire Archaeological and Historical Society*, Vol. 74, 2000, pp. 59–78

Page S. J.: 'Late Victorian Pauperism and the Poor Law in Leicester', https://www.le.ac.uk/lahs/downloads/PageSmPagesfromvoluMELX-8.pdf

Park, James Allan: 'The Trial of John Bishop Allen, for the Wilful Murder of William Lane of Leicester, Drummer in the 35th Regt. of Foot, at Thurmaston, On 25th Day of November, 1822', Gale MOML Print Editions Trials, 1600–1926.

Picton Phillipps, C. J. V.: 'Convicts, Communication and Authority: Britain and New South Wales, 1810–1830', PhD thesis, University of Edinburgh, 2002, https://www.era.lib.ed.ac.uk/handle/1842/1568

Push from the Bush: A Bulletin of Social History Devoted to the Year of Grace 1838 (Australian National University, Canberra), No. 2, November 1978

Push from the Bush: A Bulletin of Social History Devoted to the Year of Grace 1838 (Australian National University, Canberra), No. 16, October 1983

Push from the Bush: A Bulletin of Social History Devoted to the Year of Grace 1838 (University of New England, Armidale, NSW), No. 16, October 1984

Richards, Eric, Reid, Richard and Fitzpatrick, David: *Visible Immigrants: Neglected Sources for the History of Australian Immigration.* Canberra: Department of History and the Centre for Immigration and Multicultural Studies, Research School of Social Sciences, 1989

Richards, Eric (ed.): *Visible Immigrants: Two: Poor Australian Immigrants in the Nineteenth Century.* Canberra: Division of Historical Studies and Centre for Immigration and Multicultural Studies, Research School of Social Sciences, 1991

Richards, Eric (ed.): *Visible Immigrants: Four: Female Immigrants in Colonial Australia.* Canberra: Division of Historical Studies and Centre for Immigration and Multicultural Studies, Research School of Social Sciences, 1995

Richards, Eric: 'How Did Poor People Emigrate from the British Isles to Australia in the 19th Century', *Journal of British Studies*, Vol. 32, No. 3, July 1993, pp. 250–79

Rimmington, Gerald T.: 'Congregationalism in Rural Leicestershire and Rutland 1863–1914', *Midland History* (University of Birmingham), Vol. 31, 2006

Rizzetti, Janine (the Resident Judge of Port Phillip): review of James Boyce, *1835: The Founding of Melbourne & the Conquest of Australia*, 18 August 2011, https://resident-judge.com/2011/08/18/1835-by-james-boyce/

Roberts, Stephen: 'Thomas Cooper in Leicester, 1840–1843', https://www.le.ac.uk/lahs/downloads/RobertssmvoluMELXI-8.pdf

Royle, Stephen A.: 'Hinckley in the mid-nineteenth century', www.le.ac.uk/downloads

Samuel, Raphael: 'Workshop of the World: Steam Power and Hand Technology in mid-Victorian Britain', *History Workshop Journal*, No. 3, Spring, 1977, pp. 6–72

Simmons, Jack: 'Mid-Victorian Leicester', *Transactions of the Leicestershire Archaeological and Historical Society*, Vol. 4, 1965–6

Simmons, Jack: 'A Victorian Social Worker: Joseph Dare and the Leicester Domestic Mission', *Transactions of the Leicestershire Archaeological and Historical Society*, Vol. 46, 1970–1

Simmons, Jack: 'Public Transport in Leicestershire, 1814–80', *Transactions of the Leicestershire Archaeological and Historical Society*, Vol. 70, 1996

Sturma, Michael: 'Eye of the Beholder: The Stereotype of Women Convicts, 1788–1852', *Labour History*, No. 14, May 1978, pp. 3–10

Temple Patterson, A.: 'The Making of the Leicestershire canals 1766–1814', *Transactions of the Leicestershire Archaeological and Historical Society*, Vol. 27, 1951

Thurmaston Heritage Group: *Memories of Thurmaston Volume 1.* Thurmaston: Thurmaston Print Shop Ltd, 2007

Thurmaston Heritage Group: *Memories of Thurmaston Volume 2.* Thurmaston: Thurmaston Print Shop Ltd, 2011

Townsend, Claire: 'County versus Region? Migrational Connections in the East Midlands 1700– 1830', *Journal of Historical Geography*, Vol. 32, 2006, pp. 291–312

Turnbull, Gerard: 'Coal and Regional Growth during the Industrial Revolution', *Economic History Review*, New Series, Vol. 40, No. 4, November 1987, pp. 537–60

Turton, Maurice: 'Disease and Death in Nineteenth-Century Market Harborough', *Harborough Historian* (Market Harborough Historical Society), Vol. 27, 2010, pp. 25ff

Ullwood, Sarah and Putnis, Peter: 'The Crimean War and Australia's Communication & Media History', *Australian Media Traditions*, 2007, https://www.academia.edu/8989985/

Van Vugt, William E.: 'Prosperity and Industrial Emigration from Britain during the Early 1850s', *Journal of Social History*, Vol. 22, No. 2, Winter 1988, pp. 339–54

Willetts, Jen: 'Free Settler or Felon? Newcastle and Hunter Valley History', www.jenwilletts.com

Willox, John: *Practical Hints to Intending Emigrants for the Australian Colonies.* London: Houlston & Wright, 1858

Wilshere, Jonathan, E. O.: 'Leicestershire Long-Case Clocks', *Leicestershire Historian*, Old Series (Leicestershire Archaeological and Historical Society), Vol. 1, Part 7, Autumn 1970, pp. 220ff

Woollacott, Angela: 'The Meanings of Protection: Women in Colonial and Colonising Australia', *Journal of Women's History* Vol. 14.4, Winter 2003, pp. 213–21

Magazines and Newspapers

The Age, Melbourne
The Argus, Melbourne
Australasian Chronicle
Australian Historical Studies
Blackwood's Edinburgh Magazine
Chester Chronicle and North Wales Advertiser
Chester Courant
Goulburn Herald & County of Argyle Advertiser
Government Gazette, NSW
Grantham Journal
Hampshire Advertiser
Hertfordshire Guardian, Agricultural Journal and General Advertiser
Illustrated London News
Leicester Chronicle
Leicester Journal
Leicestershire Mercury
Lincolnshire Life
Liverpool Chronicle
Liverpool Mercury
London Review of Books
Louth and North Lincolnshire Advertiser
Maitland Mercury and Hunter River General Advertiser
Melbourne Punch
New South Wales Government Gazette
Northampton Mercury
Prahran and South Yarra Guardian
Prahran Telegraph

Quadrant, Australia
Stamford Mercury
Sydney Herald
Sydney Gazette and New South Wales Advertiser
The Telegraph, St Kilda, Melbourne
Victorian Government Gazette
Victoria Police Gazette
Wodonga and Towong Sentinel, Victoria
World's News, Sydney

Websites

http://adb.anu.edu.au (*Australian Dictionary of Biography*)
https://www.atlasobscura.com/articles/the-incredibly-disturbing-medieval-
    practice-of-gibbeting
https://archiveshub.jisc.ac.uk (and all Chartist websites)
https://archiveshub.jisc.ac.uk/features/apr08.shtml
https://australianmuseum.net.au
www.barossa-region.org/Australia_2/Bathurst-s-bushrangers---Ribbon-Gang.html
https://books.google.co.uk
https://www.british-history.ac.uk/vch/leics/ (*A History of the County of Leicestershire*)
https://www.british-history.ac.uk/vch/leics/vol5 (Market Harborough, Great Bowden)
https://collections.museumvictoria.com.au/items/245458
httpps.//www.coraweb.com.au
https://corpun.com
http://www.danbyrnes.com.au/blackheath/ (The Blackheath Connection)
and http://danbyrnes.com.au/networks
http://www.davesact.com/p/reid-crypt.html (David Reid memoir, as told to
    J. C. H. Ogier; also available at the National Library of Australia, http://nla.gov.au/
    nla.obj-52773898/view?partId=nla.obj-89055323#page/no/mode/1up)
https://dictionaryofsydney.org/entry/second_fleet
www.educationforum.com
http://www.fomad.org.au/history-overview.html
https://www.frameworkknittersmuseum.org.uk
https://www.genuki.org.uk
https://www.goulburn.nsw.gov.au/Planning-Information/Bungonia-heritageinvesti
    gation.aspx
www.granpapencil.net
https://www.gutenberg.org
https://www.history.ac.uk/research/victoria-county-history
http://www.historyhome.co.uk/peel/poorlaw/plaa.htm
http://www.historyworkshop.org.uk
http://historicengland.org.uk
https://www.jenwilletts.com ('Free Settler or Felon?')

http://www.jenwilletts.com/scourgers.htm

http://www.knittingtogether.org.uk

https://www.legislation.nsw.gov.au/#/view/EPI/2009/56/full (Goulburn Mulwaree Council Planning Proposal, Bungonia Heritage Conservation Area Local Environmental Plan 2009)

https://www.legislation.gov.au/Details/C1901A00017

https://www.leicester.gov.uk/ (Record Office for Leicestershire, Leicester and Rutland)

https:// www.leicestersecularsociety.org.uk

https:// www.leicestervillages.com

https://www.liverpoolmuseums.org.uk/maritime/archive/sheet/64

https://www.maritimeheritage.org (Maritime Archives & Library, National Museums Liverpool, Information Sheet 64, 'Liverpool and Emigration in the 19th & 20th centuries')

https://www.marx-memorial-library.org.uk

http://mhcongregational.church/wp/

https://museumsvictoria.com.au/immigrationmuseum/

https://catalogue.nla.gov.au/Record/3068005 ('Linking a nation: Australia's transport and communications 1788–1970'

https://www.nationalarchives.gov.uk

http://www.norwayheritage.com/articles/templates/great-disasters.asp?articleid=106&zoneid=1

http://nzetc.victoria.ac.nz/tm/scholarly/

https://www.plumstead-stories.com

http://www.pogues.com/forum/viewtopic.php?f=38&t=8312

https:// www.thepotteries.org/focus/001.htm

https:// www.prov.vic.gov.au/provenance/no5/PrahranTechPrint

www.prov.vic.gov.au

https://residentjudge.wordpress.com/2011/08/18/1835–by-james-boyce

https://roaringwaterjournal.com/tag/abbeystrewry-graveyard

https://sites.rootsweb.com/~tmi45/ (Thurmaston Heritage Group)

https://lists.rootsweb.com/hyperkitty/list/aus-vic-high-country@rootsweb.com/thread/33708194/

http://www.theshiplist.com

http://www.slaverysite.com

http://www.spellweaver-online.co.uk

http://www.stonnington.vic.gov.au (Prahran local history publications)

-Live/Indigenous-Reconciliation/Stonningtons-Indigenous-History

https://www.tolpuddlemartyrs.org.uk

https://trove.nla.gov.au/newspaper/

https://www.victorianlondon.org/ (website of Lee Jackson)

http://www.victorianweb.org

http://www.historyhome.co.uk

http://www.villagesonline.com/counties/leicestershire.aspx

https://en.wikipedia.org/wiki/History_of_Victoria

https://en.wikipedia.org/wiki/

Reports

Muggeridge, Richard M.: *Report of the Commission appointed to Inquire into the Condition of the Frame-work knitters, with Appendices*. London: The sessional Papers of the House of Lords, in the Session of 1845.

Report from the Select Committee on Transportation: together with the minutes of evidence, appendix, and index. London: HMSO, 1838

Museums, Libraries, Archives and Societies, Family History Websites

Boston Guildhall Museum
Boston Library, UK
British Library
Cheshire Archives and Local Studies
Chester Record Office
Fenland Family History Society
Foxton Canal Museum
General Register Office for England and Wales
Guildhall Library, London
Lincolnshire Archives, Lincolnshire County Council
Lincolnshire Family History Society
Lloyd's Register of Shipping
London Library
Market Harborough Historical Society
National Archives, Kew
National Archives of Australia, Melbourne
National Museums of Liverpool
North Kensington Public Library, London
Northants Family History Society
Public Record Office, Melbourne, Victoria
Record Office for Leicestershire, Leicester and Rutland
Sands and Macdougall Directories, Victoria, Australia
Society for Lincolnshire History and Archaeology
Stamford Museum
State Library Victoria
State Archives and Records Authority, NSW
Thurmaston Heritage Group
Wigston Framework Knitters Museum
York Archives and Local History Service

Index